PALESTINIANS IN SYRIA

T0317392

PALESTINIANS IN SYRIA

NAKBA MEMORIES OF SHATTERED COMMUNITIES

ANAHEED AL-HARDAN

COLUMBIA UNIVERSITY PRESS ■ NEW YORK

Columbia University Press
Publishers Since 1893
New York   Chichester, West Sussex
Copyright © 2016 Columbia University Press
Paperback edition, 2018

Library of Congress Cataloging-in-Publication Data
Names: Al-Hardan, Anaheed, author.
Title: Palestinians in Syria : Nakba memories of shattered communities /
Anaheed Al-Hardan.
Description: New York : Columbia University Press, [2016] |
Includes bibliographical references and index.
Identifiers: LCCN 2015039971 | ISBN 9780231176361 (cloth) |
ISBN 9780231176378 (pbk.) ISBN 9780231541220 (e-book)
Subjects: LCSH: Refugees, Palestinian Arab—Syria. | Palestinian Arabs—Syria. |
Arab-Israeli conflict—1993–
Classification: LCC HV640.5.P36 A38 2016 | DDC 956.04/21—dc23
LC record available at http://lccn.loc.gov/2015039971

Cover design: Martin Hinze

This book is dedicated to Syria
and its people.

CONTENTS

NOTE ON TRANSLITERATION AND NAMES

All Arabic to English translations in the book are my own unless stated otherwise. I have followed a simplified version of the American Library Association–Library of Congress Romanization Table for the transliteration of modern standard Arabic sources. This means that with the exception of the use of apostrophes to indicate *ayn* (') and *hamza* ('), I have not used diacritics to indicate non-Roman letters. Similarly, with a few exceptions, I have generally not added short vowels at the end of words, doubled consonants to indicate *al-shada* in initial letters, or transliterated the final *ha'*. I have also attempted to bring two Arabic words into common English-language use: Nakba (1948 catastrophe) and Naksa (1967 setback).

In regard to common words and names of individuals and organizations, I have used common English transliterations when available. This includes an author's name as per its preexisting English transliteration when citing their English language work. I have also used the lowercase for the definite article *al-* with the exception of the uppercase *Al-* when referring to the last name of an author whose work is available in English with an uppercase.

I have followed the Walid Khalidi–edited *All That Remains: The Palestinian Villages Occupied and Depopulated by Israel in 1948* (Institute for Palestine Studies, Washington, DC, 1992) for the transliteration of the names of destroyed Palestinian villages. The only exception is the transliteration of the names of two villages whose names were pronounced differently by its people and their descendants (Akrad al-Baqqara and Akrad al-Ghannama). I have also followed the website of the United Nations Relief and Works Agency for Palestine Refugees in the Near East for the transliteration of the names of Palestinian refugee camps in Syria.

PREFACE AND ACKNOWLEDGMENTS

Beginnings, the late Edward Said (1997, 5) wrote, are the first step in the willful production of meaning. One of the beginnings of the research project that underpins this book is in the Nakba, or catastrophe, that resulted from the establishment of the state of Israel on Palestine in May 1948. This catastrophe saw the dispossession of more than half of historic Palestine's population, some 800,000 people, the overwhelming majority between March and October 1948. This annihilation of at least four-fifths of Palestinian society as it had once existed in the conquered territories, which unfolded from the end of 1947 to the beginning of 1949 and afterward, took place alongside the obliteration of at least 531 villages and eleven urban localities (Pappe 2006a).[1]

Reclaiming and claiming history, Indigenous scholars have argued, is an essential part of decolonization (Smith 2012). The Nakba, however, is not only a historical event. It is today also a structure of Israeli settler-colonial rule in historic Palestine (Salamanca et al. 2012), one based on settler-colonialism's logic of the elimination of the Indigenous population (Wolfe 2006). Examining memories that resulted from the Nakba is therefore not about taking part in a mourning of a second order (Chow 2008). It is about acknowledgment and accountability for the atrocities and enforced statelessness that accompanied the establishment of the state of Israel in 1948. This includes the decolonization of an ongoing violent system of settler colonial domination (or total exclusion, in the case of the Palestinians expelled in 1948) that Israel has established over all Palestinian lives since 1948 (Salamanca et al. 2012; F. Sayegh 2012).

This geopolitical formulation of the research project's beginnings is intersected by yet another one, the body-political location of the researcher

(Mignolo 2011). Setting out to search for memories of the Nakba was a deeply personal endeavor. I myself am a granddaughter of the Nakba, and my family, like all Palestinian families expelled in 1948, has a history of experiencing a violent dispossession. This dispossession unfolded from Umm al-Zinat, a Mount Carmel village outside Haifa that was subsequently erased from the face of the earth, and with it our communities' existence in Palestine (Al-Hardan 2008; al-As'ad 1990). The story of the Nakba for my family, as with most Palestinian families turned refugees now unto the fourth and fifth generation, did not simply end in 1948. The enforced statelessness and lack of implementation of our right of return to what became the state of Israel resulted in repeated dispossessions and deportations. The latest of these has been encapsulated by the fate of the Palestinian refugee community in Iraq following the US invasion and destruction of that country (Al-Hardan 2009; al-As'ad 1999).

The body and the political in the body-political location of researchers do not necessarily always correspond. Closely tied to these ontological beginnings are therefore the epistemic and the structural locations of the researcher as beginnings. In February 2008, I traveled to Syria from Ireland, guided by a "situated knowledge" (Haraway 1991, 183–201) of the Nakba as central to Palestinians whose families were made refugees in 1948. The research was methodologically inspired by radical and black feminists, as well as Indigenous and decolonial theorists and activists. It was informed by theory based on everyday lived experiences, the researcher as part of, and not separate to, her research and knowledge claims, and research communities as places of conversation rather than discovery (Collins 2008; Haraway 1997; Smith 2012; Stanley and Wise 1993).

I was therefore thinking against normative research epistemologies, which have historically and politically been constituted through the European colonizers' will to power and knowledge and this will's conquered "others" (Dussel 2000; Moreton-Robinson 2004). This meant that I also had to unlearn their conceptual categories. Not being a member of the Palestinian community in Syria, I came to learn that my preoccupation with such notions as "insiders/outsiders" overlooked the "coloniality of power" in the world (Quijano 2002).[2] Also overlooked was the impact this had on the structural relations of power in the "field," constructed as a site of research, as well as on research communities understood as comprising "informants." Put another way, this is yet another beginning, one in which the body-political location of the researcher is realized within structural relations that are part of the coloniality of global power in the academy and in the world at large (Grosfoguel 2011).

In Syria, the colonial trajectory of these categories meant that they overlooked the relations of power so integral to any researcher's arrival, indeed, the very ability to arrive in a "field" from imperialist centers of power and their allies. This was the case of my arrival from a European Union that continues to sanction the settler-colonized and stateless status quo of Palestinians (Cronin 2010). They also overlooked the political agency of actors in the communities in which the research is carried out—actors, in more than one sense of the word, rather than the highly passive and problematic "informants." Finally, they also overlooked how research participants view researchers as both insiders and outsiders and how this positioning takes place within the overarching historical and political parameters of the numerous encounters that constitute research. These factors directly affect, even limit, the conversations researchers may have. This is because community members enable or otherwise affect the research through their identification, or lack thereof, with the relations of power under whose weight these encounters take place. It is these same relations that determine how these encounters are packaged as a finished product for academic consumption.

These factors also meant that I did not discover a "truth" in Syria. Rather, I was engaged in the coproduction of a truth implicated in the overarching relations of power between where I had come from and where I had come to, and between my own negotiation as a simultaneous insider and outsider within a particular historical and political moment. The resultant encounters and conversations that I had with different individuals, families, and communities cannot be "reflected" away even by the most "reflexive" researcher to arrive at some "truth" when making subsequent claims about Palestinian lives. Moving beyond reflexivity as a critical practice that simply displaces the same elsewhere requires thinking of different visual metaphors as well as the power inherent in vision (Haraway 1991, 1997). Knowledge as composed of diffraction patterns that result from recording histories of "interaction, interference, reinforcement, difference" (Haraway 1997, 273), it has been argued, is one such possibility (see also Barad 2007, 71–94). Our truth claims can therefore be thought of as a diffraction pattern of the coloniality of power and knowledge, in other words, as diffracted through the conditions in which our search and re-search unfold. These conditions are central to these claims, which are partial and always located in historical and political realities.

In my six months spent in Syria, I conducted sixty-three qualitative, in-depth Arabic-language interviews. These were with three generations of Palestinian refugees, community activists, United Nations Relief and

Works Agency for Palestine Refugees in the Near East (UNRWA) employees and General Authority for Palestinian Arab Refugees (GAPAR, Ministry of Social Affairs and Labor) civil servants.[3] They were carried out in all the UNRWA-designated camps around the capital (five out of a total of nine in Syria), in Yarmouk, one of three additional camps designated "unofficial" by UNRWA, and in six different neighborhoods of the capital or suburbs that surround the city and fall under the jurisdiction of the Rural Damascus Governorate.[4] This geographical focus is on Damascus and its environs because before the war close to four-fifths of all Palestinians in Syria lived in the Damascus and the Rural Damascus Governorates (UNRWA 2012c).

Having lived in Yarmouk Camp, I have included rewritten parts of the extensive diary I kept in Syria in order to critically contextualize, as far as that is possible, the interviews I conducted and the conclusions I reached. For anthropologists, this may come across as an incomplete and even "thin" ethnography or autoethnography, the latter understood as research about oneself or among a group that a researcher belongs to (Ellis 2004, 2009; Reed-Danahay 1997). My primary research methods, however, involved the interviews that I conducted. The reflections and observations from my stay in Damascus included here are meant to provide context to the interviews and speak, even if in a limited way, to the diffraction of the geopolitical, body-political, epistemic, and structural relations of power outlined earlier. Finally, given the epistemic premise of this book, I have also ventured into interdisciplinary terrains. I have written an intellectual history of the Nakba in Arab thought with an eye to demonstrating how Palestinians and Arabs more generally are knowledge-producing subjects, rather than mere objects of research. I have also constructed a social, political, and historical portrait of the Palestinian refugee community in Syria in order to provide the necessary background, including institutional and spatial, to the analysis of memories and histories of the Nakba in Syria.

* * *

This book was not meant to be about the catastrophes of today, but about the catastrophe of 1948. It was not meant to be about the destruction and uprooting of one of the most socially and economically integrated of the Palestinian refugee communities in the Arab world, but about the potentialities of the shared memories engendered by the historical experience of different Palestinian individuals, families, and communities in Syria. It was also not meant to be about the ongoing devastation of that country, but about the realities of multiple and different belongings to both Syria and Palestine that resulted from the devastation wrought by the establishment of the state of Israel in 1948. With so much death and destruction, past and present, hovering over this book, it has become, above all, a tribute to the reality of Palestinian refugee life in Syria that no longer is.

All the individuals who believed in and allowed the research that forms the basis of this book have been devastatingly affected by the Syrian war, now in its seventh year. Some have been killed, kidnapped, or have disappeared; others have witnessed their own children being shot; some have passed away from pain and heartbreak, others' siblings have been taken away; and some have lost homes to shelling, others have had their houses looted. The overwhelming majority have been displaced from their homes, their families torn and scattered within Syria and beyond. Some are today in Lebanon, Jordan, Egypt, and Turkey, while others have been more fortunate to survive the perilous journey to Europe. Conditions under which research for this book was made possible by many of those to whom this book ultimately belongs no longer exist. These are the families, communities, activists, and institutions in Damascus who had faith in the importance of writing about memories of the Nakba. I am deeply indebted to all those individuals, most of whose names will appear repeatedly throughout the book, and I hope that this book will at a minimum document the Nakba of today by shedding light on what has been lost in Syria.

Others to whom I am also deeply grateful for sharing their time, contacts, acquaintance, often humor, and even friendship in Damascus include the late Adnan Abdul-Rahim, whose premature death has been an irreplaceable loss to all who knew him and his community at large, and Bassam Mahmud, Basim Sarhan, Bisan Ahmad, ʿIzz al-Din Barghuthi, Hiba al-Basir, Mahir Yusifi, Makram Hijazi, Mufida al-Masri, Omar Shanbur, Shams Barghuthi, and Wisam Ahmad. I am particularly thankful to the ʿAwad and the Hershawi families, who became my own families during those lonely days that accompany research. I also wish to extend special gratitude to Ahmad Nijm, who gave me access to his priceless personal library, and to the late Ghassan Shihabi of the Shajara Institute for Oral Memory, who gave me access to the institute's resources. Ghassan's life, which was brutally cut short, was dedicated to the institutionalization of memory for the future generations, and I hope this book will ensure that these same generations know of his efforts and the institute. I am also thankful to Abdul Fatah Idris and Hamza Barqawi at the General Union of Palestinian Writers and Journalists for facilitating my research, and to Raʾid Shakir at GAPAR for coordinating my access to GAPAR and my visitor status at UNRWA.

I am also thankful to my supervisor Ronit Lentin, examiners Andrew Finlay and Liz Stanley, and friends and colleagues in the department of sociology at Trinity College, University of Dublin. These include Antje Röder, David Landy, Elena Moreo, Jean Cushen, Kathryn Breda Feehan, and Jonathan Lacey.

Most of the book was written in Berlin, where I was a postdoctoral fellow at the ICI Berlin Institute for Cultural Inquiry. There, for two years I was fortunate to be part of a colloquium group where I could present key concepts and ideas at the heart of this book and take part in a range of readings, discussions, lectures, workshops, and conferences as I was refining my arguments. I am thankful to the colloquium group members who made this possible, including Aaron Schuster, Alice Gavin, Arnd Wedemeyer, Beau Madison Mount, Benjamin Dawson, Bobby Benedicto, Brigette Bargetz, Christoph Holzhey, Claudia Peppel, Daniel Colucciello Barber, David Kishik, Gal Kirn, Kit Heintzman, Luca Di Blasi, Manuele Gragnolati, Nahal Naficy, Robert Meunier, Sandrine Sanos, Stefano Osnaghi, Volker Voltersdorff, and Zeynep Bulut. Special thanks go to Corinna Haas and the rest of the library team for facilitating my research at the ICI.

Some people who took it upon themselves to read chapters of the book in different draft forms, and to whom I am grateful for their feedback, include Bobby Benedicto, Claudia Saba, Corinna Mullin, Elizabeth Suzanne Kassab, Nell Gabiam, Rosemary Sayigh, and Sonja Hegasy. They are not, of course, responsible for any of my arguments. Parts of this preface have previously appeared in "Decolonizing Research on Palestinians: Towards Critical Epistemologies and Research Practices," in *Qualitative Inquiry* 20, 1 (2014): 61–71, republished by permission of Sage Publications. Chapter 1 has previously appeared as "*Al-Nakbah* in Arab Thought: The Transformation of a Concept," in *Comparative Studies of South Asia, Africa and the Middle East* 35, 3 (2015): 622–638, republished by permission of Duke University Press. Parts of chapters 2 and 3 have previously appeared as "The Right of Return Movement in Syria: Building a Culture of Return, Mobilizing Memory for the Return," in *Journal of Palestine Studies* 41, 2 (2012): 62–79, republished by permission of the University of California Press.

This book would not have been possible without the financial assistance of a Trinity College Postgraduate Studentship, a Trinity College Continuing Student Award and a Trinity Trust Travel Award (2006–2010), a Palestinian American Research Center Doctoral Fellowship (2007–2008), and an ICI Berlin Institute for Cultural Inquiry Postdoctoral Fellowship (2011–2013). I am also grateful to the ICI for financial assistance toward organizing a workshop, "Memories of Palestine: The 1948 Nakba," and a podium discussion,

"What Future Now? The Palestinian Refugees and the Arab Uprisings," in March 2013 in Berlin, where I had the opportunity to present and benefit from feedback on parts of the book. Finally, a Palestinian American Research Center Sami 'Amer Travel Award allowed me to organize a conference panel, "The Palestinians in Syria: Their Past, Present and Changing Realities," at the Middle East Studies Association annual meeting in New Orleans and to lecture in different North American universities on memories of the Nakba in Syria as well as the Palestinian refugees in light of the Syrian war in October 2013. I am thankful to the audiences who engaged parts of the book that I presented at these different venues and universities, and to my hosts for inviting me. These include Pamela Waldron-Moore at Xavier University of Louisiana, Christophe Corley at Minnesota State University, Denise DeGarmo at Southern Illinois University, Beverly Guy-Sheftall and Erica Williams at Spelman College, Hibba Abugideiri at Villanova University, Craig Campbell at St. Edwards University, and Lisa Adeli at the University of Arizona.

A book is always the product of many more people and events than one can ever acknowledge. Some of these people are my family, Muhammad and Wisal, the primary source of inspiration for my search for memories of the Nakba and whose own *Children of the Dew* (1990) set me off on this journey in many more ways than they can ever imagine. And Malik, who patiently saw the research from beginning to end, spread over eight years and five different countries.

PALESTINIANS IN SYRIA

INTRODUCTION

THE CATASTROPHE OF 1948, THE CATASTROPHES OF TODAY

[The Nakba anniversary] last year was different. It was a day in which the refugees' fear was broken and a day in which they reclaimed their voice and image. What took place that day was legendary, it returned hope to millions of refugees and it returned joy to the camps.

"HILM 'AWDA" BY KHALID BAKRAWI (1988–2013), DIED UNDER TORTURE IN JAIL[1]

I love it [Yarmouk Camp] a lot. I love its details. I love living in it, I don't know why. I hope to never leave it, I hope to remaining living in it, I hope that my circumstances become better and I remain living in it. If I could produce only one play per year, and to stage it in the camp only, I'd have no problem. I would be content and happy, and no one will get to know me, I don't want to become famous or become anything. I only want to remain living in this place, and to be able to work in theater and to remain an ordinary person, not more than ordinary. I don't want to live in anything other than an ordinary situation, in this situation I would be very happy. These are my hopes.

INTERVIEW WITH HASSAN HASSAN (1984–2013), DIED UNDER TORTURE IN JAIL[2]

At the end of December 2012, with the full-fledged arrival of the war, a booby-trapped car exploded in Yarmouk Camp's Rejeh Square. A picture was posted in the aftermath of the explosion on Yarmouk Camp News, a Facebook page that provides on-the-ground coverage of events in Yarmouk. Although there were no human injuries or deaths, the picture showed the extensive damage in the square and the area that surrounds it, including the al-Samadi family's badly damaged home, part of which directly faces the square.

A few days later, a second picture of the bombed-out square was circulated on the same page. This time the picture was of al-Hajj Abu Samih, the eldest member of the al-Samadi family, standing with a cane outside his half-blown-out family home, looking straight into the camera, surrounded by the ruins of Rejeh Square. The caption attached to Abu Samih's photo on Facebook read:

> In Yarmouk Camp, an old man who remains put in his home, in his street, in his camp. The explosion destroyed parts of his home, his neighborhood and his square, but he refused to leave his home. Al-Hajj Abu Samih al-Samadi, who lived through Palestine's Nakba [catastrophe], and now refuses another Nakba that would come about through his departure from the camp.[3]

During my interview with Abu Samih some five years earlier, Abu Samih spoke to me about Palestine's Nakba. The Nakba, or catastrophe, is the Arabic word that Palestinians and Arabs more generally use to refer to the establishment of the state of Israel on Palestine in May 1948 and the resulting destruction and uprooting of the major part of Palestinian society (Abu-Lughod and Sa'di 2007). Born in Lubya, Tiberias subdistrict, Abu Samih was a young volunteer with Jaysh al-Jihad al-Muqadas (Holy War Army). This was a group of local irregular volunteers loyal to Muhammad Amin al-Husayni and operating in Palestine before the entry of the regular Arab armies in May 1948 (Pappe 1992, 65; 1997; 2006b, 85–108).[4] He was shot near Ma'lul and taken to a hospital in Nazareth, from there to a hospital in Beirut, and eventually to a third hospital in Damascus because of the overcrowding. Once he reached the border with Syria, he spent the last two piasters in his pocket on a newspaper. He was eventually reunited with some members of his family, now scattered throughout Palestine, Lebanon, and Syria, and remained in one of the mosques in Damascus that put up the refugees until he moved to Yarmouk in the 1950s. In Yarmouk, he would begin to rebuild his life from nothing, and it took him twenty years, he told me, to finally emerge from the total poverty that he and his family were thrust into as refugees. Abu Samih also had an extraordinary library (AM 2012), and given his age and role in 1948, he appeared on Al Jazeera Arabic's special series on the Nakba, "A Right That Refuses Forgetfulness," which the channel began to air in the run-up to the sixtieth anniversary of 1948.

Thus, in the course of five years and against the backdrop of the devastation caused by the war in Syria, the Nakba was transformed. From a catastrophe that engulfed the Palestinians in 1948, which Abu Samih witnessed and bore witness to on its sixtieth anniversary, the Nakba became another catastrophe that would be realized by Abu Samih leaving Yarmouk at the end of 2012. At the core of this understanding of the 1948 catastrophe is that the unresolved Nakba has resulted in yet more catastrophes, given the now seventy-year statelessness of the majority of Palestinians, the refugees. Within the context of Syria, this meaning of the Nakba reflects the drastic transformations that Palestinian communities in the country are undergoing after an uninterrupted four-generation socially and economically integrated presence.

Before the war in Syria, the establishment of the state of Israel, when understood through its Palestinian patriotic and Arab nationalist significations,[5] could be articulated as a catastrophic event whose impact on the new generations of Palestinian refugees was underscored by several factors. Most important of these are an ongoing statelessness, a political claim to historic Palestine, and diverse feelings of belonging. Today, these meanings of the Nakba have been transformed. The Nakba is no longer only about a distant event in the past that continues to manifest itself through an ongoing statelessness. It is also a catastrophe taking place in the present through the destruction of Palestinian communities yet again and the severance of their temporal, spatial, material, and personal ties in Syria. Thus, Abu Samih's Facebook caption—"another Nakba"—underscores the Palestinians' attachments to their homes, camps, and communities in Syria. The al-Samadi family, like most of the people of the camp, have since left Yarmouk, and their neighborhood, Harit al-Fida'iyye, has been extensively damaged by the fighting. The war has therefore not only drastically transformed the country, and with it the Palestinian refugee community, but also changed and continues to change the significations of the Nakba.

This book examines Nakba memories and histories of Palestinians in Syria. It explores how 1948-as-catastrophe was first conceptualized in Arab nationalist thought and transformed as a result of the rise and fall of the Palestinian liberation movement. It considers the ways in which Palestinian refugee right of return activists have rejected the 1993 Palestinian-Israeli Oslo Accords' institutionalization of the separation of Palestinian liberation from the return (Chomsky 1999, 533–565; R. Khalidi 1992).[6] It explores the politically expedient memory discourses and practices around the Nakba that they have as a result created in their communities. While these efforts have led to specific and pervasive significations of 1948, including the contemporary and singularly patriotic view that 1948 is important as "the Nakba," this book turns instead to the realm of memories to examine other possible meanings of 1948. It considers significations of the Nakba beyond its purportedly static and universally shared guise popularly furthered by activists and more broadly evident in Palestinian patriotic discourses.

Drawing on multigenerational interviews with Palestinian refugees in Syria, I demonstrate how the Nakba, despite its patriotic importance, is not the primary object of the narration and transmission of memories of loss in Palestinian refugee families. Rather, the Nakba's importance lies in the ways in which its resultant temporal and spatial referents gave way to shared memories and histories around which communities in Syria would eventually crystallize despite the devastation of Palestine. These communities coalesced through the Palestine generation's own shared memories and through the shared narratives on the Nakba of the "postgeneration[s]" (Hirsch 1997; 2012, 5)—what I refer to as the "post-Palestine generations"—their children and grandchildren. And herein lies the meaning of the Nakba in Syria today: the war's destruction of these communities, the scattering of Palestinians from Syria to all corners of the world, has resulted in a catastrophe that, unlike 1948, means that the devastation may now be final.

Rather than taking the contemporary meanings and significations of the Nakba at face value, I therefore provide a counterintuitive reading of the Nakba. I do this by approaching its pervasive significations in Palestinian refugee communities as the result of shifting historical, political, and material circumstances in the Arab world. The contention that the meanings associated with patriotic or nationalist signifiers of the past are subject to change, contestation, divergent meanings, and different articulations is, however, hardly a radical or novel proposition. This contention therefore needs to be understood in the context of the new and growing literature on the Nakba in English, which tends to take the Palestinian patriotic meanings of the 1948 Nakba at face value. This is the Nakba as the establishment of the state of Israel on Palestine in 1948 and the ongoing statelessness, expulsions, and destruction of communities or settler-colonization of the remnants of Palestinian society. Important as they are, these are nevertheless only some of the meanings of the 1948 Nakba. They are also relatively new.

I also take the argument beyond pervasive yet historically contingent and shifting meanings of signifiers of patriotic or nationalist events of the past.

I do this by examining the ways in which shared histories and memories in the shadow of the afterlives of such events, particularly traumatic, speak to the possibilities of communities arising from and despite the devastation of collective shattering and uprooting. I therefore consider both Palestine and the Nakba through memory studies. This is an area of research that has been heavily dominated by German and European history, with a marked insistence on European Jewish Holocaust exceptionalism that has only recently been reconsidered through the so-called "colonial turn" in Holocaust studies (see, e.g., Langbehn and Salama 2011; Zimmerer 2004). Memory studies has also largely ignored memories and histories of violence and atrocities inflicted in the course of European colonialism (R. Sayigh 2013). This raises important questions about this body of work's ideological blind spots and Eurocentrism that have led to these exclusions, including the exclusion of the ongoing ravages of Zionist settler-colonialism in Palestine and the Nakba (Abu-Lughod and Sa'di 2007).

Syria as a case study is central to the book's arguments on memories and histories of the Nakba. Syria was home to approximately 560,000 UN Relief and Works Agency for Palestine Refugees in the Near East (UNRWA)–registered Palestinian refugees on the eve of the war (UNRWA 2012d, 2013b).[7] Palestinians who arrived in Syria in 1948, and their descendants, have been the only Palestinians who maintained their refugee status while enjoying full civic rights (bar the right to nationality and the vote) and obliged to perform duties (military service) in an Arab state to which they fled in 1948.[8] Before the war in Syria, memories and histories of the 1948 Nakba were not produced under the immediate threat of war, settler-colonization, occupation, and multiple dispossessions. This has not been the case in other Palestinian communities, particularly those in Israel, the Occupied Palestinian Territories (West Bank and the Gaza Strip, OPT), and Lebanon. In Syria, Nakba memories and histories were, four generations later, produced and diffracted through the ability of Palestinians to therefore belong in different ways and to different communities. Although these communities shared the experience of the 1948 expulsion from Palestine, they also shared the reality of having been formed and rooted in Syria for several generations.

In an in memoriam for the young actor and director Hassan Hassan, whose words in the opening epigraph are now a haunting reminder of Palestinian refugee life in Syria that no longer is, an exiled activist from Yarmouk movingly articulated the reality of his now-shattered community in this way:

> Palestine, the land we all dream of, consisted of our passion [for] life, our
> shouts during the demonstrations on Land Day, our tendency to break the

usual in our poor context (the refugee camp), with the death of Hassan under torture in Assad prisons, with the death of Ahmad Kosa before him, with the death of Ghassan Shihabi before that, with all those lives lost, Palestine now is more irrelevant to me! Countries are made of people, lands are our illusions, I dream of the right of return with my beloved ones!

(Salameh 2013)

Thus, while Palestine is a dream, a passion, a cause, the aspiration of return to this Palestine is one rooted in Salameh's community in Syria, the now-dead friends and comrades with whom these ideals were shared. It is against the context of a Palestinian past shared with others whose families were expelled in 1948, a present that was unique to those whose families happened to cross into Syria in 1948, and the different belongings and realities of communities that this made possible in Syria that this book unfolds. In it I examine the Nakba's shifting nationalist and patriotic significations, its rearticulation and mobilization by right of return activists in Syria, and the different possibilities its memories and histories have engendered among the Palestine and post-Palestine generations.

In the remainder of this introduction, I briefly sketch the history of the Nakba's contemporary nationalist and patriotic meanings and significations, the changing realities of the Palestinians in Syria in light of the war, and some of the main concepts that I deploy from an engagement with memory studies.

THE NAKBA

May 15, 2011, marked the sixty-third anniversary of the Nakba and coincided with the uprisings that had engulfed the Arab world following the revolutions first in Tunisia and later Egypt in January and February 2011 respectively. By May of that year, demonstrations and popular unrest had spread, to varying degrees and with different consequences, to Algeria, Bahrain, Iraq, Jordan, Libya, Morocco, Oman, Saudi Arabia, Sudan, Syria, and Yemen. This is more than half of the twenty-two League of Arab States members at the time.

Inspired by these unprecedented regional developments, Palestinian refugee youths planned marches of return to coincide with the sixty-third anniversary of the Nakba. The organizers envisioned these as a series of peaceful and coordinated "one-million-man" marches to historic Palestine. Through these marches, Palestinian refugees in Israel, the OPT, Syria, Lebanon, and

Jordan would exercise their right to return to their families' homes and lands in what is today the state of Israel (Fayyad 2011).

The idea of return as inherent to liberation has historically been a central, though now all but abandoned, component of the Palestinian national liberation movement. It was not historically discussed in terms of rights, but was seen as inherent to Palestinian liberation (R. Khalidi 1992). Today, the (right of) return continues to be important in Palestinian refugee communities and in direct contestation of the moribund statist project of the Oslo Accords. These Accords relegated return, and thus the refugees' hopes and aspirations, to "final status" negotiations. Given the implications of the Oslo Accords for the return, community activists invoke it as a right by using the language of human rights and international humanitarian law, especially UN General Assembly (UNGA) Resolution 194. This resolution enshrined the Palestinians' right to return to their homes and lands in the wake of the establishment of the state of Israel (UNGA 1948). They therefore invoke human rights in order to contest the way in which the return has been consistently blocked by Israel in contravention of international humanitarian law and as part of its denial of responsibility for the expulsion and destruction of Palestinian society during the Nakba (Masalha 1992, 1997, 2003).

In the end, the marches were not the marches of millions the organizers had envisioned. Nevertheless, Palestinian and Syrian youths, their access to the border area facilitated by the authorities (Bitari 2013), made a dramatic crossing into the Israeli-occupied Syrian town of Majdal Shams on the Israeli-occupied side of the Syrian Golan Heights. The march was captured on film from the Majdal Shams side, with the sound of live Israeli fire in the background (Abunimah 2011b). The footage begins with frantic warnings by the people of Majdal Shams, who plead with the advancing line of Palestinian and Syrian flag-waving youths to stop because of the danger of land mines. Undeterred, the youths continue to advance as they chant, "The people want to liberate Palestine," a play on the Arab uprisings' chant "The people want to bring down the regime." A few minutes later, we see the first youth cross into Majdal Shams, with the sounds of bullets ringing in the background. He runs up to one of the men awaiting him and is embraced and congratulated. When asked what he would like to tell his people in the Golan, the young man ecstatically exclaims: "God protect them! And we want to return to Palestine! We want to return to Palestine!" He is followed by other youths, who are also given a hero's welcome. "Yes, this is how liberation looks like," says one man from behind the camera.

This historic March of Return, which the late community activist Khalid Bakrawi eloquently wrote about, as quoted in the opening epigraph, encapsulates the three main concerns of this book. These are the Nakba, Palestinians in Syria, and memories and histories. In regard to the Nakba, the march highlights its memories and histories ongoing significance in Palestinian refugee communities, as well as their entanglement with political claims and visions of Palestinian liberation and return that refuse the separation of the two. The youths' enactment of a symbolic march of return to a concrete physical space is intelligible only within the context of the records and recollections of a forced expulsion from that space in 1948. This is because this space is for Palestinian refugees historic Palestine, or what is today the state of Israel, the object of their political claims. The march was therefore also a clear demand for acknowledgment and restitution by Israel and its powerful backers, especially the United States and the European Union, for the Nakba. It also underscored the nature of the political claims attached to the Nakba and its memories and histories. These revolve around the consequences of the forced expulsion of 1948 as ongoing, given that Palestine continues to be under Israeli occupation and that the right of return of refugees expelled in 1948 and their descendants remains to be implemented.

Given the meanings associated with 1948 demonstrated through the March of Return, the question arises, how and why have these significations of the Nakba come about? Some have retrospectively argued that denoting 1948 as a catastrophe has reduced the event to a natural disaster or calamity, obscuring questions of political will, agency, and responsibility (H. Khader 1998; Khoury 2012).[9] A more comprehensive understanding of 1948 as a *nakba*, however, comes from placing the concept in its "universe of discourse" (Foucault 1991, 2005; Said 2003, 273). This universe of discourse can be traced to the first two decades after 1948, when various authors theorized the Nakba within the context of the ascendant Arab nationalist liberation project and its related modernization discourses.

In August 1948, while the war on Palestinians was still ongoing, the Damascus-born educator, historian, and nationalist theorist Constantine Zurayk was the first to describe the outcome of the war as a catastrophe in his 1948 *Maʿna al-Nakba* (The meaning of the catastrophe) (al-ʿAzma 2003). For Zurayk, what transpired in Palestine was catastrophic because of the defeat of the combined might of the Arab armies that had entered Palestine in May 1948. It was also catastrophic because of the mass dispossession of the inhabitants of Palestine at the hands of the Haganah, the prestate Zionist fighting force and nucleus of what would become the Israeli army (Rogan and Shlaim 2007). This early conceptualization of the 1948 war on the Palestinians as a *nakba* was made in relation to the catastrophe that it posed to the project of pan-Arab unity, liberation, and decolonization, given that Palestine was part of the envisioned Arab nation ('Abd al-Da'im 1998). Although Zurayk's conception of 1948-as-catastrophe does indeed encompass the dispossession of the inhabitants of Palestine, this was not Zurayk's primary concern, for it was only part of what made the establishment of the state of Israel on Palestine a catastrophe.

These were the discursive dimensions within which the 1948 war-as-catastrophe was first conceptualized and articulated, not only in 1948 but also in the first two decades of its aftermath, when the pan-Arab nationalist project of liberation was at its peak. In these decades, the Arab, rather than Palestinian, Nakba came to be associated with a definite rupture with the old Arab order left behind by French and British colonial rule that had made the catastrophe possible in the first place (al-Tal 1959). The Arab Nakba was also associated with the promise of a new dawn to be brought about by the military coups and emergent ideological currents and movements of the time (Talhami 1998).

What this meant in practice was that ideas about the 1948 catastrophe became entangled in the militarism institutionalized in the 1950s and 1960s (Gerges 2007; al-Jabiri 1982). This was primarily the case as a result of the Egyptian July Revolution of 1952 and the emergence of Gamal Abdel Nasser as a powerful contender for regional leadership (Kerr 1971). Within this context, Nasser, who had been a major (*sagh*) in the Egyptian army in Palestine during the 1948 war (al-Tal 1959, 434–435), argued in his 1954 *Falsafat al-Thawra* (The revolution's philosophy) that the Nakba was not the cause of the July Revolution. Rather, the Nakba was catastrophic to the political realization of the Arab nation, and thus it was within the political sphere of the revolution.

Even during early Palestinian organizing in the wake of 1948—especially under the banner of pan-Arab groups such as the Arab Nationalists Movement (ANM) and the Ba'th Party—the question of the Nakba remained an Arab question and was articulated as such (Y. Sayigh 1991b; al-Sharif 1995, 48–56).[10] Only with the emergence of Fatah would Palestinians finally come to organize under a specifically Palestinian banner and articulate visions of liberation and the resolution of the Nakba within an exclusively Palestinian framework.[11] In an impressive study of Palestinian political thought, the historian Mahir al-Sharif (1995, 88–89) argues that what in fact distinguished Fatah was its "assertion that the making of the Nakba and its ongoing nature, were, to a great extent, the result of the distancing of the Palestinians from their cause, and its call to the Palestinians to take over their cause once again."

Thus, for the first two decades following the Nakba, the intellectual and political trajectory of 1948-as-catastrophe would take center stage in terms of its pan-Arab dimensions. The 1967 June War, however, transformed this meaning of the Nakba.[12] Initially, in the immediate years following 1967, a new wave of critical works addressed the new defeat primarily as being yet another catastrophe or disaster, one in a direct continuity with the first, and as having the same root causes (al-Azm 1968; al-Bitar 1968; Zurayk [1967] 2001). Indeed, Nasser himself would deem the new defeat a *naksa*, or "setback," to the project of pan-Arab unity, liberation, and decolonization (Abu-Lughud 1972). Eventually, thinking about the new defeat would come to subsume and eclipse the Nakba of 1948.

This preoccupation with the 1948 Nakba, even if only as part of the new defeat, would eventually conspicuously disappear from the post-1967 literature altogether. All eyes were now on the so-called "Palestinian Revolution" (see, e.g., 'Abd al-Da'im 1970; al-Khatib 1971; Sayf al-Dawla 1970; Tu'ma 1969). This revolution, or increased Palestinian political and paramilitary organization, took off after the Palestinian takeover of the Palestine Liberation Organization (PLO) during a process that culminated in the election of Yasser Arafat as PLO chairman in 1969 (Y. Sayigh 1992, 264). The revolution was now the site where the emergent Palestinian guerrillas were actively operating and determining how the liberation of Palestine and the return were to unfold. Later still, the resolution of the Nakba through liberation and return would itself take secondary place, with the guerrillas shifting their focus to effect reversal of Israeli gains made in 1967 (Y. Sayigh 2004).

The eventual "reemergence" of the Nakba in the 1980s as a Palestinian rather than an Arab catastrophe allowed it to take on a radically altered meaning, form, and content, one that we are more familiar with today. That the Nakba "disappeared" and "reemerged" refers to the disappearance of its Arab universe of discourse and the latter's eclipse by another one that resulted from the failure of the Palestinian national movement to deliver on both liberation and return. The Nakba, of course, did not disappear nor reemerge for those who lived through and survived 1948, nor has it done so for those who have grown up in the shadow of its memories and the material realities of its aftermath.

The emergence of this Palestinian Nakba was made possible primarily through a renewed interest in the Palestinian past by Palestinians. It took place when the PLO's decade in Lebanon was ending and the organization was subsequently evacuated to Tunis (R. Sayigh 2008b). It also came about as a result of Palestinians' own attempt to revive memories of their villages, towns, and ways of life in the Palestine that the Nakba had destroyed (Abdel Jawad 2007; Abu-Lughod and Sa'di 2007; Farah 2006). This turn to memories of historic Palestine was accelerated further by the Oslo Accords, which posed a threat to the refugees' right of return to their homes and lands. In view of this context, this turn led to a particular emphasis on Nakba memories, especially in refugee communities and the generation of Palestine, the sole remaining witnesses to the 1948 catastrophe. This generation's memories were now seen to be able to lead to the eventual reclamation of Palestine (Hammami 2010; Hill 2005).

In Syria, this focus took place largely as a result of what came to be known as the Right of Return Movement (RoRM) (Al-Hardan 2012a; Suleiman 2004). The RoRM emerged as a response to the Oslo Accords and as an attempt to undermine the agenda of the PLO and the Oslo-created Palestinian Authority (PA) in the OPT. Its focus was especially on the question of the legitimate representation of the refugees, and with that, the PLO's and PA's ability to forfeit the right of return in negotiations. Oslo, among many other things, completely excluded the refugees from the Palestinian decision-making process by giving birth to the PA in the OPT (Suleiman 2001). Insofar as the refugees are concerned, the PLO all but signed away their right of return through its abandonment of a coherent national liberation project encompassing all Palestinians. It did this by engaging in two decades of futile negotiations with Israel over "final status" issues (i.e., borders, the status of Jerusalem, and the right of return) (Swisher 2011). These negotiations merely provided a cover for increased Israeli settler-colonization of the OPT and never resulted in a Palestinian state (see, e.g., R. Khalidi 2006, 2013).

On the local level, activists began to mobilize memories associated with historic Palestine and the Nakba as resources for collective action (McAdam, McCarthy, and Zald 1996; McCarthy and Zald 1977). This particular mobilization led to the emergence of contemporary as well as popular memory discourses on the Nakba in Palestinian communities in general (Masalha 2008; R. Sayigh 2008b). Central to these discourses are notions that memory itself is a guarantor of a future return to Palestine and that the Nakba is ongoing, given the lack of its resolution. At the heart of these discourses is, therefore, a memory/return matrix as well as particular patriotic understanding of the Nakba as central to Palestinian political claims and identity. It is in and through community activists' mobilization of memories as resources and their commemorative efforts that the articulation and rearticulation of the Nakba is taking place today.

Thus, the different significations associated with the Nakba since its occurrence have resulted from shifting historical and political conditions and the response of Palestinians to these circumstances. The most important of these changes have arguably been the twentieth-century defeats of the pan-Arab nationalist liberation project and the Palestinian liberation movement. First, as noted, the Nakba was articulated as a catastrophe for Arab liberation; and later, as a catastrophe within the context of Palestinian liberation. In addition, whereas the Palestinian liberation movement once saw return as inherent to liberation, today Palestinian refugee activists have responded to the movement's abandonment of both liberation and return by tying the imperative to remember with the right of return and thus the eventual liberation. As a result, the idea of memory has come to have high political currency in Palestinian refugee communities.

Returning to the March of Return, which began this brief sketch of the Nakba, I next examine what it can tell us about the Nakba in relation to these Palestinian communities in Syria.

THE PALESTINIAN REFUGEE COMMUNITY IN SYRIA

The day after the historic march of May 2011, yet another dramatic act of return was captured on film. Hasan Hijazi, a young Palestinian refugee from Syria, traveled from Majdal Shams to Jaffa, his family's hometown. While in Jaffa, he gave an interview on Israeli television and defiantly made his symbolic act of return public before he was deported (Abunimah 2011c). In the interview, Hijazi tells the interviewer that it was his dream to come to Jaffa because "it is my town." He asserts that he was not scared of the elite Israeli Golani Brigade soldiers sitting next to him on the bus that brought him to Jaffa and that he does not recognize the state of Israel even though he is aware that he is making his declarations from the heart of the state. When the interviewer asked him whether he considers the march a victory against the state or merely a symbolic act, Hijazi tells the interviewer that it is merely symbolic because real victories come through armies.

Hijazi's interview demonstrates the power of memories and histories of the Nakba for individual Palestinian refugees (Sanbar 2001). Despite his birth in Syria, Hijazi made a claim to the town of his family's memories. Although he had never seen Jaffa in his lifetime as a refugee, his was nonetheless a return to a town that he had in many ways already seen and known, if only as a family memory, as the town of his grandparents. He had in fact known it enough to dream about returning to it, as he told the interviewer, and to declare Jaffa his town. His return to his grandparents' Jaffa was as much anchored in the narration and transmission of family memories as it was in his and his community's uprooted histories; it was ultimately a return to a town from where his family had been expelled three generations earlier. Through his declarations, Hijazi drew a clear connection between his memories, history, and political claims and aspirations, as encapsulated in a single town, Jaffa, the site of his imaginative and political attachments.

Although Hijazi's symbolic return and television interview may have been extraordinary acts during a regionally extraordinary zeitgeist, his memory claims are not uncommon among the post-Palestine generations. This is because his memory claims are ultimately articulated against the Nakba's shifting meanings and pervasive significations. Beyond this, what can Hijazi's imaginative and political attachments tell us about histories and memories in the shadow of the afterlife of the Nakba and the possibilities of communities arising from and despite its collective devastation? To begin with, though Hijazi took part in a march on the sixty-third anniversary of the Nakba, the object of his memory claims is clearly Jaffa, not the Nakba. The occasion of the Nakba anniversary is indeed the reason for the march and Hijazi does make all the necessary nods to its patriotic significations in his interview. For example, he refuses to cede legitimacy to Israeli settler-colonization of Jaffa and his family's expulsion from historic Palestine. The Nakba is, however, subsumed within the object of Hijazi's imaginative and political attachments, his family's hometown. He does not conjure up memories of 1948 and his memory claims do not simply reproduce the central place of the Nakba in the post-1993 memory discourses. Rather, his memory claims speak to the ways in which refugee families narrate and transmit their memories of the loss that resulted from the Nakba. In this narration and transmission, it is the object of loss, or families' lives, worlds, and very social existence, that is the object of memories, the Jaffa of Hijazi's family, and not the Nakba per se.

Closely related to this is the communal claim encapsulated in Hijazi's return to Jaffa. His return speaks to the Palestinian communities that once existed in the Jaffa that he dreamed of seeing and to the possibilities of communities of Jaffans that inform his memory claims despite their destruction in Palestine in 1948. These are communities that Hijazi and other refugees born in Syria have encountered through their symbolic contours, their memories. The existence of these communities itself embodies meanings of the Nakba that may at times overlap, sometimes contradict, or even contest the meanings associated with 1948 as a patriotic signifier.

Thus, in addition to the concept of memory, the concept of community is also central to the arguments of this book. Community is a multifaceted concept having different connotations in different disciplines, though it could be broadly characterized to be about notions of belonging. Generally, sociologists associate community with groups' social organizations and relations based on a locality, and anthropologists in recent years have argued for community as a form of cultural belonging, meaning-making, and identity. Political scientists emphasize community in relation to political participation in its different forms, whereas in philosophy, community is an idea and even an ideal, whether as utopia or ideology (Delanty 2010, xi). In a comprehensive interdisciplinary study of the concept of community, the sociologist Gerard Delanty (2010) synthesizes these different approaches and argues that community is an ideal as much as it is also real. This is because "community has a transcendent nature and cannot simply be equated with particular groups or a place. Nor can it be reduced to an idea, for ideas do not simply exist outside social relations, socially-structured discourses or a historical milieu" (Delanty 2010, xii).

In this book, the notion of community appears in two specific ways that I contend are also complementary and not necessarily mutually exclusive. First, community is used to explore the Palestinians' social, historical, and political experiences in Syria. Here, the emphasis is on community as specific modes of social organization and their resultant forms of belonging and imagination of social relations (Delanty 2010, 35). Thus, I approach the Palestinians in Syria as constituting a politically, nationally, and legally defined and constructed community. I demonstrate the ways in which this definition, demarcation, and construction historically took place through the bureaucratic practices of the Syrian state, UNRWA, and the reemergence of the Palestinian liberation movement after 1948. This community as case study is important because of its unique context and because to date no full-length academic Arabic- or English-language monograph examines its experiences.[13]

When discussing the Palestinians in Syria as a community, however, I imply neither that they are homogenous nor that there is one overarching community. They therefore also constitute heterogeneous communities shaped by myriad factors, including different origins in Palestine, places of abode in Syria, and economic class, among other factors. In addition, like other Palestinian refugee communities in the Arab world, Palestinians in Syria have been and continue to be shaped by the general post-1948 Palestinian experiences of statelessness and the trials of the Palestinian liberation movement. Their unique Syrian context, however, has historically set them apart as a community. This is because it has been relatively stable over the past six decades and Palestinians in Syria have enjoyed rights shared by no other disenfranchised Palestinian refugee community in the Arab world. To speak of Palestinians in Syria as constituting a community is also, therefore, to speak of heterogeneous local communities with a unique overarching historical experience as well as a connection to transnational Palestinian refugee communities.

Before the war and the suspension of all normal life in Syria, the Syrian state's relationship to its Palestinian refugee community, it has been argued, paved the way for the gradual socioeconomic integration of Palestinians into Syrian society. This took place as Palestinians were allowed to maintain a separate national identity (Brand 1988c, 621). Others have argued that Palestinians in Syria lie somewhere between an established diaspora and a transit refugee community (Hanafi 2003). The former can be characterized by communities descending from late Ottoman immigrants in the Americas, while the latter can be characterized by communities of Palestinian refugees in Lebanon, with their institutionalized temporariness and insecurity. More recently, the notion that Palestinians constitute a diaspora has itself been problematized (Peteet 2007). This is because of Palestinian refugees' closeness to historic Palestine and their former homes, the immediacy and ongoing nature of their displacement, the potential depoliticization of the term "diaspora" in relation to the right of return, and the question of identity (some Palestinian refugees rejecting diaspora as ideological invocation, resistance to displacement, etc.).

With these debates about the overall nature of the community in Syria in mind, I also use the notion of community in a second, complementary way. This allows me to explore the RoRM activists' political mobilization efforts as enabling the realization of community. In addition, it allows me to consider the generation of Palestine's shared memories and the post-Palestine generations' shared Nakba narratives as circulating in their communities. Here, the emphasis is therefore on community understood in its practice, symbolic, and communicative aspects (Delanty 2010, 102). The symbolic contours of these communities are found in their members' shared memories and histories of an expulsion from Palestine. Their realities are communicated through a shared history and refugee experience in Syria and are also constructed through activists' efforts to redress their communities' ongoing statelessness.

The different aspects of community used in this book move beyond an examination of the Nakba in Arab nationalist, Palestinian patriotic, and popular memory discourses. They allow for an understanding of the circulation of 1948's meanings in and through community members' memories and histories. These memories are constructed around the Nakba's shared yet uprooted and fractured temporal and spatial referents. As such, they embody the possibility of communities despite the devastation wrought by the establishment of Israel. This meaning of the Nakba today and the different memories of 1948 realized through community at times coexist, sometimes compete, and at other times challenge Arab and Palestinian significations of 1948.

Syria as a country is a defining factor for its Palestinian refugee community, regardless of how the latter is theorized. Palestinians made up less than 3 percent of the multireligious and multiethnic population in Syria prior to 2011. They have historically formed an important pillar of the regime's official Ba'thist Arab nationalist ideology that far exceeds the size of their community. Given this ideological connection, the regime's treatment of the Palestinian refugees in the country has provided important political capital, even though before the Ba'thists came to power the Palestinians had been granted the rights setting them apart from other Palestinian refugees (GAPAR n/a; Hinnebusch 2002). This historical and political reality arguably allowed for Palestinians' particular relationship to and sense of belonging in Syria. This is despite the fact of the Syrian Ba'thist regime's instrumentalization of the Palestine question while allowing for sieges of Palestinian camps and communities in neighboring Lebanon during that country's civil war. The treatment of the Palestinian refugees in the country notwithstanding, the Syrian regime has also had a historically turbulent relationship with the PLO (Brand 1990; R. Khalidi 1984; Talhami 2001).

This history alongside the current Syrian war also means that the Palestinians' relationship to the Syrian state and its current regime is today undergoing unprecedented transformations. The regime's current struggle for survival has not spared Palestinians from the death and destruction that have engulfed the country. It could be argued that the ways in which this refugee community was violently thrust into the war, alongside virtually all of Syria's diverse communities, came as no surprise precisely because of the Palestinians' full-fledged social and economic integration in the country ('Aziza 2012; Munawwar 2012). The long-term impact of the current war, the deteriorating humanitarian and political situation, and the uprooting, bombardment, and starvation of Palestinians in Syria is difficult to assess as it is ongoing. What is certain is that the communities of which I write, and whose memories I explore, are part of a Syria that has now ceased to exist.

Thus, the Syrian war has had a dramatic impact on the entire country, not just the Palestinians. The March of Return, having taken place only three months after the beginning of the Syrian uprising, could only take place on the Syrian side of the Israeli-occupied Golan Heights as a result of the regime's nod of approval (Bitari 2013). The youths' own political agency notwithstanding, the march may have been used by the regime to divert attention from the events beginning to engulf Syria. It may have also been a warning to Israel, and its American and European backers, of what could come should the regime fall (Shadid 2011).[14]

The Palestinians, however, had become embroiled in the uprising as soon as it began. Newspaper reports circulated in which Palestinians were accused of instigating the "rioting" in Dar'a, the town where the uprising started through demonstrations, as early as March 2011. A senior government official pointed the finger of blame at Palestinians yet again for the early "riots" in Latakia (Al-Hardan 2012b). Wisam al-Ghul, a Palestinian man from Dera'a Camp, became the first Palestinian "martyr" of the uprising on March 23, 2011, after he was killed while trying to provide aid to the demonstrators ('Aziza 2012; Bitari 2012; Hamoud 2012). Palestinians also became embroiled in the uprising from the very beginning because they lived in Syrian neighborhoods and Palestinian camps that would become battlegrounds for the Syrian army and different armed groups known as the Free Syrian Army (FSA). They also provided relief and sheltered internally displaced Syrians from nearby war-stricken neighborhoods ('Aziza 2012; Hamoud 2012).

Thus, the small Palestinian communities in Dar'a, Homs, Hama, and Latakia in particular had long been affected by the uprising. It was only toward late 2011 and 2012 with its militarization in the Rural Damascus Governorate, where four-fifths of the Palestinians in Syria lived, did the uprising begin to have ramifications for the major part of the community (Bitari 2013). Within this context, the spillover of the fighting into Yarmouk in midsummer of 2012 was both relatively late compared to other parts of the country and particularly important, given the centrality of Yarmouk and its surrounding areas to Palestinian refugee life in Syria. This happened when mortar shells fell on the camp during the fighting that raged between the FSA and the regular army in the areas that surround Yarmouk (Nayel 2013; UNRWA 2012e; Zarzar 2012a), with deadly and devastating consequences (UNRWA 2012a; Williams 2012). Partisans have been keen to portray the Palestinians in Syria as supporting one side or the other. However, to make claims about more than half a million people on the basis of the actions of individuals who may have indeed supported the uprising, especially in its early days, is implausible. Similarly, to argue that the Palestinians' proregime stance, especially after the uprising turned into an all-out war that devastated their communities, can be inferred based on the actions of some of their factions, which were hardly representative to begin with, is equally untenable.

Insofar as these factions are concerned, initially, with the exception of the Syrian regime–aligned Popular Front for the Liberation of Palestine–General Command (PFLP-GC), all maintained strict silence on the question of the Syrian uprising. Hamas broke off with the Syrian regime by leaving

Damascus, which became public at the end of 2011 (Napolitano 2013), and the PFLP-GC began arming committees to fight the FSA in Yarmouk (Bitari 2013; Hamoud 2012). The Palestinian factions did not, however, actively recruit Palestinians on a mass scale to join one side or the other prior to the air bombardment of Yarmouk at the end of 2012 and the exodus of its people ('Aziza 2012; Bitari 2013).

The arming of so-called "Popular Committees" by the PFLP-GC to battle the FSA in Yarmouk accelerated the increasing militarization of that camp and it led to lawlessness, theft of private property, kidnappings, anarchy, and insecurity (AFP 2012; UN 2012; UNRWA 2012c). Battles raged in neighborhoods directly adjacent to Yarmouk, including al-Hajar al-Aswad, al-Tadamun, al-Taqadum and al-'Uruba. On December 16, 2012, a Syrian fighter jet bombarded a mosque in the middle of Yarmouk, leaving dead a number of people who had been sheltering there (UNRWA 2012b, 2012h; Zarzar 2012b). This air bombardment marked the beginning of an exodus from the camp, the defeat of the Popular Committees, and the takeover of the camp by the FSA. The FSA ransacked private homes and vehicles and looted private properties and UNRWA facilities (UNRWA 2012f, 2012g, 2013c).

It is within the context of the full-scale arrival of the war to Yarmouk that the booby-trapped car exploded in Rejeh Square in January 2013. The situation in Yarmouk during the past five years has drastically deteriorated, with armed groups holed up inside and the army and its Palestinian allies enforcing a siege on the camp. In addition to the transformation of the camp into a devastated war zone and the four-year lack of electricity, water was also cut off toward the end of 2014 despite the then approximately 18,000 remaining residents in Yarmouk (AGPS 2015). Parts of the camp were destroyed beyond recognition, a siege economy flourished, starvation cases were reported, and snipers enforced a shoot-to-kill policy. The appearance of Islamic State of Iraq and Syria (ISIS) fighters within the vicinity of the camp in April 2015 led to most remaining residents moving to surrounding areas. According to relief workers with access to the environs of the camp, an estimated 2,000–4,000 people remained in Yarmouk in the wake of ISIS. The camp was subjected to inter–armed group fighting and barrel bombing from government forces (AI 2015). As of this writing in May 2018, the army has begun a concerted aerial and ground offensive against the camp in a bid to drive out ISIS and an estimated twenty people have been buried underneath the rubble of their homes with no rescue teams on the ground to pull out survivors. A deal has now been reached between government forces and some armed groups in the vicinity of Yarmouk that has led to the evacuation of fighters and their families to the north of Syria (AGPS 2018).

Before the pivotal air bombardment in 2012, Yarmouk and its inseparable Rural Damascus Governorate environs had an estimated population of one million people. Of this population, only 150,000 were UNRWA-registered Palestinian refugees (UNRWA 2012a, n/a-b). As the Syrian uprising became increasingly militarized, the estimated population of Yarmouk increased with the arrival of internally displaced Syrian families seeking shelter from the surrounding war-stricken areas and beyond. According to UNRWA, approximately 31,000 Palestinians who had been in Syria are in Lebanon today, having entered before the Lebanese state barred their entry. Another 16,000 are in Jordan, where entry for Palestinians was barred even earlier than in Lebanon and where some have resided in two different camps in the north. An estimated 4,000–6,000 Palestinians went to Egypt, where those attempting to board illegal boats to Europe were reported to have been shot, killed, or imprisoned (AGPS 2018; 'Ayid 2012; HRW 2012, 2013; al-Jammal 2012; UNRWA 2015; UNRWA 2018).

The Action Group for Palestinians of Syria (AGPS 2018) estimates that as of the end of April 2018, approximately 85,000 Palestinians had made their way to Europe.[15] This figure reflects the increasing number of Palestinians from Syria who are left with no exit options from the war except through the precarious journeys on the so-called "death boats" from Turkey, Egypt and Libya to Europe, sometimes with tragic consequences. The first most highly publicized death boat incident saw Italian coast guard officers turn a blind eye as a boat carrying up to 500 refugees, including children, was left to sink off the coast of Lampedusa in October 2013 (Gatti 2013). Numerous boats carrying Palestinian refugees from Syria, as well as other migrants— one boat carrying even higher numbers than the refugee boat that sank in October 2013—have since sunk in the Mediterranean.

Given the demographic distribution of the Palestinians in Syria, the entire community has been drastically affected by the war. In addition to the siege and current assault on Yarmouk, others continue to live in neighborhoods that have become war zones and in camps that have become "theaters of war" (UNRWA 2013a, 2013c, 2013d). In view of these war realities, UNRWA estimates that as of the end of March 2015, 95 percent of Palestinians in Syria were in need of humanitarian assistance, at least half having been internally displaced at least once and more than a tenth having been externally displaced (UNRWA 2015, 2018).

In terms of the UNRWA camps, AGPS (2018) estimates that at least 70 percent of Dera'a Camp is in ruins; it also continues to be inaccessible to UNRWA (2018). Latakia Camp was in the eye of the storm as early as August 2011, though as of this writing it is calm (Hamoud 2012).[16] The war had long reached the camps in Homs and Hama, given the fierce battles that took place between the army and the armed groups, especially in the former town, though as of this writing both camps are relatively calm and accessible to UNRWA. The war also reached the two camps in Aleppo: armed groups expelled Ein el-Tal's residents in April 2013, and the camp, although under the government's control today, remains inaccessible, whereas Neirab remains accessible to UNRWA and is relatively calm. Several of the camps in the Rural Damascus Governorate, including Sbeineh and Qabr Essit, were depopulated as a result of fighting. Residents have been allowed to gradually return since the government retook control of the camps following fierce battles in their vicinities. Khan Eshieh is inaccessible to UNRWA and continues to be severely affected by intense clashes in its vicinity as well as the presence of armed groups within it. The war has also severely affected Khan Danoun and Jaramana, given their proximity to war zones and their hosting of internally displaced people, even though they remain relatively calm and accessible to UNRWA (UNRWA 2013b, 2015, 2018).

Finally, according to the AGPS, as of May 2018, there were approximately 4,000 deaths. More than half of these deaths took place in Damascus and the Rural Damascus Governorates. Approximately 200 resulted from the now almost four-year siege that has led to starvation, inadequate medical care, and spread of disease in Yarmouk. As of this writing, approximately 1,700 Palestinians are imprisoned and 300 are missing (AGPS 2015, 2018).[17]

This brief sketch of the impact of the war on the Palestinians in Syria demonstrates how their fate is today tied to the fate of the country as a whole. What continues to distinguish their experience from that of their Syrian counterparts, however, is their immobility. Palestinians carry refugee travel documents and face restrictions on entering all Arab states. This leaves them with nowhere to legally seek a second refuge. Their only exit options are therefore to either flee to appalling conditions in neighboring states or make precarious journeys to Europe. Syria's future and that of all its communities remains uncertain, given the country's full-fledged and prolonged descent into the abyss of war.

NARRATIVE, MEMORY, HISTORY

It has been argued that "the past is constituted in narrative, always representation, always construction" (Hodgkin and Radstone 2003, 2). The area of narrative research is vast, with no agreed-on definition of what constitutes narrative. It has also been argued that the overlapping and at times contradictory meanings of narrative and narrative research stem from the diverse historical antecedents of narrative inquiry. As a result of these antecedents and the so-called "three waves" of narrative research, one of the main fault lines in narrative inquiry is between those who use narrative as a method and those who use narrative as on object of analysis (Andrews, Squire, and Tamboukou 2013; Georgakopoulou 2006; Tamboukou, Squire, and Andrews 2013). In this book, narrative is used methodologically. The Palestinians' past and present in Syria are explored through narratives and stories collected in Syria's Palestinian refugee community. These were related as activists shared the visions, goals, and aspirations that drive their Nakba commemorative and memorial activities and community members narrated how they remember or understand the Nakba.

Narrative is therefore a means of exploring how right of return activists use the idea of memory to further political objectives through what I refer to as "memory discourses." These are the post-1993 Oslo discourses, briefly outlined earlier, that activists have created through contesting the PLO's and the PA's policies on liberation and return. These memory discourses are thus also Palestinian patriotic discourses. Narrative is also a means through which to explore the different social articulations of memories by Palestinians in Syria. Here, it is only the generation of Palestine that is understood as narrating memories through "memory narratives" that are based on memory in its strictly referential sense. These memory narratives, which I refer to simply as "memories," drive the intergenerational narration and transmission of memories of loss, imagined as "postmemories" by the children and grandchildren of the Nakba.

Postmemories are memories that are not referential but are nevertheless imagined as one's own (Hirsch 1997, 2012). Whatever so-called memories of the Nakba second- and third-generation Palestinian refugees articulate are therefore better understood as narratives. These narratives incorporate the generation of Palestine's memories as well as the idea of a coherent and singular Nakba memory found in activists' memory discourses and Palestinian patriotic discourses more broadly. Thus, as these are not memories in a referential sense but narratives on the idea of memory, I refer to them as "narratives on (Nakba) memory."

This methodological approach enables moving from a conceptual and analytic examination of the Nakba in intellectual discourses and mobilization practices to its different meanings in memories and narratives. The emphasis is therefore not on the "authenticity" of these memories, but on the social processes inherent in remembering, the ways in which these processes occur, and what these processes tell us about the present. Moreover, although the various memories and memory-making mediums this book explores may shed partial light on the past in question, this book does not constitute an oral history of the Nakba. It also does not seek to construct an account of it, even though historians in general and oral historians in particular have used memory as an analytic concept in different ways (e.g., Gray and Oliver 2004; Passerini 2011; Perks and Thomson 2006; Winter and Sivan 2000). Rather, the main questions explored here are what, how, and why people choose to remember, imagine, or mobilize memories of the Nakba as they do. More specifically, what are the interactions among the personal, familial, communal, and public in the making of these memories? What are the consequences of these interactions and memory-making? And what may this all tell us about the afterlife of the Nakba in a quickly changing Palestinian reality in Syria?

Given this centrality of memory, I draw on the large body of work known as memory studies in order to investigate the social memory of the Nakba (Olick 2008; Olick and Robbins 1998). The works that constitute this area of research have resulted from an interest in memory at the end of the twentieth century, with intellectual antecedents in an earlier, turn-of-the-twentieth-century preoccupation with memory (Olick, Vinitzky-Seroussi, and Levy 2011; Radstone and Shwartz 2010; Rossington and Whitehead 2007). The more recent interest in memory has resulted from the poststructuralist and linguistic turns in the academy. It has also come about within the context of the collapse of the former Soviet Union, the rise of state-sanctioned commemoration and competing nationalisms, and the debates around memories of the European Jewish Holocaust and Germany's recent past (Hutton 1993; Huyssen 1995; Kansteiner 2002; Klein 2000; Winter 2001). Thus, the reasons for the rise of interest in memory are wide-ranging, and they have also become a subject of scholarly inquiry (Huyssen 2003; Nora 1989; Radstone 2000; Ricoeur 2004; Terdiman 1993).

The treatment of the concept of memory in this book is sociological. Memory is understood as a social process, the outcome of the individual recall of images from the past that gains meaning within, and is constrained by, a present-oriented societal and social context. Maurice Halbwachs, the interwar Durkheimian sociologist (Coser 1992; Douglas 1980; Vromen 1975), is often credited with socializing the concept of memory, and the translation of his works to English coincided with the late twentieth-century interest in memory (Schwartz 1996). In his *The Social Frameworks of Memory* ([1925] 1992b), Halbwachs's thesis is that no memory is possible outside a social context and that the very act of remembering is a social process. For him, remembering consists of constructing images of the past in the present by associating these images with contexts from the past. The conjuring of these images is made possible through "reasoning and comparing, and of feeling in contact with human society" (Halbwachs [1925] 1992b, 41). Remembering requires individuals to "localize" their memories in the social frameworks of the groups to which they belong: "We can understand each memory as it occurs in individual thought only if we locate each within the thought of the corresponding group . . . connect[ing] the individual to the various groups of which he is simultaneously a member" (53).

Thus, for Halbwachs, remembering is reconstructing the past, and given that this reconstruction is an activity that occurs in the present, it is bound to reflect the remembering individual's present rather than a real past. Ultimately, Halbwachs argues, not only do groups understand the past through the present, but this present also gains meaning only through these groups' collective memories. Thus, the construction of the past has a specific present-oriented social function. It is construction, rather than reconstruction, because the past is the result of competing versions of what and how events took place (Stanley 1992, 7). The shared contexts of the images conjured up from the past by individuals who belong to the same group outline the "collective" in a collective memory (Halbwachs [1925] 1992b, 54–166).

A more thorough elaboration of the notion of collective memory was to come in the form of Halbwachs's response to the notion's critics. Published posthumously, *The Collective Memory* (1980) elaborates on the title of the book and also explores the relationships between collective memory and history, time and space. In this work, Halbwachs (1980, 48–49) takes his notion's Durkheimian functionalism to its end. He does this when he argues that an individual's ability to conjure up unique memories is virtually impossible insofar as the memory of an individual is retained only because it exists within a social framework of memory common to a group. This is also one of the main points of contention regarding Halbwachs's thesis. Halbwachs arguably crosses the line separating the idea that memories are the product of individual recall within a social context to making a claim that individuals are not authentic subjects of their own memories (Ricoeur 2004, 122). Others have insisted on the cognitive and referential, arguing that there is no such thing as collective memory, only collective instruction (Sontag 2003, 85).

The critique of collective memory's functionalist dimension in particular has led to the rejection of the "collective" in "collective memory" and the appending of terms such as "social" and "cultural" to what continues to be a social understanding of memory. This approach pays as much attention to individuals as it does to the collectivities that these individuals constitute

(Bal, Spitzer, and Crewe 1999; Connerton 1989; Fentress and Wickham 1992). In addition, there is also much debate about the relationship between memory and history (Hodgkin and Radstone 2002, 2003; Hutton 1997, 2000; Le Goff 1992; Ricoeur 2004). The philosopher Paul Ricoeur (2003) has argued that this debate can be understood as one between the historicization of memory and the history of memory. Insofar as the historicization of memory is concerned, Halbwachs was unequivocal in the dichotomy he drew between history inherent in collective memory and history in a disciplinary, academic sense. This distinction is grounded in his positivist understanding of academic history. "General history," he argued, "starts only when tradition ends and the social memory is fading . . . [and] so long as a remembrance continues to exist, it is useless to set it down in writing or otherwise fix it in memory" (Halbwachs 1980, 79).

The history of memory, in contrast, is in the rise of memory as an important concept in the discipline and the study of history (Hutton 1993; Klein 2000; Winter 2001). In fact, one of the foremost figures in the so-called "memory turn" of the late twentieth century (Olick 2008), the French historian Pierre Nora, has also been a leading exponent of a "history of memory" through his work on French national history (Hutton 1993, 147–153; Juneja 2009, 18; Kritzman 1996; Nora 1996a, xv; Ricoeur 2004, 401–411). Nora's conception of the relationship between memory and history, however, is ultimately not so different from that of Halbwachs. This much is evident in Nora's *lieux de mémoire*. These are sites or realms of memory, depending on the context (see, e.g., Nora 1989, 1996a, 1996b, 1996c, 1997, 1998, 2001, 2006, 2009, 2010).

Insofar as the relationship between memory and history is concerned, this book complicates this purported dichotomy that stands in for another one: orality (i.e., memory) versus literacy (i.e., history). It does so by drawing on the historian Patrick Hutton's reading of Francis Yates's (1999) study of the Renaissance period's "art of memory." Hutton (1993) argues that history can be understood as an art of memory because it mediates the encounter between two moments of memory. These are repetition, which concerns the presence of the past in the present, and recollection, which concerns present efforts to evoke the past. It is in the opening between these two moments, he contends, that historical thinking becomes possible.

The copresence of memories and histories of the Nakba is explored further in this book. This copresence is inherent in the Nakba's competing significations. These significations are demonstrated through reading the transformation of the Nakba in Arab nationalist thought, an analysis of activists' memory discourses, and an examination of community members' own memories and narratives on memory. Taken together, these different layers of analysis demonstrate the presence of the Nakba in the present, as embodied in the symbolic contours of different communities in Syria, and the evocation of Nakba memories in referential and nonreferential forms (memory discourses, narratives on memory). History and memory therefore coexist in the myriad meanings, evocations, and possibilities that the Nakba encapsulates today.

SYNOPSIS

In chapter 1, I analyze the Nakba's universe of discourse through its conceptualization as a pan-Arab nationalist catastrophe, transformation after 1967, eventual disappearance as an Arab Nakba, and reemergence as a Palestinian affair. In chapter 2, I set the historical, political, and social context of the Palestinian refugee community in Syria, paying attention to the role played by institutions, including the Palestinian liberation movement, the state, and UNRWA, in shaping this community. Chapter 3 examines one of these institutions, the RoRM, and the ways in which its emergence post-Oslo has furthered politically expedient memory discourses that center on notions of a Palestinian Nakba.

In chapters 4, 5, and 6, I move from this institutional examination of the ways in which the idea of memory is used and mobilized to an examination of community members' memories, histories, and narratives of the Nakba. I pay attention to these as articulated against and in conversation with the Nakba's various universes of discourse, including the Arab and the Palestinian, the activist and the patriotic. In chapter 4, I analyze the central role of the Palestine generation in the narration and transmission of Palestinian refugee memories of loss that resulted from the Nakba. In chapter 5, I turn to an analysis of the Palestine generation's communities and memories, and examine what the embodiment of meanings of the Nakba in these communities may tell us about the afterlife of 1948. Finally, in chapter 6, I take up second- and third-generation refugees' postmemories of loss and narratives on Nakba memory.

CHAPTER 1

THE NAKBA IN ARAB THOUGHT

I remember those days in which I used to sit in the trenches and think through our problems. Al-Faluja was under siege, and it came under concerted and horrific tank fire and warplane shelling at the hands of the enemy. During those times, I repeatedly told myself that "here we are besieged in this hole, we have been deceived, our fates have been determined by greed, machinations and secret desires, and in the end we were left here with no weapons and under fire." When these thoughts would cross my mind . . . I would then tell myself "our homeland [Egypt] is here, it is another Faluja. What is happening to us here is a microcosm of what is happening over there. Our homeland has been besieged by problems and enemies as well, and has been deceived. It has been pushed into a battle it wasn't prepared for, and its fate was also determined by greed, machinations and secret desires, and it too has been left over there under fire with no weapons!"

GAMAL ABDEL NASSER, *FALSAFAT AL-THAWRA* ([1954] 2005: 12–13)

Our planes, tanks and artillery will raze your village, bombard your houses and break your backs. . . . If you want to avoid a catastrophe [nakba] and a disaster [musiba], and to survive inevitable death, surrender as the noose has tightened around your necks.

PAMPHLET DROPPED BY ISRAELI ARMY WARPLANES ON
THE PEOPLE OF AL-TIRA, HAIFA, JULY 1948

The notion of 1948-as-catastrophe is as old as the Nakba. The Nakba, however, did not necessarily always embody the meanings today associated with 1948. An understanding of the conceptualization, articulation, and transformation of 1948-as-catastrophe comes from placing the notion in its "universe of discourse" (Foucault 1991, 2005; Said [1978] 2003, 273). Here, "discourse" conveys a structured system of meaning, embodied in and reinforced by language implicated in nondiscursive practices of power. Accordingly, to be understood, the Nakba's universe of discourse needs to be examined within the context of the historical and political changes that took place in the Arab East in the first two decades following 1948. These decades saw Arab nationalist thinkers, pre-1948 Palestinian leaders, early historians, officers who took part in the battle for Palestine, and nationalist leaders and activists write about the cataclysmic events that shook the Arab East. They also collectively theorized and gave meaning to 1948-as-catastrophe in light of the ascendant Arab nationalist liberation project and its related modernization discourses.[1]

This Arab Nakba's universe of discourse was gradually eclipsed as a result of the defeat of the June War (1967). The new defeat briefly took precedence as the new Nakba/Naksa (setback), before the Nakba in both its old and new Naksa guises disappeared from the literature altogether. The discourses around the Arab Nakba were then eventually replaced by the emergence of yet another universe of discourse, one concerned with the Palestinian Nakba that we are more familiar with today. This change took place as a result of the transformation of the Palestinian national liberation movement, the declassification of Israeli government archives pertaining to the 1948 war on Palestine (Kabha 2007; Masalha 1991, 2011; Said 1998), and Palestinians' own attempt to revive memories of destroyed places, communities, and worlds in a process accelerated in the wake of the Oslo Accords (Abdel Jawad 2007, 2008).

Today there is a body of interdisciplinary multilanguage literature on the Nakba that is also growing.[2] This literature largely sees the Nakba in its contemporary a priori meaning, as the 1948 war for Palestine and the resulting mass dispossession and destruction of the major part of Palestinian society. In this literature, the universe of discourse of 1948-as-catastrophe is also largely ignored, with a few token references to the first use of the term "catastrophe" to describe the 1948 war or the first multivolume Arabic-language history of the events that unfolded during the Nakba. One of this literature's shortcomings is therefore in its treatment of Palestinians specifically and Arabs more generally as mere objects of knowledge. As such, they are studied and analyzed without serious consideration of their intellectual output as subjects of history and theory.

In this chapter, the Nakba is interpreted in a way that goes against the grain of contemporary understandings of 1948 and challenges the writings on contemporary colonized and neocolonized societies that lack serious consideration of their intellectual and theoretical production (Dussel 2000). This approach does not, a priori, accept that the Nakba has consistently or universally implied the subjection of the Palestinians to a catastrophe in 1948 (see, e.g., CPE 1984b). It is also neither a historical nor a historiographical overview of the 1948 war on the Palestinians, a subject on which there is an abundant and wide-ranging English- and Arabic-language literature (see, e.g., Kabha 2006b; Pappe 1999; Rogan and Shlaim 2007; Shlaim 1995). Rather, it presents a limited review of Arab intellectual discourses that circulated in the aftermath of 1948 and the political and historical realities that made these possible and to which these discourses, in turn, also responded. This analysis provides the backdrop for the subsequent examination of activists' memory discourses and mobilization practices, which are a response to these same changed political realities. It also provides the backdrop for the subsequent examination of Nakba lived and transmitted histories, memories, and narratives. These in part constitute an engagement with the different meanings of the Nakba that have circulated since its making.

CONCEPTUALIZING THE PALESTINE WAR: AL-NAKBA, THE ARAB CATASTROPHE

Constantine Zurayk is often credited with first using the term *nakba* to describe the then-ongoing war on the Palestinians and its outcomes in his *Ma'na al-Nakba* (The meaning of the catastrophe) ([1948] 2001, 1956). Zurayk was a historian, an educator, and an interwar-generation Arab nationalist thinker whose intellectual legacy includes a large number of books, edited collections, translations, and articles. He received a PhD in philosophy from Princeton University in 1930 and took up the position of assistant professor of history at his alma mater, the American University of Beirut (AUB). Upon the independence of Syria, he served as the first envoy on the first Syrian delegation to Washington, D.C. (1945–1947), and on the Syrian delegation to the UN Security Council in the critical pre-1948 years (1946–1947). He was also the rector of the University of Damascus (1949–1952) and vice president, acting president, and dean at the AUB during the 1950s. In 1950, he was elected to the executive board of the UN Educational Cultural and Scientific Organization, where he served for four years. He also served on the executive board and later as the head of the

International Association of Universities (1955–1970) and was a founding member and head of the Board of Trustees of the Institute for Palestine Studies in Beirut until 1984 (al-'Azma 2003, 5–6; Kassab 2010, 65–74; W. Khalidi 2009, xiii; Steppat 1988, 12–19).[3]

Given this background, Zurayk's analysis of 1948 is grounded in his experience as an educator, his pan-Arab nationalist commitments, and his intricate knowledge of Arab politics in the pre-Nakba years. These factors combined shed light on the different ways in which Zurayk's reflections on 1948 in his small book were particularly important. In addition to influencing a new generation of nationalist activists and students in the wake of the Nakba, Zurayk was probably also partly privy to the politics of the Arab states as they formulated their wartime policies against the backdrop of their own interests and rivalries. These were formed with an eye to the spoils of Palestine and the balance of power in the region. This was an important reason for the catastrophic defeat of the Arab states in Palestine in 1948 (Rogan and Shlaim 2007).

In his brief foreword, Zurayk ([1948] 2001, 197) begins by telling the reader that his examination of the calamity of the Arabs in Palestine is an attempt to think through "the suffocating crises" that has enveloped the Arab nation. His foreword frames the rest of his mediations in an explicitly pan-Arab framework, and it is within this context that his mediation on the war-as-catastrophe unfolds in the rest of his small book. In the first part, Zurayk sets out what he sees as the "gravity of the catastrophe" (199), and it is here that he first uses the term *nakba* when he states: "The defeat of the Arabs in Palestine is neither a mere setback nor a simple passing evil. It is a catastrophe [*nakba*] in every sense of the word, and a calamity that is greater than any other that has afflicted the Arabs in their long calamity and tragedy ridden history" (201).

Zurayk ([1948] 2001, 201–204) uses *nakba* to describe the war on the Palestinians, in the first instance, in relation to the performance or lack thereof of the seven Arab states that entered Palestine after the Zionist movement declared the establishment of the state of Israel. The term is also used in relation to the Arabs' consequent colossal failure and the human and material losses and loss of morale as manifested in, inter alia, the dispossession of the inhabitants of Palestine. The gravity of the catastrophe for Zurayk is further compounded by the Arab states' inability to thwart the Zionist movement despite the justness of the Palestinian cause. He does recognize, however, that the enemy the Arabs faced was the Zionist movement not only in its physical colonialist manifestation in Palestine but also in its alignment with imperialism. In light of this, Arabs must look inward, he contends, toward their own weaknesses and failures, accept their share in the making of the Nakba, and learn from their mistakes. This response is all the more urgent, given that the establishment of the state of Israel is the beginning of what Zurayk projects to be a long-term battle with colonialism in Palestine.

It is this call for introspective critical self-reflection that Zurayk ([1948] 2001, 207-209) diligently carries out in *The Meaning of the Catastrophe*, making the case for the special duty of the intellectual in this regard, especially in times of national calamities and disasters. With this sense of urgency and duty, Zurayk sets out both short- and long-term fundamental solutions to the catastrophe. He argues that the short-term remedies include raising immediate awareness of the real and imminent danger that Zionism poses; an immediate investment in state-based military, economic, and political capabilities; Arab unification; the enlistment of popular forces as a resource for the struggle against Zionism; and, finally, bargaining with the "Great Powers" in the greater interests of the Arab nation (213–224).

Despite these immediate solutions, however, Zurayk ([1948] 2001) argues that the battle with Zionism is ultimately a long-term one because the root cause of the catastrophic defeat is based on the regressive pan-Arab condition. Of paramount centrality to this condition is the continued lack of the political Arab nation despite its existence in both the geographic and the linguistic sense. As a result, the only way for the resolution of the war-as-catastrophe is through "a total and fundamental change in the Arab condition, an all-encompassing revolution in all our ways of thinking, working and living" (221). This is a process that encompasses short- and long-term modernization plans. These include industrialization, separation of state and religion, scientific training, and learning from the achievements of other civilizations. The goal of these plans is a unified Arab national progressive entity. Ultimately, Zurayk concludes, "the catastrophe [*nakba*] that has befallen us today is thus a marker of our internal state of affairs" (238).

The Meaning of the Catastrophe is a remarkable text of its time. This is because it appeared with a clear future-oriented vision when compared with other contemporaneous texts that were the last echoes of the world that the Nakba itself had destroyed. Zurayk places the Nakba's making at the doorstep of the Arab states while being acutely aware of the collusion between Zionism and European and American imperialism. He also sees the eventual resolution of the Nakba as ultimately a pan-Arab affair predicated upon the Arab states' ability to radically transform and modernize their social, economic, and political systems and to unite. The meaning of the Nakba for Zurayk ([1948] 2001, 227) is not "the superiority of one nation over another, but rather, the distinction between one system and another." Thus, for him, the Zionist movement is part of the modern world, while the Arabs still lack the most basic modern political necessities such as a unified nation-state, national economy, and military.

It is within these parameters that Zurayk first argued that the 1948 war on Palestine and the Palestinians was a *nakba*. His book therefore sheds light on the discursive dimensions within which the 1948 war-as-catastrophe was first conceptualized and articulated in 1948. This conceptualization of 1948-as-catastrophe would become implicated in the changes that resulted from the end of direct French and British colonial rule and the deposition of the post-"independence" regimes they left behind. These political realities, in turn, allowed for the articulation and rearticulation of the Nakba in different ways in the first two decades of its aftermath.

Before turning to these post-1948 political realities and the shifting meanings of the Nakba, I examine the different ways in which the 1948 war was articulated and understood in its aftermath through texts that were contemporaneous with Zurayk's own. These are the texts of the pre-1948 generation of Palestinian leaders that constitute their attempts to come to terms with the consequences of what were ultimately their colossal failures in Palestine.

EARLY WORKS, 1948–1967

PALESTINIAN EVALUATION AND HISTORICIZATION OF THE DEFEAT

The post-1948 era saw the reality of an Arab Nakba materialize through successive military coups that overthrew the ancien régimes that presided over the catastrophic Arab defeat in 1948. It also saw the publication of Palestinian Arab texts that belonged to a pre-1948 experience and worldview. These were texts of men who were mostly either directly or indirectly involved in the pre-1948 Palestinian national movement. These texts, broadly speaking, attempted to explain the reasons for the Nakba (see, e.g., Alami 1949a, 1949b; Darwaza 1959, 1960; al-Ghuri 1955, 1959; Hanna 1948; al-Hawwari 1955; al-Husayni 1956; Tuqan 1950; Zuaʻiter 1955, 1958). Two of these men also published early histories of the war on Palestine (al-ʻArif 1956–1962; al-Khatib 1951, 1967).

What the majority of these men also shared was the fate of banishment or exile that their thirty-year failed direct or indirect leadership had wrought upon the Palestinians. Despite this shared context, these texts—especially those of a reflective or explanatory nature—reveal very little, if any, introspective critical reflection on Palestinian Arab policies and actions, rather than those of the Arab states, which allowed for and led to the Nakba. The self-criticism that does exist is mostly general and limited. This can be seen, for example, in Musa Alami's '*Ibrat Falastin* (The lesson of Palestine) (1949a, 1949b). Alami worked in the British colonial administration and as a result played a limited political role under British colonial rule (Hourani 1988). In his small book, he argues that there were two phases to the battle of Palestine:

> In the first phase the burden of defense was thrown on the shoulders of the Palestinians. . . . The fundamental source of our weakness was that we were unprepared even though we were not taken by surprise . . . that we proceeded along the lines of previous revolutions . . . [and] that we worked on a local basis. . . . Our arms were poor and deficient. . . . Our aims in the battle were diverse.
>
> (Alami 1949b, 374)

According to the historian Mustafa Kabha, Muhammad Nimr al-Hawwari, was the first and perhaps only member of the pre-1948 generation to point the finger of blame directly at the man who was at the helm of the Palestinian national movement under the British, al-Hajj Amin al-Husayni. Perhaps he was able to do so as his *Sir al-Nakba* (The catastrophe's secret) was published in 1955 in Nazareth after he was allowed to return by Israel.[1] Kabha (2006a) argues that the book's implications are that the secret of the Nakba, or its cause, is al-Husayni himself. Others have argued that "social auto-criticism permeates Palestinian and Arab discussion of the [1948] war . . . [like] criticisms of disorganization, disunity, self-interest, and 'backwardness'" (Hasso 2000, 491). Self-criticism did indeed exist, and it ranged in scope from Alami's and others' more general assessments of the causes of failure to al-Hawwari's more direct assigning of responsibility for this failure. It can be argued, however, that these early texts lack a thorough and systematic Palestinian Arab self-criticism of the leadership's failures rather than the more prevalent and general Palestinian or Arab criticism. This is not a lack in terms of who the author of a text in question was but who or what the object of criticism was. As a result, what the pre-1948 generation of men did not produce was a thorough analysis of the failures of the Palestinian national movement during its brief thirty-year leadership under British colonial rule in Palestine (see, e.g., R. Khalidi 1996, 192–201; 2007).

The degree and quality of Palestinian Arab self-criticism shed light on what could and could not be articulated immediately after the 1948 catastrophe. This is because while the Nakba may indeed have been partly the result of the Palestinians' own failed leadership under British rule (R. Khalidi 2007), it was also the outcome of inter-Arab disunity, rivalry, and alliances against Transjordanian regional ambitions in particular (Al-Rasheed 2007; Gerges 2007; Landis 2007; Rogan 2007; Shlaim 2007; Tripp 2007). These texts were therefore also constrained within this particular historical moment and its associated intellectual, geographical, and political limitations. In light of this, these texts shed light on the milieu of the major capitals of the Arab East, where most of the texts were published, and the discourses circulating in these capitals in the years immediately after 1948. Rather than examining these texts for the degree and quality of the pre-1948 Palestinian leadership's self-criticism, it is therefore more instructive to focus on what they tell us about the discourses that the authors were engaging.

Of particular importance in this regard is Muhammad Amin al-Husayni's *Haqa'iq 'an Qadiyyat Falastin* (The Question of Palestine facts) (1956). This is because al-Husayni was at the helm of the pre-1948 Palestinian national movement in Palestine until an arrest warrant issued by the British during Thawrat Falastin al-Kubra (1936–1939), the Palestinian uprising against the British (Swedenburg 2003), forced him to leave Palestine. Al-Husayni's book is a collection of ten extended essays that initially appeared as responses to a series of questions put forth by the editor of the Egyptian *al-Masri* newspaper. In his foreword to the first edition of the book, published in 1954, al-Husayni (1956, 6) states that the colonial and Zionist "lies and fabrications" were successfully spread in the Arab world. This was particularly the case during the first year of what he calls the "disaster" (*al-karitha*) and "the Palestinian migration" (*al-hijra al-falastiniyya*) to the neighboring Arab states. The lies and fabrications that al-Husayni alludes to can in part be discerned through the editor's questions, especially those with a more accusatory tone. They point the finger at Palestinian leaders, including al-Husayni, and the people of Palestine more generally, for bringing the disaster upon themselves.

This finger-pointing includes accusations that the people of Palestine willfully gave up their homeland, especially through land sales to Zionists. It also implies that they did not defend their homeland during British rule more generally and in 1948 in particular, and were working for the Zionists to whom they sold Arab military interests (al-Husayni 1956, 8). The accusations also underscore that factional and local disagreements engendered disunity among the Palestinian leaders, which led to their inability to compromise with the British and accept any of the solutions they put forth, the cause of the eventual disaster (27). Furthermore, the Nakba is portrayed as having resulted from the Palestinian leadership's passivity and its rejection of Britain's offers, including partition (46). Further implied is that it was the 1946 Arab League–created and al-Husayni–headed Arab Higher

Committee, the Palestinian representative to the Arab League (al-Hut 1981, 531–545), that ordered the Palestinians to leave after adoption of the UN General Assembly Resolution 181 of November 29, 1947 (al-Husayni 1956, 59).[5]

In the last essay, al-Husayni puts forth what he argues are the main reasons for Palestine's disaster and suggests ways in which to resolve it. He also divides these reasons into "external" (the Zionists, the British, colonialism) and "internal" causes. Here, a serious reckoning with the faults and errors of the national movement by a man who was at its helm prior to his exile in the aftermath of the destruction of half of Palestinian society is nonexistent. The role of the British and the Zionists and the mostly ambiguous criticism of the Arab states for their roles notwithstanding, one must conclude that self-criticism is nowhere to be found because al-Husayni still had hopes to lead the Palestinian national movement after the Nakba. Thus, his *Question of Palestine Facts* seems to be an attempt to vindicate the defeated former vanguards of the Palestinian national movement rather than to present a thorough reflection on their failures.

Beyond this lack of self-criticism, the series of questions and al-Husayni's defensive responses throughout shed light on the various meanings associated with the Nakba and the discourses on 1948 that were circulating during the early 1950s. To begin with, the term *nakba* for 1948 was not universally used when the book was first published in 1954; al-Husayni's preferred term is *karitha*. Second, the case can made that the idea of the 1948 war on the Palestinians as a Zionist-inflicted catastrophe was not universally accepted in the years immediately following 1948. In fact, what seems to have been associated with the Nakba is the notion that the Palestinians brought the catastrophe upon themselves through either selling land to Zionists, not putting up a fight, or instructing their own people to leave.

The political scientist Saleh Abdel Jawad (2006a, 75) has argued that the historical Arab "narrative categorically rejects Israeli allegations that Arab leaders ordered Palestinians to evacuate their villages, even if, in some cases, residues of this myth remain in the popular discourse, mainly because Palestinian refugees listened to Israeli-sponsored, Arab-language radio, which was used to wage psychological war." Nevertheless, when reading al-Husayni's text, these accusations seem to have formed a part of the meaning of the Nakba, or *karitha*, in some Arab circles during the early years. The thorny question of leaving (or remaining in) Palestine is an issue still alive in the Palestine generation's memories and the post-Palestine generations' narratives. Moreover, the Israeli state has used these accusations in order to deny its role in the expulsion of the Palestinians. These accusations and their enduring importance, however, do not absolve Israel from its primary responsibility for the mass dispossession of Palestinians or the atrocities it committed in 1948 (Masalha 2003).

There were also two early attempts to historicize the Nakba by two individuals who belonged to the same pre-1948 generation of leaders (CPE 1984a; al-Samadi 2007). The first is Muhammad Nimr al-Khatib's *Min Athar al-Nakba* (The catastrophe's aftermath) (1951), republished in 1967 as *Ahdath al-Nakba aw Nakbat Falastin* (The events of the catastrophe or Palestine's catastrophe) in the wake of the June War. There has been a recent revival of interest in the latter book, given that al-Khatib provided what was probably the first written account of the Tantura village massacre in the Haifa subdistrict. This was one of approximately seventy documented Nakba massacres (Abdel Jawad 2007; al-Khatib 1951, 118–120), whose notoriety happened to come to light in English because it was the subject of a lawsuit in Israel in 2000 (Esmeir 2003; Pappe 2001). The other book is 'Arif al-'Arif's six-volume *al-Nakba: Nakbat Bayt al-Maqdis wa al-Firdaws al-Mafqud* (The catastrophe: The catastrophe of Jerusalem and the lost paradise) (1956–1962). This book is an encyclopedic documentation of the military, political, and diplomatic events that shook Palestine, covering the period from the passing of UN General Assembly Resolution 181 until the last armistice agreement between Syria and the Israeli state on July 20, 1949.

In al-'Arif's early attempt to historicize the war, he also defines the Nakba, when he argues: "How can I not call it [the book] 'The Nakba'? We have been afflicted by catastrophe, we the Arabs in general and the Palestinians in particular, during this period of time in a way in which we have not been subjected to a catastrophe in centuries and in other periods of time: our homeland was stolen, we were thrown out of our homes, we lost a large number of our sons and of our young ones, and in addition to all this, the core of our dignity was also afflicted" (al-'Arif 1956, 3).

The title of al-'Arif's book therefore derives from the idea of the Nakba as a catastrophe for the Palestinians and Arabs, the details of which he documents in the first four volumes.[6] However, the emphasis is clearly not only on the Palestinians but also on the Arabs, for both groups have been afflicted. The pan-Arab link remains important and the Nakba cannot be understood outside this context. Thus, as early as 1956 the term *nakba* had already encapsulated various, competing meanings—as a catastrophe to pan-Arab nationalism, as a catastrophe brought about by Zionist and imperial collusion, and as a catastrophe self-inflicted by the Palestinians' own leaders or the people themselves. The Nakba was also referred to as "the disaster" and "the Palestinian migration."

Thus, when read together, texts that circulated in the aftermath of 1948 shed light on the multiple and at times even contradictory significations of 1948 as a *nakba*. These multiple significations were articulated within discourses circulating in response to the changing realities of the time. The changes in the political map of the Arab East, realized through successive military coups in Egypt, Syria, and Iraq, were arguably the most important and defining features of the new post-Nakba Arab reality. These coups allowed the pan-Arab dimension of 1948-as-catastrophe to gain further prominence, particularly in the first two decades following the Nakba.

THE DAWN OF A NEW POST-NAKBA ARAB ERA

In a seminal study of the reemergence of the post-1948 Palestinian national movement, the political scientist Yezid Sayigh (2004, 25) argues that the Nakba coincided with the beginning of three significant historic processes in the Arab region: "the formation or consolidation of independent national states, the emergence of a distinct Arab-state system, and the replacement of colonial domination with US-Soviet rivalry." The Nakba was therefore both the end and the beginning of two distinct chapters in the history of the post-Ottoman Arab East. These were the end of direct colonial rule through the League of Nations–sanctioned mandate system, on the one hand, and the beginning of U.S. imperial domination and Soviet influence in the region, on the other hand.

Coming at both the beginning and the end of these critical historical junctures, the Nakba sent tremors across the Arab East. Understood in retrospect, one of the most important aftereffects of these tremors was the institutionalization of militarism in the Arab world. Although this institutionalization allowed for the further articulation of the pan-Arab nationalist significations of 1948-as-catastrophe, it also gave these significations yet another dimension that departed from Zurayk's Arab Nakba in significant ways. This is because "the tension and conflicts between the civilian-military leadership during the Palestine War were partly responsible for the armed coups d'état that shook the Arab world to its core after 1949" (Gerges 2007, 156). Within this context, the texts to emerge during the dawn of this new post-Nakba era reflected this schism and were grounded in the various political currents and movements rising to prominence, hand in hand with the military men, after 1948 (see, e.g., al-Bitar [1965] 1973; G. Nasser [1954] 2005; Qamhawi 1956; al-Tal 1959).

One of the Nakba's most significant political tremors shook Egypt, where as early as 1952 the Free Officers led a military coup dubbed the "July Revolution" and deposed the British era monarchy (Y. Sayigh 2004, 25–26). Gamal Abdul Nasser emerged as the leader of the Free Officers and eventually Egypt (Badeau 1959; Gunther 1959; Kirk 1959; R. Robinson 1959). He had been a major (*sagh*) in the Egyptian army brigade under siege in the village of al-Faluja in the Gaza subdistrict from October 1948 to February 1949 (al-Tal 1959, 434–435). Syria, in contrast to Egypt, would see more than one military coup by the time of the July Revolution in a pattern that would mark its politics for the next two decades (Hinnebusch 2002, 25). In 1958, Iraq followed suit with a military coup that overthrew the British era monarchy, led by Abdul Karim Qasim, among others. Qasim, an officer in the Iraqi army, would later emerge as the leader of the 1958 Iraqi Revolution and would lead Iraq until 1963. King Abdullah of Transjordan, which eventually became Jordan, was assassinated in Jerusalem as early as 1951. Though he was succeeded by his son, his grandson, King Hussein, became de facto leader in 1952 and foiled a failed military coup in 1957 (Y. Sayigh 2004, 26–33).

One text to emerge during this era that demonstrates the extent of the changing ideological and political realities in the Arab world is Abdullah al-Tal's *Karithat Falastin: Mudhakkarat 'Abdu Allah al-Tal, Qa'id Ma'rakat al-Quds* (Palestine's disaster: Memoirs of Abdullah al-Tal, leader of the Battle of Jerusalem) (1959). Al-Tal was a colonel in Transjordan's Arab Legion during the war on Palestine and was appointed military governor of Jerusalem in October 1948 (al-Tal 1959, 355–358). He also took part in the Transjordanian and Zionist secret meetings and negotiations that began at the end of 1948 (437–544). After learning of King Abdullah's intention to send him away as a military attaché to a foreign embassy, he resigned in June 1949 (586). He secretly left Jordan five months later, eventually arriving in Egypt, where the authorities, according to him, granted him political asylum (598). While in Egypt, al-Tal was tried in absentia for his alleged role in the 1951 assassination of King Abdullah (Rogan 2007), a topic mentioned only in passing in his book (al-Tal 1959, 587–599).[7]

Although al-Tal (1959, 599) began publishing what he knew of Transjordan's collusion with Zionism as early as March 1950, it was nine years later, according to the date of his foreword, that he would finally publish what he intended to be the first part of his memoirs.[8] This book's most important contribution is al-Tal's disclosure of the secret negotiations and agreements between Transjordan and leaders of the Zionist movement prior to the entry of the regular Arab armies into Palestine. He also discloses those he personally took part in before the formal Rhodes Armistice Agreements between

Israel and neighboring Arab states in 1949. Crucially, he supports his claims with a collection of personal and secret letters, correspondences, and telegrams that he had access to as King Abdullah's trusted military governor (see, e.g., al-Tal 1959, 64–74, 437–466, 467–486, 487–544).

The publication of al-Tal's book at the height of the 1956 Suez War and in Egypt[9] demonstrates the extent of the rupture with the ancien régimes that presided over the Nakba and the subsequent centrality of Nasser and Nasserism (Kerr 1965, 1971; Torrey and Delvin 1965).[10] His exposing of Transjordan's duplicitous role in the making of Palestine's Nakba is also testament to the ways in which the various discourses associated with the Arab Nakba were being molded by the changing political visions brought about by the military coups. Al-Tal's foreword captures the relationship between the Arab world's changing political realities and the parameters of its discourses on 1948, when he tells the reader:

> When I wrote those memoirs, some ten years ago, the Arab nation was passing through one of the most dangerous periods of disintegration and disunity. . . . [It was] a period during which some Arab leaders helped the colonists establish a criminal state in the heart of the Arab homeland. . . . There is a stark difference between the period during which these memoirs were written and the period during which these memoirs are being published. . . . [We are now in] a stage which allows for reassurance and hope for comprehensive Arab unity.
>
> (al-Tal 1959, ii)

Al-Tal's book is thus part of the clear demarcation line that was being drawn between those who allowed for—indeed, colluded in bringing about—the Nakba and those who now promised a new dawn of Arab unification, decolonization, and independence. For Nasser, his supporters, and Arab nationalists of various creeds, what this dawn meant in practice was that "the liberation from colonialism and its collaborators . . . [came to be seen as] the correct path towards the liberation of Palestine. . . . 'The path to Tel Aviv passes through here' [was a] banner for 'Arab revolutionaries' in every Arab capital beginning in the mid-1950s" (al-Jabiri 1982, 122).

Nasser's own meditation on the July Revolution in his *Falsafat al-Thawra* (*The Philosophy of the Revolution*) ([1954] 2005, 1959) demonstrates how the meaning of the Nakba came to encapsulate, in the first instance, the need for Arab unification and liberation, the path toward the liberation of Palestine. In the English language translation of his book, Nasser (1959, 26) argues that "it is not true that the revolution of July 23rd started on account

of the results of the war in Palestine." He refers to the "myth, now completely refuted, that the Egyptian army in Palestine was defeated because
it had been equipped with defective arms by corrupt politicians" (Abdel
Jawad 2006b, 79). He does this in order to underscore his unequivocal
rejection of the Nakba as cause for the revolution. He argues that "had
the officers endeavored to avenge themselves because they were cheated in
Palestine or because the defective arms strained their nerves and because
they suffered . . . the whole affair would not have deserved to be called a
revolution" (G. Nasser 1959, 27). For Nasser, Palestine and its Nakba, among
other factors, "may have accelerated the flood but they could never be the
original source" (31).

The revolution, Nasser (1959) argues, was the cumulative result of the
Egyptian people's aspiration for independence and self-determination.
Where Palestine and its Nakba do figure for Nasser are in terms of their
encapsulation of the political pan-Arab space of the revolution. As he puts
it, "The fighting in Palestine was not fighting on foreign territory. Nor was
it inspired by sentiment. It was a duty imposed by self-defense" (G. Nasser
1959, 63). This self-defense makes Palestine a part of what Nasser refers to
as the "Arab circle" (62), of which Egypt and its revolution are also a constitutive part.

In view of this, Palestine's Nakba was therefore a catastrophe to the project
of the becoming of the Arab nation in the political sense, or independence
and unification. Reflecting on the relationship between his experiences in
the Egyptian army in Palestine and the subsequent Egyptian revolution,
Nasser tells us that after the siege in al-Faluja, "I came home with the whole
region in my mind one complete whole…. one region, the same factors and
circumstances, even the same forces opposing them all" (G. Nassar 1959, 65).
Rather than bringing about the July Revolution, Palestine's Nakba brought
home the extent to which 1948 was a pan-Arab Nakba, and its resolution
was therefore possible only through unification and decolonization. In other
words, this was the liberation, in the first instance, of the Arab circle.

Nasser clearly conceived Palestine as integral to the pan-Arab political
sphere of the revolution and of the Nakba as brought about by imperialism
and its Zionist ally—the same forces to which the revolution responded. This
shares similarities with and yet departs from Zurayk's 1948-as-catastrophe.
The similarities lie in the pan-Arab nationalist vision of liberation. The significant departure is the discrediting of the old social and political classes
while legitimizing the military as the new saviors of the Arab world (Gerges
2007, 157). Thinking about the Nakba therefore also became part of building
the necessary military force capable of eventually decisively defeating Israel

(al-Jabiri 1982, 116–135). Thus, the discursive dimensions within which the Nakba was articulated as early as 1954 were shifting yet again, to contain yet more meanings, as they responded to the quickly changing political realities and currents on the ground.

These early years also saw Palestinians politically organize as part of the emergent Arab nationalist movements of the time. The two most significant of these were the Arab Nationalists Movement, greatly influenced by Zurayk's ideas, and the Ba'th Party (Gordon 1969; Y. Sayigh 1991b; al-Sharif 1995, 48–56). The Nakba, as central to the Palestine question, occupied an important place in these different movements and their political literature, but only as part of the broader question of Arab liberation (al-Sharif 1995, 48–56). This was still the case when calls began to be made to organize Palestinians qua Palestinians for the battle of liberation through the emergence of Palestinian armed groups against the backdrop the "Arab-Arab conflict" (al-Sharif 1995, 83; see also Y. Sayigh 1998). This is because these calls were still made within the context of a broader Arab struggle for liberation. As Naji 'Allush, a member of the Ba'th Party who would later join Fatah, put it in his *Al-Masira ila Falastin* (The march to Palestine) (1964), "The establishment of a revolutionary movement, the organization of the Arabs of Palestine, and the release of their energies is important and necessary for the liberation of Palestine as long as this organization remains aware of the parameters of its struggle, and comprehends that it is first and foremost a struggle for [Arab] unity and liberation" ('Allush 1964, 222).

Only with the emergence of the Palestinian Patriotic (National) Liberation Movement, or Fatah, in 1957 were calls made for "a total Arab battle that takes a regional Palestinian face as a cover for itself" (al-Sharif 1995, 91). This call to bring Palestinians on board as Palestinians to the battle of liberation and to focus on the liberation of Palestine as the path toward Arab liberation would realize itself only in the aftermath of the June War. The outcomes of that war, "by discrediting Arab authority and weakening state control, created the opportunity for the rise of the Palestinian guerrillas as regional actors" (Y. Sayigh 1992, 244). This second defeat also led Palestinians to assume the task of Palestinian liberation and resulted in the eventual eclipse of the 1948 Nakba in Arab thought.

THE JUNE WAR AND THE NEW NAKBA/NAKSA

The years immediately following the June War led to a wave of critical works, articles, and lectures that attempted to come to terms with the new defeat and were written by nationalists, Marxists, and Islamists (e.g., al-Azm 1968, 2011; al-Bitar 1968; al-Hafiz 1979; al-Munjid 1968; Zurayk [1967] 2001). This new defeat was seen as yet another catastrophe or disaster, one with the same root causes as the Nakba of 1948. Nasser referred to the outcomes of this new round of fighting as a *naksa*, a setback, to the project of pan-Arab unity and liberation (Abu-Lughud 1972). Although the works that emerged in the aftermath of 1967 assessed the new defeat in different ways, what they shared in common was linking 1967 and 1948.

Thus, thinking about the new defeat would come to subsume and eventually eclipse the Nakba of 1948. Once the Palestinian guerrilla groups took over the Palestine Liberation Organization (PLO) and eventually the task of liberation, preoccupation with the 1948 Nakba, even if only as part of the new Nakba/Naksa, conspicuously disappears from post-1967 literature. By the early 1970s all eyes were fixed on the Palestinian Revolution, the site where the guerrillas were actively participating and determining the ways in which the liberation of Palestine was to unfold (see, e.g., CAUS 1993, 1996). Eventually the resolution of the Nakba via the liberation of historic Palestine would itself take secondary place, with the Palestinian guerrillas' focus now aimed at reversing the Israeli gains made in 1967 (R. Khalidi 1992). These political changes also signaled the beginning of the disappearance of the Arab Nakba's universe of discourse, which would eventually lead to the reemergence of the 1948 Nakba in a new and exclusively Palestinian discursive guise.

Zurayk's *Ma'na al-Nakba Mujaddadan* (The meaning of the catastrophe anew) ([1967] 2001) was one of the texts to emerge in light of the second Arab defeat by Israel. The title of his book, as well as his main argument, link to his first book on the Nakba. He begins the sequel by explicitly making this link, stating that whereas the first disastrous battle took place in 1948, "today, after nineteen years, the second battle has erupted and the new disaster [*al-karitha*] is no less horrific than the first, and its anticipated outcome will be no less severe for the Arab people; the event and its outcomes seem to be greater and more detrimental" (Zurayk [1967] 2001, 996). Quoting from his first book, he insists that he described the first defeat as a Nakba because it was indeed "a catastrophe [*nakba*] and not a setback [*naksa*], and like it, and indeed more vicious than it, is what we have now been afflicted with" (996). In his insistence on 1948 and 1967 as catastrophes rather than mere setbacks, Zurayk seems to be directly contesting Nasser's response to the latest defeat.

Zurayk ([1967] 2001) summarizes what he wrote about the meaning of the defeat of 1948. He also uses the sequel to emphasize yet again the scientific and state-based transformations that Arabs must undertake to transform their societies and, ultimately, their abilities to confront Zionism. Thus, the central thesis of the second book is that the reasons for the new catastrophe are the same as those for the catastrophe of 1948. For Zurayk, the outcomes of both wars are fundamentally tied to Arab societies' ongoing lack of modernization and unity. Once again, he argues that the core of the problem in 1967, like the core problem he analyzed in 1948, is based on Arab and Israeli societies belonging to "two different civilizational epochs" (997). The former is "premodern" and "backward," whereas the latter is modern, unified, and technologically, scientifically, organizationally, and industrially advanced. In conclusion, Zurayk quotes from his first book in order to underscore the "old meaning [of the Nakba] anew" (1031), without which there will be no resolution of the new Nakba.

Another important book written as a response to the new defeat was the Marxist philosopher Sadik Jalal al-Azm's *Al-Naqd al-Dhati Ba'd al-Hazima* (Self-criticism after the defeat) (1968, 2007), published in English translation in 2011. This book provides grounds for comparison with Zurayk's nationalist position on the new Nakba/Naksa. Al-Azm's (2011, 38) central thesis, like that of Zurayk, is that the defeat of 1967 is "tied directly to the prevalent economic, cultural, scientific and civilization conditions in the Arab nation, i.e., it was a reflection and expression of those conditions." He advances this argument by comparing the reasons for the Russian defeat during the Russo-Japanese War (1904–1905) with those for the Arab defeat during the June War. For al-Azm, the main difference between the two, which is also the most telling manifestation of the regressive civilizational condition of the Arabs that led to their defeat, is the Arabs' evasion of responsibility.

This insistence on the prevalent evasion of responsibility extends to the naming of the new defeat a *nakba*. Rather than singling out Zurayk, al-Azm names the then-head of the Department of Philosophy at the Lebanese University, Kamal Yusif al-Hajj. He argues that the very use of the term "catastrophe" constitutes an evasion of responsibility because "whoever is struck by a disaster [*nakba*, plural *nakabat* in the original] is not considered responsible for it. . . . [T]his is why we ascribe disasters [*nakabat*] to fate, destiny and nature" (al-Azm 2011, 40). In addition to rejecting 1967 as yet another *nakba*, al-Azm also rejects Nasser's *naksa* and singles Nasser out for criticism. In his June War fortieth-anniversary edition foreword, he argues that when initially publishing his book, he insisted on using "defeat" in opposition to "setback." His was an attempt to name "the defeat by its name publicly and clearly, without any attempt to hide or dilute the effect of the fire and napalm on its victims" (17).

Thus, the main task of *Self-Criticism* is to engage in the far-reaching autocritique that, according to al-Azm, the Arabs had not only failed to do but remain incapable of doing, given their cultural, social, and political state of affairs. The self-criticism in the book is far-reaching. It ranges in scope from his analysis of the myriad ways in which the evasion of responsibility took place (al-Azm 2011, 45–72), to a psychosocial analysis of certain Arab social characteristics that were responsible for the defeat (72). He also provides an assessment of the importance of the Vietnamese model and modernization to the Arab struggle against colonialism and imperialism (including Zionism) (87–91). Finally, he critiques the "socialist Arab revolutionary movement" in general and Nasserism's "middle roadism" in particular (110). In conclusion, al-Azm ties the defeat of 1948 to 1967, foregrounding the role of class and its relationship to the Arab elites responsible for both defeats. It is this emphasis on class as well as his clear critique of Nasser that distinguishes his book from that of Zurayk. Looking to the emergent Palestinian guerrillas, al-Azm concludes that only a leadership committed to the cause of its people will be able to translate the sacrifices of the guerrillas into mass popular mobilization. This mobilization's purpose would be to engage in a comprehensive armed and cultural struggle in order to transform the Arabs' condition during a decisive historical stage (136).

In an interview given in the late 1990s, al-Azm argued that intellectually, "the Arab World witnessed the emergence of a strong leftist wave immediately after the 1967 defeat, which extended to the 1973 October War" (Talhami 1997, 117).[11] This wave also coincided with the short-lived preoccupation with the new Nakba/Naksa, before thinking of the Nakba and its meanings conspicuously disappeared from the literature. This disappearance can be understood through linking the opportunity that the June War provided for the emergent Palestinian guerrillas to take an independent military course in relation to the liberation of Palestine.

Thus, the changing political reality's relationship to the intellectual terrain was first translated through the outcomes of the June War understood as a new Nakba/Naksa. By the mid-1970s, however, this intellectual preoccupation with the Nakba, if only as part of the new defeat, would become subsumed by the guerrillas' revolution. This is because the Palestinian Revolution, especially for Arab nationalists, itself subsumed the struggle for Arab unity and liberation and came to encapsulate the hopes previously appended to the latter struggle and its related discourses. As the Palestinian movement's emphasis on liberation and return gradually transformed, and as the regional order within which it operated also changed, the Arab Nakba would become a discourse of the past. The Nakba would eventually reemerge in the intellectual and activist response to these changed political realities, but under a different Palestinian guise.

THE PALESTINIAN NAKBA

Whereas the June War saw the eclipse of the Arab Nakba and its eventual disappearance from Arab thought, the 1980s saw a renewed intellectual interest in the Nakba. This took place in two ways. The first was through Palestinians' own attempt to revive memories of their communities and ways of life in the Palestine the Nakba had destroyed (Abdel Jawad 2007; Farah 2006; R. Sayigh 2015). This interest in memories of historic Palestine was accelerated further by the Oslo Accords, taking place within the context of the threat the Palestinian leadership posed to refugees' right of return to their homes and lands (Al-Hardan 2012a). It also took place alongside the partial declassification of Israeli government archives in the 1980s (Abdel Jawad 2006a, 2007). Moreover, it occurred within the context of the general rise in political, popular, and scholarly interest in memory that began in the 1980s and mushroomed after the collapse of the former Soviet Union (Klein 2000; Olick 2008). In view of these different factors, this renewed interest in the Palestinian past led to a particular emphasis on Nakba memories, specifically in refugee communities. Renewed interest also led to an emphasis on the generation of Palestine, the sole surviving witnesses to the Palestine now threatened by the Palestinian leadership. It is within this context that the Nakba today exists with radically altered significations and in a Palestinian universe of discourse.

In an article that maps six decades of Palestinian oral history, the anthropologist Rosemary Sayigh (2015) notes that early informal attempts to record the pre-Nakba past by Palestinians in the wake of 1948 have ironically been lost to the record.[12] The institutional development of Palestinian attempts to memorialize their communities and the catastrophe are usually traced to Birzeit University's research center in the Occupied Palestinian Territories (OPT) (R. Davis 2007; Slyomovics 2007). In the mid-1980s, the center published its first anthropological monograph in The Destroyed Palestinian Villages book series. The aims of the series, summarized in its first volume and replicated in subsequent volumes on different communities, was to ethnographically reconstruct the annihilated communities of pre-1948 Palestine (Kanaana and al-Ka'bi 1986, 59, cited in Slyomovics 1991, 386). There was therefore from the beginning an emphasis on "how respondents [from the community in question] perceived events . . . [through] oral testimonies"

(Abdel Jawad 2007, 62). Shut down in the late 1980s by an Israeli military order, the research center resumed its work in 1993. The new director of the center and the series, Saleh Abdel Jawad (2007), historicized the otherwise anthropological monographs. He foregrounded the use of oral histories of the Nakba as well as the 1980s declassified Israeli government archives in order to cross-check oral testimonies with archival material and secondary sources (62–63). Books on the destroyed villages also took on popular semi- and nonscholarly forms written by activists and individuals in exile and have become a topic of scholarly research in English (R. Davis 2010; Khalili 2004, 2005; Slyomovics 1998).

The publication of these books took place alongside Palestinian oral history initiatives within historic Palestine and beyond, with an emphasis on pre-1948 Palestine as well as the Nakba (R. Sayigh 2015). Even the Palestinian Authority mobilized memories in 1998 during its official commemorations of the fiftieth anniversary of the Nakba through print sources, public events, and official radio stations (Hammami 2010; Hill 2005). In addition, these oral history initiatives took place through non-PA-affiliated organizations in the OPT, like the Palestinian Diaspora and Refugee Center (Shaml) and the Resource Center for Palestinian Residency and Refugee Rights (BADIL). It also took place through the Right of Return Movement in Syria and else- where as well, as through individual efforts (R. Sayigh 2015).

These Palestinian attempts to revive memories of the pre-1948 past and the Nakba were also followed by a scholarly interest in Palestinian memo- ries, in English and Arabic, as well as more recent oral history works on the 1948 Nakba (El-Nimr 1993; Kabha 2006b; Masalha 2005; Slyomovics 1998; Swedenburg 2003). However, not until 2007 did scholarly interest in Pales- tinian memories lead to a groundbreaking collection on the social memory, rather than oral history, of 1948 (Saʿdi and Abu-Lughod 2007). Today, there is a small but growing body of interdisciplinary literature on the Nakba.[13]

Concurrent with these developments, the renewed intellectual interest in the Nakba in the 1980s also resulted from the Israeli government's par- tial declassification of archives that pertain to the war on the Palestinians. This spurred an ideologically and methodologically varied group of so- called Israeli "new historians" and "sociologists" to reconsider the received Zionist narratives about what happened in Palestine during the Nakba (e.g., Morris 2001, 2004; Pappe 1992, 2006a; Shlaim 1988). The main conclusions that this group brought to the English-language academic sphere have been examined through the Arab Nakba's universe of discourse. These include the Arab coalition's heterogeneous, uncoordinated, and competing war aims; the Zionist movement's knowledge and full exploitation of this reality; and the movement's military advantage over the Arabs throughout the official phase of the war (Shlaim 2007, 80; 1995). In short, this reconsideration of both the politics and the military operations during the war demolished the myth of Israel standing alone against the combined might of the Arab states against all odds. It underscored the convergence between the interests of the Zionist movement and the Transjordanians at the expense of other coalition members and Palestinians in particular (Shlaim 2007, 100). There is, however, nothing new or remarkable about such claims, except that it is Israelis, rather than Palestinians and Arabs, articulating them and being heard when doing so.

Thus, the Nakba of 1948 became plausible in English only after it was articulated by the colonizers. Their scholarship, designated "new," was merely articulating what Arab intellectuals, historians, and political leaders and activists had been saying all along. The reception of their scholarship as "new" is therefore telling of the constellation of colonial power relations that underpin when the history of the vanquished is finally allowed to enter its annals, under whose terms, and with which form and with what content. It is also indicative of the inherent power in who is allowed to determine what events are deemed historical and which routes the history of the vanquished must traverse to finally be considered plausible, if only partly so. This is because the Israeli state's Zionist ideology continues to be fundamentally predicated on the denial of the Nakba and thus of Palestinians' existence (Massad 2000).

As a result of the "new" Israeli scholarship, what is today no longer debatable in English-language scholarly circles is that the mass dispossession of at least four-fifths of the Palestinian Arab population did indeed take place in the conquered territories in 1948. In addition, this dispossession unfolded with the destruction of at least eleven urban localities and the obliteration of at least 531 villages (Pappe 2006a). Apart from collectively shedding light on the events surrounding the Nakba, however, these historians disagree on the moral and ethical implications of their endeavors insofar as acknowledgment and restitution are concerned.

It has in consequence been argued that given the Zionist ideological grounding of these historians, with the exception of Pappe, their work is informed by a "profound contradiction" (Said 1998; see also Lentin 2010; Masalha 2011). It is true that their work has collectively challenged the dominant Zionist narratives about an "empty land," from "time immemorial," "independence," and "redemption," especially in English-language scholarship (Finkelstein 2003; Said and Hitchens 2001). However, the profound contradiction lies in the implications of their arguments. These range from those who, despite their own findings, argue that the expulsions were born of war and not design (Finkelstein 1991; Masalha 1991; Morris 1991) to those who argue that "while it was morally wrong to expel Palestinians, it was necessary to do so" (Said 1998). The most notorious of the Israeli historians, Benny Morris, is for example contemptuous of the testimonies of Palestinian Nakba survivors and Palestinian and Arab historians' work on 1948 (Whitehead 2002). He has also argued that it was necessary to inflict a catastrophe on the Palestinians in order to ensure the establishment of the state of Israel in 1948 (Shavit 2004).

Pappe, in contrast, is both an ideological and a methodological exception among these historians. He has written what is the most vivid construction of the Zionist onslaught against the unarmed civilian population of British-ruled Palestine. He uses declassified Israeli government archives, and to a lesser extent Palestinian oral testimonies, to argue that what transpired after the Zionist leadership adopted Plan Dalet in March 1948 amounted to a concerted policy and campaign of the "ethnic cleansing" of the country. He has called for the political and moral confrontation of the (ongoing) Nakba through Israel's acknowledgment of its war crimes and its crimes against humanity and the implementation of the refugees' right of return (Pappe 2006a, xiii).

Most recently, genocide scholars have taken up the subject of the Nakba by building on Morris's and Pappe's scholarship in particular. For example, Martin Shaw (2010) problematized Pappe's use of ethnic cleansing to characterize Zionist policies and actions in 1948, given the notion's deployment of perpetrator language and its ambiguous relationship to the legal notion of genocide. This ambiguity, Shaw contends, can serve to narrow genocide to only one of its possible outcomes—that of total human extermination. Shaw (2010, 1) argues for an "international historical perspective" on genocide that focuses on genocide's aims rather than means and distinguishes genocidal violence from other types of violence in its targeting of civilians and its pervasive destructiveness. Within this broadened scope, he argues, the widespread destruction of Palestinian society in 1948 is partly genocidal. This is not because Zionist leaders had, in a narrow definition of what constitutes genocide, a master plan to exterminate Palestinians, though the intent to remove the population was there. Rather, it is because "its specific genocidal thrusts developed situationally and incrementally, through local as well as national decisions . . . a partly decentered, networked genocide, developing in interaction with the Palestinian and Arab enemy, in the context of war" (19).

Shaw's article led to an email exchange with Omer Bartov (2010), an Israeli Holocaust and genocide scholar, that was published in the *Journal of Genocide Research*. Put briefly, Bartov argued that while some form of ethnic cleansing may have taken place in Palestine in 1948, he took issue with Shaw's broad sociological definition of genocide. He questioned its implications for juridical utility and Shaw's conflation of ethnic cleansing with genocide. Bartov concluded that the ultimate goal of Shaw's argument is to delegitimize the state of Israel and to foreground the Palestinian right of return to their homes and lands (see also Beckerman 2011).[14] Shaw's arguments have also been taken up by politically sympathetic scholars, who have argued that he focuses on 1948 as a singular event at the expense of ongoing Israeli policies that can be characterized as genocidal (Rashed and Short 2012). He has also been criticized for his exclusive focus on European nationalism for his genocide framework, taking an international historical perspective at the expense of the inherent relationship between settler-colonialism and genocide (Docker 2012). Shaw has responded to his critics, and the conversation has continued (Shaw 2013; Rashed, Short, and Docker 2014).

Regardless of how the Palestinian Nakba has been conceptualized, what is certain is that the debates over the nature of the war crimes that took place in 1948 are still ongoing in English. This is because the mass forcible dispossession that set the Palestinians apart from other colonized people in the post–World War II decolonization era is yet to be morally or politically acknowledged and resolved. The consequences of the Nakba, or the ongoing Israeli system of settler-colonial rule over historic Palestine, are therefore realities of the present and not merely the past. They are manifested in Palestinian communities' ongoing violent subjugation by the Israeli state and their dispossession from their lands to make room for Israeli Jewish settlers (Gordon 2008; Masalha 1997; Roy 2007). Finally, the Palestinian activists and community members whose visions, aspirations, memories, and narratives are examined in the subsequent chapters of this book did not need this scholarship to become aware of the atrocities inflicted upon them and their families by the incipient Israeli state. It took six decades for the Nakba to undergo transition from (ongoing Israeli) denial to an Anglophone scholarly acceptability, minus its moral and ethical implications in relation to the right of return. This is therefore a fact to be framed in terms of the relationship between global power, colonialism, and knowledge production.

CONCLUSION

In the seven decades since 1948, first Arab nationalist and later Palestinian patriotic discourses on the Nakba have been entangled with and produced within the context of Arab regional politics and history. The defeat of the

Arab nationalist liberation project in 1967, as encapsulated in Nasser and Nasserism in particular, gave way to a short-lived preoccupation with the new Nakba/Naksa that the defeat was seen to embody. This was followed by a marked retreat in the Arab Nakba's two-decade-old universe of discourse, the disappearance of the Nakba from Arab thought, and its eventual reemergence as part of a new discourse. This reemergence was largely the outcome of changes in the Palestinian liberation movement, Palestinians' memorialization of their past, and the partial opening of Israeli archives that pertain to 1948.

The notion of 1948-as-catastrophe's appearance, disappearance, and later reemergence in a different guise has been examined in relation to discourses. This was considered through the reading of different texts and a brief discussion of contemporary Palestinian efforts to commemorate the lost homeland and the Nakba. It is therefore important not to conflate this discursive reading of the transformation in the various meanings of the Nakba with memories and narratives of 1948 by Palestinians. A catastrophe responsible for the wholesale destruction of societies and communities does not simply "appear" and "disappear" for those who were massacred, terrorized, raped, taken as prisoners of war, or expelled and turned into refugees. This is especially the case when these refugees still lack acknowledgment and restitution for the crimes committed against them by the perpetrators. The issue at stake is thus one of power, and the question that needs to be asked is why it has taken so long to listen to Nakba memories and testimonies in an alleged age of "never again" for anyone after World War II. In addition, we must ask, how and why can this listening continue to take place without the moral and ethical implications enshrined in international humanitarian law?

Finally, this discursive reading of the Nakba provides the starting point from which to examine how Palestinian refugee activists have taken up the Nakba, understood in its exclusively Palestinian guise, in order to further specific political goals in their communities post-Oslo. It also provides the starting point from which to understand Nakba memories, histories, and narratives of 1948 in Syria. This is because memories of the Nakba circulate, not in a social vacuum, but against the backdrop of the seven-decade-old Arab nationalist and later Palestinian patriotic discourses. These discourses have implications for what Palestinians choose to remember and even forget. There is, however, another important and equally necessary starting point for understanding the memories and histories of the Nakba in Syria. This is the Palestinian refugee community's historical, political, and social experiences in the country. These experiences continue to play an important role in the different articulations of the Nakba in light of the Syrian war today.

CHAPTER 2

THE PALESTINIAN REFUGEE COMMUNITY IN SYRIA

When they [the generation of Palestine] would speak, I used to say to myself "why did they leave, why did they listen to what the Jews said." Now, in my current circumstances, they are saying that there might be a war, given that now you can feel the atmosphere of war, politically, I mean, if there is a war, God forbid, I wouldn't leave my house. Not because of bravery, I won't leave my house because I've been stung before, a house has already been left, and the successive generations were destroyed.

MANAL, THIRD-GENERATION PALESTINIAN REFUGEE MOTHER FROM SAFAD

The Palestinian is shelled in the resistance axis states, placed in the camps of death in the moderate states and barred from entering the Arab Spring states. Yet they still ask him to sing: The Arabs' homelands are my own!!!

YARMOUK CAMP NEWS FACEBOOK PAGE, "AL-FALASTINI" (2013)

The emergence of a Palestinian Nakba has been most recently tied to the historical, political, and social experience of Palestinian refugee communities. It is this same experience that led to the rise of the Right of Return Movement (RoRM) and its post-Oslo memory discourses. Similarly, it is this experience that plays a central role in the ways in which Palestinian refugees invoke their Nakba memories and narratives.

These overarching commonalities in the experiences of Palestinian refugee communities in the Arab world, however, have also been differently shaped by the country of the community in question.

For Palestinians in Syria, their experience in that country has been as important as Palestine and the Palestinian past in their recalling of memories of a shared past in a shared present. This chapter examines this Syrian Palestinian refugee experience, with the making of their community—and their communities—as a central point of departure. "Community" is here understood as modes of social organization and resultant forms of belonging and imagination of social relations (Delanty 2010). This is, on the one hand, the Palestinian refugee community that was politically, nationally, and legally defined and constructed through the bureaucratic practices of the Syrian state, the UN Relief and Works Agency for Palestine Refugees in the Near East (UNRWA), and the reemergence of the Palestinian national liberation movement after 1948. These are also, on the other hand, heterogeneous Palestinian refugee communities with different origins in Palestine, different places of abode in Syria, and different socioeconomic class and status that compose and define the larger community.

The making of these communities is examined through an interview-based portrait of the common experiences of the early years and changing Palestinian spatial realities in the Damascus and Rural Damascus Governorates. It is also assessed through the role of the Syrian state, UNRWA and the Palestinian liberation movement, the three key institutions that have been central to Palestinian refugee life in the country. These different historical, political, and social factors—including their institutional and spatial dimensions—have together defined, constructed, and demarcated the Palestinian refugee community in Syria. This, however, has not been a one-way process. Palestinians in Syria have, on their part, also constructed their everyday lived communities within historical and political opportunities and constraints.

THE DEMARCATION OF COMMUNITY: THE EARLY YEARS, THE STATE, AND UNRWA

Estimates of the number of Palestinian refugees arriving in Syria during the Nakba range from 75,000 to 100,000 (Rizqallah 1998, 59; Y. Sayigh 2004, 37–46). The Syrian state registered approximately 95,000 at the end of 1948

(GAPAR n/a, 10). The great majority came from northern Palestine. The Safad subdistrict was the main place of origin, followed by the Tiberias, Haifa, Acre, Nazareth, and Jaffa subdistricts. (Tiltnes 2006, 16). Although most came during 1948, Palestinians continued to arrive in Syria following the Nakba. For example, some members of the 'Arab al-Shamalina tribe, Safad subdistrict, were repatriated to their lands that fell under the jurisdiction of what was deemed a "demilitarized zone" as a result of the 1949 armistice agreements. They were, however, expelled for the second and final time in 1951 (see also Suleiman 1994, 154).[1] In addition, during the Suez War (1956), Israel used the increased tension on its border with Syria as a pretext to expel for the second and final time the Safad subdistrict tribes of Akrad al-Baqqara and Akrad al-Ghannama. Members of these two tribes had previously been expelled in 1948 to Syria and then repatriated to become "internal refugees" after the armistice agreements (Falah 1993, 54–56). According to the General Authority for Palestine Arab Refugees (GAPAR, Ministry of Social Affairs and Labor), the highest state body responsible for Palestinians in Syria, some 17,000 refugees were not registered by UNRWA, given their post-1948 expulsion. GAPAR also lists the people of another village by the name of Zayta as yet another example (GAPAR n/a, 7–8).

A number of Palestinians arrived after the Israeli occupation of the remainder of Palestine during the 1967 June War. This war also saw the occupation of the Syrian Golan Heights by Israel, which led to the internal displacement of up to 17,000 Palestinian refugees who had initially sought refuge there (UNGA 1967).[2] Palestinians also came to Syria following the expulsion of the Palestine Liberation Organization (PLO) from Jordan in 1970 during what is known as "Black September" and then in 1982 after the Israeli invasion of Lebanon ('Ayid 2012).[3] Most recently, Palestinian refugees came from Iraq following the US-led invasion in 2003. The overwhelming majority have been undocumented because they were not allowed to legally enter Syria. A handful of these families were moved to al-Hol Camp in al-Hasaka Governorate (Al-Achi 2010; Al-Hardan 2009; Gabiam 2006). The fate of Palestinians from Iraq who were in Syria on the eve of the uprising is largely unknown.

The Nakba meant the destruction and dispersal of entire communities, as well as the annihilation of half of Palestinian society as it had once existed. The most basic social unit of the family was itself uprooted and scattered. Different family members sought refuge in various states and acquired different political and legal statuses, many never to see each other again. Umm

Ya'rub, a teacher involved in nationalist organizing in al-Rama, Acre subdistrict, who left Palestine at the age of twenty-six, told me of the separation her family endured:

When the Zionists reached al-Rama, my mother immediately told me . . . she wanted me to flee from the other side [of the village]. So I told her: "Mother, I am not one to run away" . . . and her answer was: "This is not running away, because we all know what the outcome would be should you remain here." . . . My mother, she remained there forever. . . . They feared for the youth, because they took the youth. . . . Later, my brothers Nicola and George followed [to Syria]. . . . I had a sister, she remained there [too].[4]

With the exception of the minority who could afford to resettle in second homes or purchase or claim host-country citizenship, what the Nakba wrought on most Palestinians was a mass uprooting and pauperization that came through an abrupt "refugee-ization" (Brand 1988b, 1–21; R. Khalidi 1996, 177–186; R. Sayigh 2008a). The sentiment of starting from scratch was echoed by many Palestine-generation interviewees who had been expelled or fled with nothing. Although under the impression that they would return to their homes in a matter of days, they were to find themselves subsisting on the goodwill of the Red Cross, their Syrian hosts, or relatives and acquaintances. With bitter irony, Abu Ahmad, who left Safad at the age of eighteen, put it this way: "When we first came we thought that we were staying for a week, ten days, a month; it was only later that we realized that the whole situation was messed up. We didn't become refugees; we became beggars."[5]

The inability of anyone to foresee the magnitude of the calamity that unfolded and the assumption that the Arab states would offer rescue, amplified by inflated rhetoric (Zurayk [1948] 2001, 201), played an important role in these initial expectations. During my interview with Abu Samih, I asked how he could have continued to hope for Arab rescue after having witnessed the fall of some of Palestine's major towns during his time as a volunteer in the Muhammad Amin al-Husayni–loyal Jaysh al-Jihad al-Muqadas (Holy War Army). He said: "We used to say that this was all temporary, that the Arab armies will eventually reclaim it. . . . [We believed this] because of [what was said on] the [radio] stations, so and so says, 'The cannons [shall] speak,' and so and so says, 'We will attack.' In the end, it was all talk, nothing more."[6]

The late Umm Rim also related the sentiment of Arab and particularly Transjordanian betrayal and disappointment to me. Umm Rim was a young woman from Tiberias completing her education at the Teachers Training College in Jerusalem at the time of the adoption of UN General Assembly Resolution 181 at the end of 1947. The sentiment of betrayal, she told me, was circulated in the form of a popular song attributed to women Haganah recruits shortly after the Nakba: "We are the daughters of the Haganah, the seven kings won't be able to capture us; we spend our mornings in Haifa and our afternoons in Amman" (*Nihna banat el-hagana, saba' emluk ma btilgana; el-sobih fi Haifa wa ba'd el-duhur fi 'Amman*).[7]

Until early 1949, Arab host governments were responsible for the refugees, assisted by "public subscriptions, voluntary agencies and the UN Disaster Relief Project" (Howard 1966, 31). In Syria, the Red Cross provided immediate relief to the arriving refugees. This included providing tents and food rations critical to the survival of many who had fled the onslaught with nothing. The late Abu Khalil of Yaquq, Tiberias subdistrict, told me:

> We first came to the Golan . . . to an area known by the name of al-Butayha, it is on the border with Palestine. . . . [After four or five days] the Red Cross arrived and they brought us some cheese. . . . Later, they said gather yourselves in . . . Kafr Alma village. . . . That became the gathering point. . . . They [eventually] gave us tents, and about a month later, they began giving out flour, and dates, these kinds of things, and a bit of lentils. . . . We stayed there for two years.[8]

Whereas some like the late Abu Khalil came directly to Syria on foot, and others on boats from the coastal towns and villages of Palestine, yet others came via eastern Palestine, Jordan, and Lebanon. In Lebanon, the authorities transported Palestinians in overcrowded cattle trains to the center and north of Syria, where refugee camps were eventually established (Al-Mawed 1999). Tent camps were set up in various open-air sites, like the ones in the Golan described by Abu Khalil. Others found shelter in places like the abandoned army barracks outside Aleppo, the citadel in Busra, and the different Ottoman era *khan* (in the singular; inn) around Damascus. In Damascus itself, some were also hosted for extended periods in public institutions like schools and mosques. Others lodged with family or acquaintances, and the more well-to-do rented at their own expense.

Umm 'Izz al-Din, at thirty-five a survivor of the Tantura village massacre in the Haifa subdistrict (JPS 2001), recounted her early days as a refugee in the Busra citadel during a particularly harsh winter:

We stayed for fifty-five days. I lost my mind, I said, "What is this!" The Hawranis [the people of the Hawran, a region of Syria bordering Jordan] had no food or vegetables or anything; they were living on bulgur . . . and lentils. . . . The people of Tantura eventually received permission to go to Damascus . . . [where] we were placed in mosques. There were seventeen different mosques with refugees. Al-Muʻalaq mosque is still around. . . . The people of Lubya were in al-Muʻalaq mosque . . . there were one hundred families. . . . We stayed there for seven years. . . . We were the first people to rent [private lodgings].[9]

In January 1949, the Syrian government set up the Palestine Arab Refugee Institution (PARI), renamed GAPAR in 1974, as the highest state body responsible for Palestinians. In addition to being in charge of Palestinian refugees' affairs, it also oversees the Syrian operations of UNRWA, which began in May 1950 (UNGA 1949). Together with and under the supervision of PARI, UNRWA was responsible for providing the Palestinians in Syria with their basic needs, including shelter, food, education, and health care, in the years immediately following the Nakba (GAPAR n/a, 8–10). For the past seven decades UNRWA's mandate has been renewed, and it continues to operate in the Palestinian refugee community in Syria to provide what are arguably "responsibilities traditionally assigned to national governments in the field of education, health and social services" (al-Husseini 2000, 51). Thus, UNRWA has been and continues to be an important actor in the Palestinian refugee community in Syria, a role that has given the refugees a certain visibility during the war. Historically, Palestinian refugees have qualified for UNRWA's services from the Syrian state as well.

The second director of UNRWA, the American diplomat John B. Blandford Jr., devised what became known as the Blandford Plan. This plan sought money for a three-year combined relief and reintegration project, to be logistically carried out with the help of local governments, in order to allow refugees to become self-supporting and pave the way for their economic integration in the host countries. It was adopted by UN General Assembly Resolution 513 in January 1951 and it was part of the initial UNRWA reintegration and resettlement drive that came to a halt by the end of the agency's first decade of operation (Bowker 2003, 123–153; Buehrig 1971, 147; al-Husseini 2000, 52; M. Shadid 1981, 62–63).

In Syria, this plan found favor with some of the military men who had come to power in the repeated military coups that were a hallmark of Syria's postindependence history (Hinnebusch 2002). As early as 1949, Husni Za'im, the chief of staff of the Syrian army—who came to power in a coup in March before being deposed by yet another coup in August of the same year—began secret negotiations with Israeli agents. In the process, he offered to resettle up to 300,000 Palestinians through Western financing in a way that would economically transform and develop the Jazeera region of the country (Shlaim 1986). Attempts to implement the Blandford plan during this period in Syria took place through encouraging the resettlement of Palestinians in self-supporting farming and cattle-rearing communities. This took place in the al-Ramadan area on the outskirts of the eastern desert region in return for their renunciation of UNRWA relief. By 1954, some twenty to twenty-five families had been resettled there. However, the project failed as within months the families spent the capital they were supposed to invest in their new lands, and some were unable to farm altogether, for not all refugees came from rural localities. Soon UNRWA gave up on the project before PARI brought the enterprise to an end (Suleiman 1994, 156–157).

The al-Ramadan project, retrospectively, became the one-off exception to the rule in Syria. The system that eventually prevailed was the allotment of state land by PARI, in cooperation with UNRWA, to the Palestinian refugees. They were subsequently allowed to build and own their private home structures on the land until implementation of their right of return.[10] The al-Ramadan Camp, defined as a camp by GAPAR but not by UNRWA (GAPAR n/a, 19), continues to exist, housing a small resident community of UNRWA-registered Palestinian refugees.[11] Like the rest of the country, al-Ramadan also became embroiled in the Syrian war (AGPS 2013a, 2014).

The first League of Arab States (LAS) resolution on Palestinian refugees was adopted in 1950. The league urged member states to cooperate with UNRWA without prejudicing the final solution to the Palestine question, the refugees' right of return and right to be compensated for their losses (GAPAR n/a, 10). Subsequently, LAS issued numerous resolutions in the first post-1948 decade that called on member states to issue Palestinian refugees with travel documents to facilitate their mobility (but not to naturalize them) and to ease work restrictions (Brand 1988b, 25–26). The most comprehensive resolution would come through the 1965 Casablanca Protocol. The protocol called on member states to allow Palestinians the right to employment on par with citizens and the freedom of movement within Arab states. This movement was to be facilitated by granting Palestinians valid travel documents and treating these documents as national passports issued by LAS members (LAS 1965).

Given that LAS resolutions are nonbinding, they were largely ignored. The political and legal status and rights of Palestinian refugees were eased or restricted differentially depending on their host country. In Syria, the easing of work restrictions for Palestinians began as early as November 1948, when Palestinian drivers and fishermen were granted the right to practice their professions (GAPAR n/a, 23). By September 1949, legislation was passed that allowed Palestinians access to public sector employment; further legislation during the early years made additional jobs accessible (Brand 1988c, 623; GAPAR n/a, 23–29). In 1955 Palestinians were issued with restricted travel documents that required a reentry permit (GAPAR n/a, 26); before this, Palestinians had state identification cards as well as UNRWA and PARI ration-entitlement booklets (Brand 1988c, 623; al-Husseini 2000, 53). The most comprehensive Syrian legislation with regards to Palestinian refugees in the country was passed a year later. This is Law 260, adopted in 1956, which became the basic law that governed and continues to govern the state's relationship to the Palestinians. Article 1 of this law reads, "The Palestinians residing in the Syrian Republic as of the adoption of this law are to be regarded as Syrians in origin in relation to all the laws and regulations that have thus far been adopted, viz. employment, work and trade rights and military service, while retaining their original nationality" (GAPAR n/a, 40).

Law 260 in essence as well as in practice granted the Palestinian refugees who were present in 1956 rights shared by no other Palestinian refugee community in Arab host states. The nationality clause means that the only right they lack is the right to vote. In 1963, the reentry permit requirement for Palestinians was removed (GAPAR n/a, 27). This, along with Law 260, gave Palestinians in Syria rights on par with Syrian nationals. There are, however, limitations placed on property ownership to one property per refugee and the ownership of land (Takkenberg 1998, 167–169). The official reason for this is the state's compliance with LAS resolutions that call on member states not to encourage Palestinian refugee resettlement.[12] In reality, however, loopholes exist, and thus there are ways in which to circumvent these restrictions.

Today this group of Palestinian refugees who arrived in 1948 and were present in 1956—the majority of Palestinians in the country on the eve of the war—have the right to private and public sector employment and state education, including higher education. Men over the age of eighteen are drafted and subject to compulsory military service. This service is carried out in the Syrian branch of the Palestine Liberation Army (PLA), formed as part of the PLO in 1964. The PLA, also known as the Hittin Brigade, is today part of the regular Syrian army (Brand 1988c; Y. Sayigh 1989). The state issues Palestinians with "temporary residency cards for Palestinian refugees" that in reality do not need to be renewed; they are temporary only in that legally, Palestinians are refugees who are meant to return to their homeland one day.

Not all Palestinians, however, arrived in the country before 1956. Thus not all Palestinians who are refugees in Syria enjoy the rights granted by Law 260. The most obvious segment of Palestinian refugee society that is excluded from the law and whose host state is Syria are the people of Akrad al-Baqqara and Akrad al-Ghannama, as well as their descendants. This is because they were expelled to Syria after the adoption of Law 260. In addition, Palestinians in Syria who were registered in other host states, like Lebanon, and those who carry Jordanian passports or were denationalized by Jordan following Black September are excluded from Law 260. Estimates of Palestinians in Syria excluded from Law 260 on the eve of the war stood at 100,000 out of a total population of some 600,000, of which half a million were UNRWA-registered 1948 Palestinian refugees (Salayma 2012).

Despite the unparalleled rights enjoyed by Palestinians as refugees in Syria, all Arab states impose numerous restrictions on the mobility of Palestinians. This discriminatory treatment was most recently seen in how Lebanon and Jordan initially facilitated the entry of Syrian refugees fleeing the war but restricted that of Palestinians fleeing Syria (AI 2013, 2014; HRW 2012). The Palestinians' immobility, coupled with the discriminatory treatment by Arab states, was an important topic in my interviews and conversations in Syria, especially with the new generation of Palestinian refugees. In a 2005 UNRWA-commissioned Geneva and Louvain University quantitative survey of 2,000 Palestinian refugees in UNRWA's different areas of operation, the data on Palestinians in Syria stand out. Their responses were exceptional in that they placed less emphasis on lack of rights, access to services, and discrimination than did other Palestinian refugees, and more on their immobility (Al-Husseini and Bocco 2009, 282).[13]

This historical, political, and legal sketch of the early years in Syria underscores common Palestinian experiences in the country over the years. These experiences are the basis for the realities of lived day-to-day Palestinian communities in Syria. Through these everyday lives and interactions, Palestinians were to become members of different communities. These encompassed Arab, including Syrian Arab, students, coworkers, neighbors, and even family members through marriage or local community members through abode. This took place as Palestinians went to Syrian state schools and universities, worked in the public and private sectors, and owned and lived in properties in Palestinian camps, in small Palestinian communities outside the camps, or in Syrian-majority areas. At the same time, the state's bureaucratic instruments and practices served to demarcate and construct Palestinians as legally, politically, and nationally constituting "a community." Thus, the Palestinians in Syria were to gradually become a distinct community composed of refugees who nevertheless enjoyed rights on par with Syrian citizens.[14]

Another important institution that enabled the making of a distinct Palestinian refugee community in Syria is UNRWA (Bocco and Takkenberg 2009; Gabiam 2016; Hanafi, Hilal, and Takkenberg 2014). The UN agency's operational mandate first defined who constitutes a Palestine refugee (UNRWA n/a-a). Through its humanitarian, institutional, and bureaucratic practices, it would come to further demarcate and embedd its operational mandate's definitions over the years (Feldman 2012; UNRWA n/a-c). Further, it is the intersection between the policies and practices of the state and UNRWA that has played a central role in the making of a distinct community. This can be seen most clearly in the field of education: UNRWA provides education in its schools until the ninth grade, after which students continue their secondary education in state schools. Throughout their schooling years, students study the Syrian Ba'thist Arab nationalist curriculum, which includes topics like Palestine and the Nakba. The UNRWA schools are staffed by Palestinians— whether in camps or in Palestinian communities outside the camps—and have a Palestinian-majority student body.[15] The state's Ba'thist curriculum and UNRWA's Palestinian-majority educational framework have together provided a central institutional context within which the overlapping national and local communities and, most important, their histories are defined and reproduced.

It is such intersections of these two institutions in particular that have played an important role in creating a distinct Palestinian refugee community in Syria and have facilitated common histories and memories. Underscoring this point is not to suggest that Palestinians in Syria have merely been passive recipients or simply constructs of the state and UNRWA. It is true that the state allowed the establishment of the camps, played an important role in demarcating community, and even co-opted Palestinians, especially through GAPAR or its relationship with the PLO. The Palestinians themselves have however also created and given meanings to their lived communities. This is most clearly evident in the rise of the Palestinian liberation movement, which has posed a challenge to the state in the past.

Similarly, UNRWA's humanitarian construction of a community of refugees was for the purpose of facilitating its humanitarian mission, such as dispensing aid or providing services. Its local Palestinian-majority staff have worked within these internationally determined parameters, it has been argued, to "appropriate, renegotiate or subvert humanitarian classifications and practices, and challenge the intentions and interests of more powerful actors" (Farah 2009b, 392). The field of education is once again important in this regard. For example, on the sixtieth anniversary of the Nakba, in 2008, Palestinian UNRWA teachers were working with RoRM activists in Yarmouk in order to incorporate into the curriculum the histories, memories, and knowledge of places of origin in historic Palestine (R. Davis 2010, 64–67). This demonstrates that the bureaucratic making of community is not a one-way process.

Another important factor in the construction of a community in Syria has been in the intersection of state and UNRWA practices and policies in the field of housing. Historically, UNRWA, in collaboration with and under the supervision of the state, facilitated the construction of Palestinian refugee camps and extended its services to those who lived beyond camp borders in small Palestinian communities known as *tajamu'at*. The construction of these camps has been important in physically creating Palestinian refugee communities. Nevertheless it is the inhabitants of these localities who, through their shared everyday experiences and interactions, including circulating common memories and histories, gave meaning to and shaped these localities (see, e.g., Peteet 2005).

CHANGING PALESTINIAN SPATIAL REALITIES

Today there are nine "official" UNRWA-defined camps in Syria. Five of these are administratively located in the Rural Damascus Governorate and now surround the capital, given that the city has expanded and engulfed its once-rural surroundings since their establishment. The camps that surround Damascus are Jaramana, Khan Danoun, Khan Eshieh, Qabr Essit (also known as al-Sayida Zaynab), and Sbeineh. These camps, which I visited and where I conducted interviews, are today under government control following fierce battles, with residents gradually returning (Sbeineh, Qabr Essit), are war zones (Khan Eshieh), or are severely affected by the war (Jaramana, Khan Danoun) (UNRWA 2018). The four other UNRWA camps are in the south, center, and north of the country. In the south is the now approximately 70 percent destroyed and inaccessible Dera'a Camp (composed of two sections, known as the 1948-established 'Aidin and 1967-established Taware')

(AGPS 2015). In the center of Syria are the Hama (also known as ʿAidin), and Homs (also known as ʿAidin) Camps, today calm though severely affected by the war. Finally, in the north is Neirab Camp in Aleppo, which remains calm but like virtually every locality through which the war has passed, is severely affected by it (UNRWA 2015).

A further three camps are "unofficial," according to UNRWA—though all are recognized as camps by GAPAR. This definition is based on UNRWA's role in solid waste collection, which determines whether the agency defines a camp as official or unofficial. In reality, however, UNRWA cooperates with GAPAR regarding basic camp infrastructure services even in the UNRWA-defined and therefore "official" camps.[16] The unofficial camps include Ein el-Tal (also known as Hindarat) and Latakia (also known as ʿAidin or al-Raml) in Aleppo and Latakia Governorates respectively. Armed groups depopulated Ein el-Tal in April 2013 (Dayyub 2013) and it has since come back under government control, now approximately 80 percent destroyed (AGPS 2018). Latakia Camp is today calm after having been severely affected by the war in August 2011 (UNRWA 2015). The third of these unofficial camps, Yarmouk, where I lived for six months, lies within the administrative boundaries of the Damascus Governorate and as such is part of Damascus proper. Yarmouk has been particularly hard hit by the war. This is because of its infiltration by the armed opposition, its strategic location as a gateway to southern Damascus, and the ongoing siege that has been imposed on the camp by the Syrian regime and its Popular Front for the Liberation of Palestine–General Command (PFLP-GC) allied faction since July 2013 (Bitari 2013). This siege has now extended to cutting off water and electricity even though approximately 18,000 Palestinian refugees remained in the camp prior to the appearance of the Islamic State of Iraq and Syria (ISIS) in and within the vicinity of the camp in April 2015 (AGPS 2015; UNRWA 2015). Estimates of the number of people who remain in Yarmouk today in the wake of the government offensive against ISIS stands at fewer than 1,000–2,000. A deal has now been reached by the government to evacuate armed groups and their families from the vicinity of Yarmouk to the north of Syria (AGPS 2018). GAPAR lists a further two localities as camps: al-Ramadan in the Rural Damascus Governorate and Jilin Camp/ Mazarib community in the Darʿa Governorate (GAPAR n/a: 19), all severely affected by the war (see, e.g., UNRWA 2014).

The UN agency extends its three main services of health, education, and social support to UNRWA and state-defined camps as well as Palestinian communities outside the camps. The latter are localities with substantial Palestinian refugee residents, sometimes locally referred to as "camps."

Some of these have today been completely depopulated. In the Damascus and Rural Damascus Governorates, these gatherings before the war were located in al-Hajar al-Aswad (bordering Yarmouk Camp), al-Husayniyya, al-Qabun, Barza (Hittin Camp), Duma, Dummar, Hay al-Amin (also known as Alliance, Old City quarter), Hosh Blas, al-Mazza, Jdaydat 'Artuz, Drusha, Jubar, and Rukn al-Din (Salayma 2012). Many of these localities have been substantially depopulated and severely affected by the war, and UNRWA's services have been either totally or severely disrupted (AGPS 2015). Finally, Palestinians also live outside these localities in Syrian-majority areas, whether in towns or in the countryside.

As is clear from this sketch of the geographical and spatial distribution of Palestinian refugees in Syria, Damascus is a significant location for Palestinian refugee life in the country. More than half of the UNRWA-defined camps surround the capital, and given the geography of the city, it could be argued that these camps are part of the greater Damascus metropolitan area. Furthermore, Yarmouk, which is a suburb of Damascus proper, was home to roughly 150,000 UNRWA-registered Palestinians before the exodus at the end of 2012. This means that just under half of the Palestinians in the capital and approximately one-third of the Palestinians in the country as a whole lived in this one locality. Another quarter or so of those who resided in the capital did so in the five UNRWA-defined camps. The rest lived in communities either in the city, its suburbs, or its rural outskirts, ten of which were big enough to be served by differing numbers of UNRWA schools, health centers, and relief distribution services.[17] Others resided in other areas of the city. This geographic importance of Damascus and its environs to approximately four-fifths of the Palestinians in Syria also explains the severe impact on the community brought about by the full-scale militarization of the uprising in the Rural Damascus Governorate in late 2011.

Yarmouk was unlike any of the camps in Syria and was dubbed "diaspora capital" ('asimat al-shatat) by local researchers and activists because of its former exceptional demographic and economic status (Abu Rashid 2013; Al-Mawed 2002; Gabiam 2009). It officially came into existence in 1957 (UNRWA n/a-b), though land distribution began as early as 1954–1955. It has been noted that the mid-1950s "saw the beginning of the process of the transportation of the Palestinians from the mosques, schools, hospitals and the new community that was referred to as 'Alliance Camp' (al-Amin quarter) [in the Old City] to a new community by the name of Yarmouk Camp" (Al-Mawed 2002, 21). Before the transformation of Yarmouk into a war zone, it was home to two bustling main commercial streets, one the namesake of the camp and the other Falastin (Palestine), both served by a number of transportation routes and frequented by people from all over Damascus. Unlike other refugee camps, which have only GAPAR offices, Yarmouk also had its own GAPAR-controlled and -administered local council (Hanafi 2011, 40–41).

The Palestinians in Yarmouk had become a minority on the eve of the war's arrival. This is because the camp had expanded well beyond the original state-allotted land and had become an integral part of the surrounding Rural Damascus Governorate localities. The estimated population of Yarmouk and its environs was approximately one million inhabitants (UNRWA 2012a). It is in the neighborhoods that surround Yarmouk, including al-Hajar al-Aswad, al-Tadamun, al-Taqadum, and al-'Uruba, many of which are indistinguishable from the original camp boundaries to visitors, that the fighting between armed groups and the regular army began. Yarmouk's apartment buildings, both in the original part of the camp as well as in its sprawl, were home to working-class Damascenes, rural-urban migrants, Gypsies, Syrians displaced from the Golan, and Iraqi and Palestinian Iraqi refugees who came following the US invasion of that country in 2003 (al-Samadi 2013).

Within this context, the fact that there was a Ministry of Culture–run Arab Cultural Center in Yarmouk, a feature of Damascene neighborhoods, and nine Ministry of Education–run secondary schools made Yarmouk similar to other neighborhoods of the city (Hanafi 2011, 41). What distinguished Yarmouk from them, despite the mixed and once-vibrant demographic reality, was its Palestinian character, with the names of streets and quarters reflecting places of origin in historic Palestine. Commercial businesses carried Palestinian names, and Palestinian political posters were conspicuous. The only remnants that hinted at Yarmouk's origins as a camp were the alleyways of the original 2.1 square kilometers of Yarmouk. These alleyways are today indistinguishable rubble, even to those intimately familiar with the camp. Once a far cry from the narrow alleyways of the UNRWA-defined camps, the alleyways of Yarmouk were generally wide enough to allow for the passage of cars. If Yarmouk is considered an integral urban suburb of Damascus, not a camp, then approximately three-quarters of Palestinians in the capital lived outside the camps on the eve of 2011, given their prewar concentration in Yarmouk and its environs.

The UNRWA-defined camps that surround Damascus were unlike Yarmouk (UNRWA n/a-b). Their standard of living, including infrastructure, was substantially lower than that of Yarmouk. The poorest homes in Jaramana Camp, itself cut in two by the Damascus airport highway, which forms a substantial hazard for residents, still have corrugated iron roofs. Given how these camps developed—from tents into mud houses and later concrete structures—their meandering alleyways are sometimes less than two meters apart. Khan Eshieh and Khan Danoun, the two most remote and rural UNRWA camps in relation to Damascus, have unpaved and unlit alleyways. They have lacked sewage disposal and water network systems since 1948. In 2008, the construction of a new system in cooperation with the European Union began (EU 2009, 27). This was part of UNRWA's overall Infrastructure and Camp Improvement Program, launched in 2006, which it extended to other refugee camps in Syria, Lebanon, and the Occupied Palestinian Territories (OPT) (Gabiam 2012, 2014; Misselwitz and Hanafi 2009; Tabar 2012).

None of these camps, however, were sealed urban spaces; rather, they had become an integral part of the areas in which they were established, which partly explains why they could not remain neutral during the uprising, as was the initial stance of most Palestinian factions (Salayma 2012). Thus, the camps were always open spaces in relation to movement, commerce, residence, and kinship. They also were home to poorer rural-urban Syrian migrants as well Syrians who had been displaced from the Golan in 1967.[18]

For example, Sbeineh Camp, of which 70 percent is today estimated to have been destroyed, according to the Action Group for Palestinians in Syria, was from the outside almost indistinguishable from the adjacent Masakin Sbeineh neighborhood. Masakin Sbeineh was home to Syrians displaced from the Golan as well as Palestinians who had moved there. These demographic realities and the differences between the two adjacent areas were not immediately visible to the visitor walking down the main street of Sbeineh Camp/Masakin Sbeineh. Only the blue UNRWA welcome sign, posted at the entrance of all UNRWA-defined camps, marked one part of this urban space as a camp. These signs and the distinctly narrow and meandering alleyways of Palestinian camps, visible only once inside, were perhaps the only two markers that betrayed the origins of the UNRWA-defined Rural Damascus Governorate camps. The same could be said of Qabr Essit Camp, an almost indistinguishable part of what was a bustling commercial area catering to pilgrims to the shrine of al-Sayida Zaynab.

This sketch of changing Palestinian refugee localities in Syria demonstrates the ways in which the state, hand in hand with UNRWA, enabled geographically situated Palestinian refugee communities in and outside of the camps. However, as they did with other state and UNRWA policies, Palestinians also carved their own communities within the parameters of historical, political, and social opportunities and constraints (see also Farah 2003). These communities are further explored in subsequent chapters through their own grassroots institutions' memorial political mobilization efforts and through their symbolic contours in the form of shared histories, memories, and narratives.

What this sketch also demonstrates is that unlike for Palestinian refugees elsewhere, particularly Lebanon, the geographical boundaries of Palestinian communities in Syria were fluid. This is as a result of policies and everyday realities of communities that deemed the larger community to be composed of both the same peoples (Arabs with equal civic rights) and others (Palestinians, refugees). Before the war, third-generation Palestinian refugees articulated this reality through an ambivalent sense of belonging—that is, at once belonging to Syria and also to something else, Palestine. Thus, the social and economic integration of Palestinians into the fabric of Syrian society, while ensuring their distinct Palestinian and refugee identity, often translated into feeling different, multiple, and even ambivalent belongings to both Palestine and Syria. Today this fluidity is articulated through Palestinian refugees' yearning for their destroyed communities and a return to them. These multiple belongings are often superficially misunderstood as displaced Palestinians from Syria being really Syrian rather than Palestinians, a not uncommon assumption in Lebanon, home to approximately 31,000 Palestinians from Syria.[19]

The third and final institution that has also enabled these multiple belongings and has historically played an important role in how Palestinians themselves have carved their own histories, political opportunities, and communities is the Palestinian liberation movement. It has been argued that the camps were once important recruiting grounds for this movement and significantly "benefited a military resistance project" (Farah 2009a, 80). Syria has been no exception, and it is to this movement—its history, its transformation, and the marks it left behind—that I now turn.

THE PALESTINIAN NATIONAL MOVEMENT IN SYRIA

It has been widely argued that the early years following the Nakba "consisted of 'lost years' between 1948 and the emergence of the Palestine Liberation Organization in 1964, during which the Palestinians seemed to many to have disappeared from the political map as an independent actor, and indeed as a people" (R. Khalidi 1996, 178). Far from being lost, however, these early years, consisted of reviving or reconstituting "women's, teachers', students' and workers' organizations as well as charitable societies . . . the natural heirs of the pre-1948 institutions" (Brand 1988b, 4).

These early years were therefore "a critical formative period for the later development of the quasi-governmental institutions that later emerged" (4).

Examples of this early Palestinian political organizing can be found in an account by Zafir bin Khadra' (1999), who helped establish the Syrian branch of the Arab Nationalists Movement (ANM). In his account, Bin Khadra' states that he helped found an early clandestine group, Palestine's Children (Abna' Falastin), formed by first-year University of Damascus students during the 1953–1954 academic year. One of the founding members of this group was Mahmoud Abbas. The group's activities included secret meetings, dissemination of publications, and organization of demonstrations. One of the main goals of the group was to organize around the right of return, equal rights, and military enlistment. In 1956, Palestine's Children contacted another Palestinian group, The Heroes of Return (Abtal al-'Awda), based in Homs Camp, which was organizing around the same goals. Two years later Palestine's Children's members dissolved the group as they parted ways (Bin Khadra' 1999, 120–124).

The General Union of Palestine Students (1959), the General Union of Palestine Workers (1963), and the General Union of Palestinian Women (1965) were popular instruments of mobilization that characterized the early post-1948 years (Brand 1988a, 30). They were, however, weak and only marginally active in Syria (Brand 1988c). This is because Syrian unions and other instruments of popular mobilization have always been open to Palestinians. Insofar as the Palestinian unions were concerned, this resulted in a duality of their purpose, whether for organizing or through providing a space for the expression of Palestinian identity. In addition, Palestinian organizations, like their Syrian equivalents, have since 1963 been subject to the Ba'th Party's stringent control (Brand 1988c).

After the PLO, created by the Gamal Abdel Nasser–dominated LAS summit in 1964, subsumed the Palestinian unions, Palestinian mass organizing in Syria became contingent on the relationship between Syria and Egypt. Similarly, the ability of extra-PLO groups like Fatah and the ANM to organize—including through enlistment, training, and the procurement of arms—was also contingent upon this relationship. Further, the creation of the PLO's PLA units in Iraq and Syria was a result of inter-Arab politics, as well as the attempts by the Iraqi leader Abdul Karim Qasim to outbid Nasser by playing the "Palestine card" (Y. Sayigh 2004, 25–142). Finally, the Ba'th Party also attempted to co-opt Palestinian fighters shortly before the 1967 June War through the establishment of its own Vanguards of the Popular War of Liberation—the Thunderbolt Forces (al-Sa'iqa). It did this at its party congress in 1966 for the purpose of waging a "people's war" against Israel (Brand 1988c; Y. Sayigh 2004, 184–188). It has been argued that the relaunching of al-Saʻiqa in 1968 was tied to the power struggles among the Baʻthist military officers ruling Syria (Y. Sayigh 2004, 184–185). At its height, al-Saʻiqa had up to 5,000 recruits (Brand 1988c, 626). It underwent an internal power struggle that unfolded in tandem with the power struggle among the Baʻthist military officers and was purged in 1970. The eventual Syrian withdrawal from Lebanon following the Israeli invasion in 1982 saw the remaining Saʻiqa fighters defect en masse to Palestinian guerrilla groups (Brand 1988c, 626).

The years before the June War also saw the establishment of a brief union between Egypt and Syria (1958–1961) through the United Arab Republic (UAR). This union had direct bearing on the Palestinians in Syria (and the Gaza Strip) through Nasser's codification of the Palestinian Arab Nationalist Union (al-Ittihad al-Qawmi al-Falastini) (PANU) in 1958. This was done in part as a counterweight to attempts by Muhammad Amin al-Husayni to revive the Arab Higher Committee (al-Sharif 1995, 81–84). The institutional framework provided in PANU's constitution included "local and regional councils and higher executive councils (all with offices and employees) . . . and a budget" (Brand 1988b, 27). Elections to PANU took place in 1960 throughout the UAR, including the Gaza Strip, marking "the first time Palestinians had exercised the right to vote in direct elections" (27). However, PANU never had any real active political role, given the nature of Nasser's domination of the UAR. Its existence came to an end with the end of the union in 1961 (28).

After 1967, Syrian policy toward the guerrillas—who took control of the PLO in 1969—became a central issue in the power struggles within the regime's top military echelons (R. Khalidi 1984). The immediate outcome of the June War opened the way for the various Palestinian guerrilla groups to actively engage in the armed struggle they had launched three years earlier. Two months after the new Arab defeat, the guerrillas began organizing and mounting armed operations from what had become the OPT. The swift Israeli crackdown meant that the fighters were dealt a military and organizational blow. However, it has been argued that "reports of their losses showed them to be virtually the only organizations on the ground and . . . actively resisting occupation" (Y. Sayigh 1992, 258). This further increased their popularity and also meant that they would quickly assume the task of liberating Palestine in light of the 1967 defeat.

The first post-1969 phase of the liberation struggle saw the guerrilla groups launch an armed struggle for the declared purpose of the liberation of historic Palestine, of which return was an inherent part, and the establishment of a democratic state for all its inhabitants. Two crucial events would change the course and the goal of the armed struggle. The first was the expulsion of PLO fighters and their families from Jordan in a bloody crack-down during Black September in 1970. The second was the joint Syrian and Egyptian offensive in their respective Israeli-occupied territories during the 1973 October War, which was thwarted by Israel. Black September forced the PLO first into Syria and later into Lebanon, where it would remain until 1982. The October War paved the way for Arab and international recognition, through the Non-Aligned Movement, of the PLO as the sole and legitimate representative of the Palestinian people (Y. Sayigh 1986). Subsequent regional and international events, especially the Egyptian abandonment of the Arab front and treaty with Israel in 1979 (Y. Sayigh 1991a), would also play a detrimental role in the changing course of the PLO's armed struggle.

It has been argued that the Arab and international recognition accorded to the PLO led it to scale down its demands, "to renounce its 'revolutionary' character and accept the legitimacy of the existing Arab order" (Y. Sayigh 1986, 101). As a result, in 1974 the PLO adopted the "stages" or "phases program" in which the goal of the armed struggle was no longer the wholesale liberation of historic Palestine but, rather, its liberation in stages (R. Khalidi 1992). In Syria, Hafiz al-Asad and the officers who came to power in the aftermath of Black September opposed independent Palestinian political initiative and uncontrolled military activity, which they saw as clashing with Syria's regional interests. Armed clashes occurred during Lebanon's civil war, when Syria intervened against the PLO-Lebanese leftist coalition in 1976 after they had gained the upper hand against the right (Brand 1988c; Y. Sayigh 1989). Although relations were restored, the final parting of the ways occurred after Syria stood by during Israel's war on the PLO and its siege of Beirut in 1982 (Y. Sayigh 1983a, 1983b). This siege ended after the airlifting of the PLO's entire 15,000 civil and military personnel from the city. The headquarters of the PLO and Fatah were relocated to Tunisia in the wake of 1982, while the PLO's civilian and military personnel were dispersed.

It has been argued that Syria's 1976 intervention in Lebanon constituted an attempt to insert itself as an arbiter between the different sides in a way that would serve its own foreign policy interests relating to Israel in particular (Hinnebusch 2014). In these terms, its intervention against the PLO-Lebanese leftist coalition was in part to stop the emergence of a block that could have provided Israel with grounds for military intervention in Lebanon. It also allowed Syria to place its own army in the east of Lebanon and to protect itself from this possible threat (Hinnebusch 2014, 223). In accordance with these interests, Syria also played a critical role in harnessing the "anti-Arafat opposition" during the Lebanon years (Brand 1990). This opposition developed into a full-blown mutiny and drove the remaining

Fatah forces from Lebanon in 1983. The Syrian government openly supported the secessionists during the intra-Fatah fighting that broke out in Lebanon, and it subsequently cracked down on Fatah cadres in Syria, imprisoning up to 2,000 activists (Brand 1988c; R. Khalidi 1984; Sayigh 1988).

As a result of this crackdown, PLO and Fatah institutions in Syria—the former semidefunct, the latter operating indirectly through charitable or educational enterprises prior to the war—never fully recovered and remained marginal to Palestinian life in the country on the eve of the uprising.[20] In addition, Syria hosted the anti-Fatah and anti-PLO factions, which after the Oslo Accords came to be formally known as the Alliance of (Ten) Palestinian Forces (Strindberg 2000). In the 1990s these factions were also joined by the anti-Oslo Islamist opposition, the most significant of which was the political bureau of the Islamic Resistance Movement, known by its acronym Hamas. However, Hamas broke off from the regime during the uprising and changed its policy regarding its previous ally and the uprising toward the end of 2011 (Napolitano 2013).

Thus, the crackdown on the PLO and Fatah began the process of their peripheralization in the Palestinian community in Syria. This coincided with the overall decline in the PLO's influence in what had been its main constituency, the refugee communities, after its evacuation from Beirut and the loss of its civilian and military quasi-statist base in Lebanon. The onset of the first intifada, the Palestinian popular uprising against Israeli occupation in the OPT in 1987, and the PLO's adoption of its "Declaration of Independence" in 1988 accelerated the process of separation between the liberation movement and its former core refugee constituencies (Y. Sayigh 1989, 247).[21] In addition, the beginning of the Oslo Accords in 1993 saw the shift of the liberation movement's center of gravity to the OPT and, arguably, the Palestine question's center of gravity was also shifted. The negotiations and the capitulations to Israel essentially transformed the PLO, through the Oslo-created Palestinian Authority, into a subcontractor of the Israeli occupation (Chomsky 1999, 553–565). This further entrenched the gulf between the Palestinian liberation movement and the refugees. It has also led to the common perception today that the PLO has in effect abandoned a coherent anticolonial national liberation project that includes the refugees and their political claims to the right of return.

It is therefore through this historical experience of the liberation movement that Palestinians in Syria have marked the national parameters of their communities. Unlike in neighboring Lebanon, there were always limits to this. In addition, the policies of the state meant that in certain instances the PLO had a dual purpose (e.g., in the provision of social services). On the eve of the uprising, what did have a presence in terms of Palestinians' own political mobilization and community organizing were civic organizations. Some of these were autonomous, and some were more directly tied to Palestinian factions. Common to these organizations was their emergence to fill the absence in PLO institutions and to combat the post-Oslo political marginalization of the rights of Palestinian refugees. It is within this context that some of these political factions and civic organizations together formed what has, in light of the Oslo Accords and the threats they posed to the Palestinian refugees in particular, come to be known as the RoRM. It is in and through the RoRM, I contend, that Palestinians in Syria were trying to stake a claim in Palestinian politics, especially by contesting the separation of liberation from return. In the process, they articulated the Palestinian Nakba's contemporary universe of discourse.

CONCLUSION

Toward the end of 2012, a month before the bombardment of Yarmouk and the exodus of its residents, PA president Mahmoud Abbas gave an interview on the Israeli Channel 2 television station. Abbas, whose mandate to govern had expired four years earlier, declared that he has the right only to visit rather than to live in his hometown of Safad. Responding to the interviewer's question as to whether he considered Safad to be Palestine, Abbas asserted that Palestine comprises its 1967 borders, with East Jerusalem as its capital. "Now and forever," he continued, "this is Palestine for me, I am a refugee, but I am living in Ramallah, I believe that the West Bank and Gaza [are] Palestine, and other parts [are] Israel" (Mondoweiss 2012).

Three months later, after the full-scale arrival of the war to the biggest Palestinian community in Syria, Abbas was eager to portray his principled defense of the refugees' right of return. In an interview on the new post-uprising pan-Arab news network station Al-Mayadeen, he revealed that he had asked the UN secretary-general to seek Israeli permission for Palestinian refugees fleeing Syria to enter the OPT. Given that Israelis made the entry of refugees conditional upon their renunciation of their right of return, Abbas told the interviewer that he had (heroically) refused the Israeli offer. In an implicit reference to his earlier Israeli television interview, which led to demonstrations and condemnations in the OPT (Sherwood 2012), Abbas asserted that his stance on his own personal right of return did not contradict his defense of the Syrian Palestinian refugees' rights (Ma'an 2013a). A statement issued by the Israeli Prime Minister's Office, which followed this interview, denied Israel having agreed to the entry of Palestinian refugees fleeing Syria. The UNRWA commissioner-general, on his part, stated that his agency was unaware of any such deal (Ma'an 2013b).

Abbas's statements on Israeli television added nothing new to what was already in the public domain insofar as the Palestinian leadership's rescinding of the right of return in all but name is concerned (Swisher 2011). His cynical attempt to portray himself as the defender of the refugees and their rights in his Arabic interview merely served to underscore the extent of the Palestinian leadership's political bankruptcy. While this leadership is now publicly on record for having abandoned the refugees as a political constituency and this constituency's political rights, the expired-mandate president had no qualms in proclaiming that in the name of rights he had long abandoned, he had blocked the entry of Palestinians fleeing a war.

The hypocrisy of Abbas's unhesitant use of the fate of Palestinians in Syria to score political points demonstrates the contemporary nature of the Palestinian leadership and its relationship to Palestinian refugees. This is the case even if the Israelis had indeed consented to allow Palestinians to enter the OPT—which is highly unlikely, given Israel's track record on the right of return issue (Fischbach 2003; Masalha 2003). Abbas's statements shed light on the unbridgeable gulf between an unaccountable leadership and a long-abandoned constituency. This gulf has widened in view of the crisis of the community in Syria, who are today leaderless and unrepresented during a calamity of unprecedented proportions. The Palestinian refugees, who were first excluded from the decision-making process during the Oslo Accords, have therefore yet again been failed by their leaders, with dire consequences.

Thus, it is within this context of the Palestinian refugee community's historical, political, and social experience examined in this chapter and the transformation of the Palestinian national liberation movement that the RoRM emerged in Syria. In response to the leadership's policies, activists sought to utilize memory to politically mobilize their communities on the eve of the uprising. In the process of doing so, they gave new patriotic meanings to the 1948 Nakba, understood as the singular catastrophe of the people that needs to be resolved, and ought to be resolved, through the imperative to remember in order to return.

CHAPTER 3

THE RIGHT OF RETURN MOVEMENT
AND MEMORIES FOR RETURN

It is our duty then to write down the events that took place, as they took place, and to note them as they are before time weaves its strings of forgetfulness around them.

'ARIF AL-'ARIF, *AL-NAKBA: NAKBAT BAYT AL-MAQDIS WA
AL-FIRDAWS AL-MAFQUD, 1947–52*, VOL. 1

On May 15 of every year, a speaker on the podium bores us to death with quotations from Israeli founding leaders who once said that our "old will die and the young will forget." We are pleased with ourselves and we clap as we remember our Nakba and as we disprove this meaningless Zionist saying in one depopulated village or another. This is our great achievement after sixty-five years of the defeat: we remember.

MAJD KAYYAL, "FALASTIN: AL-NAKBA AL-MUSTAMIRRA"

Before the transformation of the Syrian uprising into an all-out war, the Right of Return Movement (RoRM) was politically organizing and mobilizing in the Palestinian refugee community. Through its activities, it was giving form, content, and meaning to the Nakba within a Palestinian universe of discourse. This universe of discourse may have had its roots in its Arab nationalist predecessor, but it is nevertheless also clearly distinct from it.

The RoRM has been defined as a protest movement composed of different community-based initiatives that aim to politically mobilize and organize around the defense of the refugees' rights (Suleiman 2004, 265–266). It emerged in Syria, as has been the case in other places with Palestinian refugee communities (Aruri 2001a, 2001b; Jaradat 2001; Masalha 2008). Its emergence was primarily a response to the unprecedented threat, following the 1993 Oslo Accords, to the refugees' right of return as legally enshrined in UN General Assembly Resolution 194 (UNGA 1948). Many activists, however, described the US-Israeli attempts to impose a final-status settlement on the Palestine Liberation Organization's (PLO) negotiations with Israel at the Camp David summit in 2000 as the turning point that led to the mushrooming of RoRM groups (Swisher 2004). This is because it was at that stage that the threat was perceived to be on the verge of becoming a reality. The RoRM therefore needs to be understood within the context of its emergence as a result and in direct contestation of the transformation of the Palestinian national liberation movement. For activists, this transformation is most clearly manifested in the Oslo Accords' institutionalization of the separation of Palestinian liberation from return, and the inauguration of the now-failed Palestinian statist project in the Occupied Palestinian Territories (OPT).

Given its operation within this Palestinian national arena of contention as well as in Syria, the RoRM also aimed to fill a local leadership and institutional void left behind by the crackdown on the PLO and Fatah in the 1980s. This means that the RoRM in Syria undoubtedly also needs to be understood within the context of the Palestinian political experience in that country, including the fact that the RoRM's constituent groups operated only with the state's approval. This approval was derived from Syria's own national and foreign policy interests. After the collapse of negotiations with Israel over the Golan Heights in 2000, these interests translated into support for Palestinian groups like Hamas and Islamic Jihad during the second Palestinian intifada, the uprising against Israel that began in 2000. The Syrian regime did so while simultaneously taking part in new rounds of Turkish-brokered negotiations with Israel over its own occupied territories in the Golan (Hinnebusch 2014, 226–227).

The RoRM was therefore tolerated within what were deemed acceptable limits and boundaries conducive to Syria's own interests. It did nonetheless operate in a sphere that could be characterized as a "space (as independent as possible from the direct interventions from the state, private business and family realms) for voluntary collective deliberations and actions that function as a source of autonomy" (Challand 2008, 399). Within this autonomous yet restricted space, activists sought to undermine the agenda of the PLO and the Oslo-created Palestinian Authority. They did so especially on the former's claim to legitimate representation of the refugees as it barters their rights with Israel, and thus its ability to forfeit the right of return in negotiations.

In the process of translating this Palestinian national arena of contention into their local communities, RoRM activists sought to build what they termed a "culture of return" as a way in which to impede the ability of negotiators to sign away their rights. An important facet of this culture was the mobilization of memories associated with historic Palestine and the Nakba as resources for collective action (Beinin and Vairel 2011; Della Porta and Diani 2006). One goal of this mobilization was to harness the new generation of refugees' Palestinian political identification and to organize these refugees around, and ensure their continued political claims to, the right of return.

Given this historical and political backdrop, the RoRM's mobilization placed particular emphasis on the Palestine generation, the sole remaining witnesses to the Palestine that the leadership was seen as now willing to negotiate away, and this generation's memories. Thus, in engaging the Palestinian national arena of contention through the resources available in their communities, activists also constructed and advanced what I term "memory discourses." In these discourses the idea of memory as a politically expedient category came to be highly valued, as has been the case in other Palestinian communities in the OPT and beyond (see, e.g., Hammami 2010, 241; Hill 2005, 2008). This high value associated with memory is derived from activists' linking of memories of pre-1948 Palestine and the Nakba with the imperative to remember in order to return. The activists were thus in effect utilizing as well as furthering the return's high political currency in their own communities in order to carve a leadership role for themselves and to ensure the return's continued importance for the new generations.

The RoRM's memory discourses, which on the sixtieth anniversary of 1948 were pervasive and therefore popular, have therefore foregrounded particular significations of the Nakba. They did this through a memory/ return matrix that advances the central Palestinian national concerns of RoRM activists. These activists' success in advancing the memory/return matrix largely lay in their capitalizing on the high currency that the right of return has in Palestinian refugee communities. They therefore also furthered this importance of the return through their practices, rather than merely invented it (see, e.g., Allan 2007; 2014, 37–67). However, how the RoRM's target constituencies—the members of local Palestinian refugee communities—understood these discourses and took part in the RoRM's mobilization practices were open to interpretation. Thus, the different meanings of the Nakba and the importance ascribed to memories in the RoRM's memory discourses were never without co- or even resignification, and sometimes contestation, in the RoRM activists' own communities.

THE PALESTINIAN SPHERE IN SYRIA
AND THE RIGHT OF RETURN MOVEMENT

The Syrian crackdown on the PLO in the country following the 1983 intra-Fatah fighting in the north of Lebanon left a Palestinian national and institutional void in Syria (Brand 1988c, 1990; R. Khalidi 1984; Y. Sayigh 1989). This was deepened by the Oslo Accords and the "return" of the PLO to the OPT. The permutation of the PLO into the PA as a result of the accords further marginalized the PLO's Palestinian refugee constituency living beyond the OPT, once the core of the Palestinian liberation movement and the site from where it politically reemerged after 1948. Given this political and historical context of PLO-Syria relations and what the PLO's "return" meant for Palestinian refugees living beyond the OPT, the prewar Palestinian sphere in Syria was as much heir as it was also a response to these historical realities. It could therefore also be characterized as a post-Oslo oppositional Palestinian sphere in which the PLO and Fatah had little, if any, role to play. This was as a direct result of their history in Syria and their role in the transformation of the Palestinian liberation movement after 1993. It is in this vibrant Palestinian sphere that the RoRM emerged and operated, and the movement was only one of its components.

In his study of the relationship between civil society and international donors in the OPT, the political sociologist Benoît Challand (2009, 27) has challenged Eurocentric conceptions of civil society. In particular, the assumptions "of progress that discourses of civil society entail, the questionable autonomy or independence vis-à-vis the state, and the cultural rootedness of the concept in European history." He therefore moves away from conceptions that argue for civil society as a sphere independent of and distinct from the family, business, and state spheres. Instead, Challand builds on the ideas of the philosopher Cornelius Castoriadis to argue that civil society should be defined as a sphere for autonomous collective decisions and actions. These can be measured in terms of this sphere's "capacity of auto-institution" or "the possibility to choose and define its own laws . . . according to its chosen cognitive and ideational means" (35).

He also critically reviews Arabic literature on civil society and contrasts the recent adoption of the notion of civil society (*al-mujtama' al-madani*) with the longer tradition in Arab thought of the notion he translates as "civic society" (*al-mujatama' al-ahli*). The adjective "*ahli*" is derived from the noun "*ahl*." This can be translated as "family, inhabitants and natives and may even be used as a translation of citizen: it designates members of a group that are tied by close association and a shared space . . . [that is] a sort of sub state realm of communal life" (Browers 2006, 100–101). Certain proponents of a liberal conception of civil society in Arab thought set up *ahli* society in dichotomous opposition to *madani* society (see, e.g., Browers 2006, 92–124). There have been recent arguments that it was civic society that was the in-between sphere in Syria that came to the fore during the early days of the uprising (al-Azm 2012). Others have noted that the Syrian regime in fact harnessed *ahli* society, given that it is essentially "primordial," in order to neutralize the more politically threatening civil society (Fu'ad 2014; see also Elvira and Zintl 2012).

Challand's (2009, 55) analytic move gives less or no "attention to the 'civil' in civil society and does not presuppose any particular form of polity (democracy or not, state present or not)." Rather, his emphasis is on this society's "possible contribution towards the definition of a project of political autonomy" (193). His argument is compelling as it provides a lens through which to understand the vibrant and multifaceted Palestinian sphere that I encountered in Syria. This is because to begin with, all activists I interviewed, whether directly involved in the RoRM or not, used *ahli* rather than *madani* or used the two interchangeably in order to describe their group or the sphere within which they or their organization operated. Also, the multifaceted nature of this sphere meant that it included "political" (Palestinian political factions' initiatives), "civic" (independent initiatives), "commercial" (initiatives that had a commercial facet to ensure autonomy and survival), and even "kinship" (family village memorial initiatives) society. Finally, RoRM activists, who composed only one component of this sphere, were at the forefront of the initial relief-oriented response to the displaced Syrians who arrived in Palestinian refugee camps to seek a safe haven as the militarization of the uprising escalated. Later still, they were to be at the forefront of the relief of their devastated communities. These different factors make the absolute theoretical distinction between *madani* and *ahli* society, even the setting up of civic society as the in-between, untenable.

This Palestinian sphere in Syria could be said to have constituted a space that by and large contributed toward a project of political autonomy. That the groups operating in this sphere did so only under the blessing, observation, and restrictions of the Syrian state restrained but did not lessen their contribution to Palestinian self-organization. Some factions in this sphere, like the Popular Front for the Liberation of Palestine's (PFLP) splinter group PFLP–General Command (PFLP-GC), have historically been closely linked to the Syrian regime and are today actively fighting alongside it. The alliance between one component of this sphere and the regime underscored the sphere's heterogeneity rather than dependency. It also underscored the latter's own considerations and interests that at times, though not always, coincided with those of Palestinian factions. Finally, activist groups that composed this sphere were not contending against a state, a key component of a traditional conception of civil society. Rather, they were contesting a national liberation movement seen as having abandoned its liberation agenda. This sphere was therefore primarily a space of Palestinian civic activism that nevertheless also encompassed Palestinian factions and their institutions.

Insofar as financing is concerned, international donors have the ability to set the agenda and curtail the capacity of civic organizations' political autonomy (Challand 2009). However, this was not an issue in Syria as a result of Law 93, which in 1958 put the registration, operation, and relationship of independent associations to foreign funders under the tightly regulated jurisdiction of the Ministry of Social Affairs and Labor. This process is overseen and controlled by the security services, further curtailing international funding bodies' influence (Sawwah and Kawakibi 2013, 23). Law 93 also means that some groups that operated within the Palestinian sphere were not registered at all. Others operated on a commercial basis in order to circumvent registration restrictions, ensure financial independence, and guarantee continued survival. Thus, it is within the context of this multifaceted Palestinian sphere in Syria, with all its overlaps of civil, civic, political, commercial, and at times even kinship societies, that the RoRM emerged and operated. It continued to do so until the full-scale militarization of the uprising and the ongoing war in Syria.

Given the centrality of Damascus and Yarmouk Camp to Palestinian refugee life in the country, many RoRM activists were headquartered in this camp and in the capital. However, their activities extended to other camps and suburbs in and around the capital and, indeed, to Syria as a whole. What follows is a brief introduction to the RoRM constituent groups whose activists I interviewed and whose headquarters or offices I visited. This introduction is not meant to provide a comprehensive map of all the RoRM's constituent groups that were operating in the Damascus area. Rather, the point is to stress the groups' heterogeneity and the multifaceted complexity of an aspect of the Palestinian sphere within which they operated.

Some RoRM groups were directly affiliated to factions, like the PFLP's Refugees and Right of Return Committee (RRRC). Another example of a group directly affiliated to a faction was the Democratic Front for the Liberation of Palestine's (DFLP) electronic online portal, the 194 Group. It was formed as a research group in 2001 and housed in the headquarters of the DFLP's main publication, *Al-Hurriya*.[1] Some factions, like Islamic Jihad, saw the movement as essentially futile; others, like the PFLP-GC, were not part of the RoRM at all. Fatah was also not a part of the RoRM given its history in Syria and weak presence in the country. Other groups had a looser factional affiliation through funding, like the Palestinian Return Community–Wajeb (Duty), established in 2006 and perceived as a Hamas front by community members. A Wajeb activist I interviewed insisted that this was not the case, as the group is nonfactional and open to no-strings-attached financial contributions from any donor. He did acknowledge, however, that Wajeb and Hamas have a common Islamist outlook and conceded that Hamas is Wajeb's biggest funder.[2] Today the main Wajeb activists who ran the group are no longer in the country.

Other groups were staffed by former members of factions, some of whom continued to have relationships with the PLO. An example of this is Ai'doun, an advocacy and pressure group established in 2000 in Lebanon and Syria. It used as its headquarters the semidefunct PLO Media and Cultural Affairs Office for free and solicited donations for its activities. Ai'doun activists who remain in the country are actively involved in the relief of their devastated communities. Other RoRM groups partly involved commercial initiatives, which allowed them to fund their activities and secure autonomy from political factions. An example of this was Dar al-Shajara publishing house, linked to the Shajara Institute for Oral Memory, which was active in commemoration.[3] Its founder and director, the late Ghassan Shihabi, was murdered by a sniper in Yarmouk in January 2013 while driving back into the camp with his wife and twin daughters after the PFLP-GC gave him clearance to reenter (see also C. Nasser 2013). Dar al-Shajara was subsequently looted, its books removed, and the disks on its premises smashed.[4] Finally, some "groups" represented fewer people, lacked the resources of bigger groups, and could comprise only one or two persons.

The beginning of right of return–oriented initiatives as a response to Oslo was underscored by the late director of al-Shajara. According to him, the publishing house began as the "Committee for the Defense of Palestinian National Culture," founded in 1994 by eighty-three intellectuals, journalists, and writers. The committee's financial difficulties led him to create Dar al-Shajara as a commercial enterprise.[5] Some RoRM activists, acknowledging that Oslo raised the alarm, emphasized the failed Camp David final-status negotiations of 2000 as a turning point. When I asked an activist in Ai'doun why it took so long after the accords for activists to finally translate their alarm into action on the ground, he explained:

> Politically speaking, since 1993, when Oslo was signed . . . the primary and essential Palestinian issues . . . refugees, Jerusalem, the borders, and the issue of the settlements—the very bases of the solution—they were all postponed. . . . And hence the fear began in 1993, but it became frantic horror in 2000 when Clinton decided that he could not finish his presidency without achieving a solution . . . [and so] they took Arafat and put him in a corner for fifteen days [at Camp David], with a lot of pressure in order to sign an agreement.[6]

The Camp David summit was therefore a watershed in the rise of the RoRM in Syria, as it was in other refugee communities that also began to organize around the right of return. Even political factions, especially those that opposed or had reservations about the Oslo Accords, like the PFLP, see themselves as part of this movement. An activist in the PFLP's RRRC explained that

> insofar as Syria is concerned, the return movement grew out of civic initiatives [al-mubadarat al-ahliyya] and independent committees after the Oslo Accords. There were truly popular feelings among the refugees concerning the unfolding of something threatening their rights and interests. So several committees were formed; the committees were personal or collective initiatives. And then it reached the stage where all the Palestinian factions formed a committee in order to defend the right of return, especially when the refugee issue was being discussed within the framework of the multilateral negotiations.[7]

RoRM activists therefore primarily see themselves as operating within a Palestinian national arena of contention that is transnational. The transnational character of this arena derives from activists' visions, aims, and practices, connecting them to Palestinian groups outside Syria. For example, Dar al-Shajara, in its Shajara Institute for Oral Memory commemorative guise, was part of the Palestinian Oral History Network. Ai'doun, for its part, is a member of the Global Palestine Right to Return Coalition. The transnational character of the RoRM's arena of contention also stems from primarily articulating a collective political struggle against the PLO and Israel, as the object of their claims.

While expounding further on the difference between factional and nonfactional right of return committees, the PFLP's RRRC activist stated, "So when the fear began [after Oslo], this worry, it began—like I said—these committees began to crystallize in order to tell the Palestinian negotiator: we are here and we are present, to try and pressure and to prevent this negotiator from offering concessions, and to address public opinion, that there is no solution without the refugee issue."[8]

Given that the RRRC is directly linked to the PFLP, an argument could be made for the inevitability of the primacy that the RRRC attributes to the national arena of contention. However, other nonaligned RoRM activists also pointed out the primacy of the national arena. For example, the Ai'doun activist stated, "We started off on the basis that, like I told you at the beginning [of our interview], the right of return is in danger, we have to get active defending this right in the face of this threat, by making the stakeholders of this right aware [so that] they don't give it up, and to form a lobby group to pressure the Palestinian negotiator."[9]

Another important point highlighted in both interviews can be read in the way both activists stressed what they termed "public opinion" and "stakeholders." In other words, both emphasized that they are not only defending Palestinian refugees' rights but also attempting to position themselves as community leaders and representatives. Their aspirations are directly related to the history of the PLO in Syria, its transformation post-Oslo, and the Palestinian institutional and leadership void in the country.

Despite these realities, however, RoRM groups were commonly not mass membership based, even though there were important intergroup differences in their activities, scope, and influence. Although there are no statistics to support this claim, the impression imparted to me through my meetings with RoRM activists and discussions with community members who participated in their activities was the top-down nature of the RoRM's visions and activities. That is, their visions and activities were formulated by the groups' members, voluntary or paid, and implemented in their own local Palestinian communities.

The RoRM groups did, though, commonly aspire to be grassroots organizations, given both the arena in which they operated and their self-positioning as community leaders and representatives. The Wajeb activist articulated the group's emphasis on the grassroots connection this way:

> We don't want to stay isolated from the street, we don't want to remain isolated from the people, we have to be in touch, so I tell some committees, and some of the institutions that are present in all the camps, prioritize this activity over any of your other activities: visit people in their homes, and be in touch with the youth, in their gatherings, in their get-togethers, in their late nights, this is much more important than any other activity. . . . I always say, the personal and individual connection is much more important than any of our activities. . . . This is very important for achieving your goals, in order to push through your vision, in order for you to in fact create a condition that reacts [to your ideas], because in the end, you have a vision but you don't want to continue singing this vision alone.[10]

Thus, going to people's homes, staying in touch with community members, and spending time with the youth involve more than just merely advancing the right of return. These social activities are also an attempt to build a space from which to lead and to claim legitimate grounds for the representation of the interests of the Palestinian refugees in Syria in opposition to the PLO and the PA. It is therefore somewhat unsurprising that the older RoRM activists were former cadres of various Palestinian political factions and see the movement as a continuation of national activism by other means. When discussing the founding members of his group, the Aïdoun activist noted that most "have left organized work, but we never left national work, never. Our activities were always ongoing, but the commitment to a party or to a specific faction ended, so some people [in Aïdoun] are former members of the factions."[11]

Thus the local, national, transnational, and even international all figure in the RoRM activists' aspirations and goals. As the Aïdoun activist continued later in our discussion in relation to what he saw as one of the achievements of the RoRM:

> The right of return has been advanced as an issue more so than before, before what was advanced was liberation, a state, and so forth. Given the spread of return committees all over the world, it has now become an issue that is advanced. . . . Basically, just talking about it, or if there

is a threat to it, there is an immediate mobilization against that threat. So the return committees have put forth issues [on the table]. Of course they didn't achieve anything that is important, but the issue of the right of return has become an issue that is discussed on the Arab level, on the Palestinian level, and on the international level.[12]

When these interviews are read together, a fairly straightforward narrative of the RoRM emerges: The military-oriented, Fatah-dominated PLO recognized Israel's right to exist on the Palestine belonging to the refugees but in return did not get its desired statelet in the now-truncated OPT. This betrayal marginalized the refugees, once the core of the Palestinian liberation movement, and threatened their legally enshrined right of return (Suleiman 2001). The RoRM groups arose in response and geared their activities toward claiming a stake for refugees in Palestinian national politics (R. Sayigh 2008b). Operating in local communities within the broader context of grassroots nationalist commemoration (see, e.g., Khalili 2004, 2005, 2007), RoRM groups largely aimed at mobilizing the refugee communities in order to prevent the PLO and PA from negotiating away the right of return.

However, what the RoRM represents or aims to be and achieve depends largely on how it is perceived and understood in the communities within which it operates. In Syria, the abundance of RoRM groups—fully or partly independent, faction affiliated or not—led to popular perceptions of these groups as private right-of-return "corner shops" [dakakin] that "trade" on the right of return. Theorists of social movements have argued that activists are rational actors, that they are social entrepreneurs who mobilize resources for collective action (McCarthy and Zald 1977; see also Goodwin, Jasper, and Khattra 1999; McAdam, McCarthy, and Zald 1996).[13] The commonly held belief that RoRM initiatives constitute "corner shops" through which activists "trade" highlights the importance that the return has among Palestinian refugees. Given this high currency, the exchange value for activists when "trading" the right of return in their communities lay in filling an institutional void and taking on a refugee leadership and representational role in the Palestinian national arena of contention.[14]

Extending the entrepreneurial metaphor further, one way in which RoRM activists ran their shops and traded was through advancing what they termed a "culture of return." This culture is essentially a political identity project. It revolves around a shared homeland that once belonged to the refugees, its unlawful and violent usurpation in 1948, and the need for the rectification of this historical and ongoing injustice. This rectification needs to take place through organizing around, and insisting on, the refugees' now-threatened collective and personal right of return. Given the aims and aspirations of RoRM activists, the most important resources at their disposal in order to advance this culture of return were memories of historic Palestine and the Nakba. Through this mobilization of memories as resources for the return, RoRM activists also gave the category of memory itself a newfound importance by directly linking it to the return in their communities.

I now examine how RoRM activists' notion of a culture of return led to particular discourses around memory. I then turn to how activists' memory mobilization practices foregrounded particular Palestinian patriotic understandings of the 1948 Nakba as part of these discourses.

FROM THE NATIONAL TO THE LOCAL: BUILDING A CULTURE OF RETURN

During our discussion of the group's beginnings, the Ai'doun activist related that one of the group's founding principles was based on

> spreading the culture of return [*thaqafat al-'awda*] among the Palestinian refugees, and to implant the hope that despite the difficult circumstances, and despite the imbalance in power to the advantage of our enemies, we shouldn't lose hope and [ensure] that a hope and a conviction continues to exist among the new and young generations, that they have a right in Palestine, and that they won't give up this right, and that they call for its implementation, even if time passes, and even if the current circumstances don't allow for the return of the refugees.[15]

The visions formulated in the national arena of contention therefore directly lead to the emphasis on building a culture of return for the new generation of refugees. Thus, when translating the national arena of contention through the culture of return, activists were striving to ensure that newer generations of refugees were aware of both their right to return and the need to exercise it. What they were essentially formulating and advancing is therefore a political identity envisioned and advanced because of the current impossibility of return and the potential impact of the passage of time on the rights of the refugees. As a political project, the culture of return is primarily oriented toward the future and firmly situated within its post-Oslo historical and political moment.

The notion of a culture of return, and its advancement, was widespread in RoRM circles. For example, the PFLP's RRRC activist articulated the same elements of the culture of return as the Ai'doun activist

> with the growth of the culture of civil society [*al-mujtama' al-madani*], many Palestinian activists, through their connections with civic organizations [*munazamat ahliyya*], and nongovernmental organizations, began spreading a kind of culture that is concerned with the popular or civil [*al-madani*] dimension in order to withstand this issue [the threat posed to the right of return], and not only through the slogans of armed struggle or the right of return as a national cornerstone. They began to work on the ground. . . . in order to stop the winds of pessimism and hopelessness and the culture of compensation from spreading in our camps.[16]

Time as working against the right of return is also a notion central to the culture of return. This is because the RoRM's object of claims is the historic Palestine of the refugees that is becoming ever more temporally distant. This distance is made acute by the fact of the passing of members of the Palestine generation while new generations come of age under the shadow of the Oslo Accords. These new generations have no lived knowledge or direct connection to their homeland, which has been Hebraicized by Israeli settler-colonialism (Benvenisti 2000). Most important, they have come of age in an era in which Palestinian leaders have been willing to rubberstamp their stateless and dispossessed reality and Israel's facts on the ground. When asked to further articulate the culture of return, the Ai'doun activist put it this way:

> The culture of return means . . . that the right of return is a personal right, and a collective right, this is your right that isn't going to disappear . . . through the passage of time, and no one ought to manipulate it. I want to make the young Palestinian person understand that this personal right shouldn't be touched, [that] Mahmoud Abbas cannot give up the right of your father—whether it is to a house or a *dunam* of land in Palestine—on your behalf, because this is a personal right.[17]
>
> If you don't personally give it up—you—then the political leader won't be able to give it up. . . . Part of the culture of return . . . [includes the] United Nations' resolutions that were adopted by the United Nations General Assembly, and one of them is Resolution 194. . . . I would make him understand these issues, I need to put it to him that if you don't willfully give up your right in Palestine, no one can give up that right for you, and this right is not only a personal right, but it is an inheritance right,

for your children and grandchildren, so it is the right of the children and the grandchildren to demand this right. . . . And within the culture of return, there is a focus on Palestinian identity, [for] we are a people, an Arab people, but we have specific characteristics that are unique to us. . . . So these issues that enhance Palestinian identity, I want to focus on them, not because of a parochial regionalism, but on the basis of the crystallization of Palestinian national identity. All these issues are part of the culture of return.[18]

Clearly then, through the culture of return and its various components activists were addressing the nemesis of memory, "forgetfulness." This forgetfulness relates, in a political sense, to the possibility that younger refugees might relinquish their political rights as a result of a combination of factors that have been noted. These include the passage of time, the threat of the right being negotiated away, and the lack of Palestinian institutions that can advance and harness the young refugees' national identification and continued political claims and demands. Thus, to counter the threat of forgetfulness, activists predicated their culture of return on the imperative to remember, giving memory itself a central place in their mobilization-derived memory discourses. It is this imperative within the broader political vision of a culture of return that has led to the notion of "memory as a guarantor of return." This is essentially a memory/return matrix at the heart of the RoRM-created and -harnessed memory discourses in Palestinian refugee communities in Syria.

In view of this, an important way in which activists translated their culture of return into concrete community practices in order to achieve their goals was through the mobilization of memories of historic Palestine and the Nakba as resources for collective action. An example of such activities can be seen in the publication of oral history–based books on destroyed villages and towns in Palestine. These books were central to the discursive reemergence of the Palestinian Nakba in the 1980s. Recent English-language scholarly interest in these books refer to them as "memorial books," rather than the Arabic "destroyed villages books" (kutub al-qura al-mudammara). This is in reference to similar books created by European Jewish Holocaust survivors and Armenians to memorialize the authors' towns and villages that no longer exist (Slyomovics 1998, xiii; see also R. Davis 2007, 2010).

In Syria, Dar al-Shajara was the leading, though not sole, publisher and distributor of these books. Wajeb, for example, also published destroyed villages books. There were also individual efforts by nonaffiliated individuals to publish these books. Commonly, these books employ memories to construct oral history–based accounts of pre-Nakba life in historic Palestine. The late director of Dar al-Shajara explained the rationale for their publication:

> Within the context of us wanting a specifically Palestinian book. After that, the idea began developing more specifically about why isn't it about Palestinian memory per se, why isn't it about the destroyed Palestinian villages, why isn't it about this huge heritage that is now on the threshold of forgetfulness, which day after day people are forgetting, and when you ask a child in school, "What village are you from?" They tell you, "I am from Yarmouk Camp" or "I am Palestinian," but he doesn't know where he is exactly from.[19]

This rationale for publishing books on destroyed localities in Palestine articulates the most important facets of the culture of return. It also emphasizes the direct relationship between the threat of forgetfulness and the creative use of memories to combat this threat.

In my conversations with community members, the issue of authorship, extent of readership, and reception of these books was controversial. Some people claimed that the books are nothing more than glorified family histories. That there was controversy, debate, and ultimately interest in these books testifies to the activists' success in both creating and advancing the memory/return matrix. However, how community members have understood the RoRM's memory discourses and practices and even the memories they mobilized has remained open to interpretation.

In the remaining part of this chapter, I further explore the meanings RoRM activists have appended to the memory signifiers they mobilized through their grassroots oral history recordings. I also demonstrate the interpretatively open nature of the RoRM's memory discourses through community members' participation in and impressions of activists' public village commemorations.

THE MOBILIZATION AND INTERPRETATION OF MEMORIES AS RESOURCES FOR THE RETURN

One way memories have been mobilized as a resource for the return is through activists' recording of oral histories (see, e.g., Wajeb n/a). These recordings are intended to preserve the Palestine generation's memories for the younger generations and to ensure the continued existence of a counternarrative to the Israeli state's denial of the Nakba even after its last witnesses pass away. During our discussion of Wajeb's Documentation and Oral History Section, the Wajeb activist stated that

the Section asked all Wajeb's camp-based committees [in Syria] to work on surveying the elderly. Every elderly person who witnessed the Nakba, who lived during the Nakba period and is able [to recollect]—meaning, that they were at the time cognizant of the unfolding events—should have his name, telephone number and the village from which he comes, his address and so on, recorded. We now have the addresses of most of the elderly, in all the Syrian camps, and we have now begun paying visits, in a slow and gradual manner. We are going to those who are older than the others because of the age issue, and the life and death issue; we are racing against time.[20]

Similarly, the Aïdoun activist's discussion of his group's Oral History Unit, which began in 2007, emphasized that his group worked along these same lines, even though in retrospect its work failed to materialize to the same extent as that of Wajeb. He said:

We are focusing on the first years of the Nakba so that those who lived through them do not die before we get to them. Now for example, when we come to the experience of being refugees, they [the Oral History Unit] can for example talk to me, and people from my generation. . . . We lived through being refugees, and we lived through the tents and so forth, and how the camp was, all these issues. So those people can still be found and still have some time ahead of them, right? This generation, the generation that [lived through events] from approximately 1946 to 1950, this period, we want to try and cover it [first].[21]

The question of time in both activists' discussion of their groups' oral history recordings once again conjures up the threat of forgetfulness. The fight against forgetfulness is, in short, a race against time. This is unsurprising, given that remembering and the very ability to speak of memories are anchored in temporal referents. Social groups' relationships to time are socially constructed and have meaning only insofar as they serve a particular purpose for the group. With regard to time and memory, Halbwachs (1980, 127) has argued that "time is real only insofar as it has content—that is, insofar as it offers events as material for thought. . . . substantial enough to offer the individual consciousness a framework within which to arrange and retrieve its remembrances." The RoRM's emphasis on the Nakba means that activists have advanced the Nakba as a marker of their communities' time (i.e., before and after the dispossession, the ongoing *nakba*).

Remembering and speaking of memories are also anchored in space. The relationship of groups to space, like time, is also socially constructed. By prioritizing the Palestine generation's Nakba memories, RoRM activists have in effect also transformed the Nakba into Halbwachs's (1980, 131) notion of an "extraordinary event." Such events are "also fitted within this spatial framework [of memory], because they occasion in the group a more intense awareness of its past and present, the bonds attaching it to physical locale gaining greater clarity in the very moment of their destruction". The Nakba as an extraordinary event marks time before and after the homeland, and it also marks the homeland, historic Palestine, as such. It also encapsulates the reasons for the distance and uprootedness from the homeland. Thus, given the overall objectives of the culture of return, the RoRM have mobilized the Nakba in a way that is politically conducive to its demands for justice.

The Nakba has therefore been constructed as a marker of time and space in the RoRM's communities, as anchored in concrete commemorative practices and memory discourses. The pervasiveness and popularity of these discourses and the meanings of their memory signifiers were striking in Damascus. My research and its importance were often associated with "*al-dhakira al-shafawiyya*" (oral memory) in my everyday encounters. This also indicated a familiarity with the RoRM's mobilization of memories and the importance of this mobilization's associated memory/return matrix.

While discussing oral history work, the Ai'doun activist articulated his group's understanding of the category of memory in this way:

> We have, insofar as the units are concerned, if I give you an hour or an hour and a bit, I can't really tell you everything. But I told you we have specialist working-units and we have geographical working-units. Part of the specialist working-units, we have the Oral History Unit, and this is concerned with the issue of memory. Of course it has a camera, and it has a recorder, and it goes to the elderly—we of course began to feel strongly that oral memory in fact completes Palestinian history, because the written history is written, and you know how history is written, and how it is filtered. So we began to feel that a very big part of those who lived as young people in Palestine is passing away, that is something normal. For example, someone who left at the age of twenty, as a young fighting man, or during an age when he was cognizant [of unfolding events], now he is eighty years old, those are a very small minority. So during those [first] two years, we rushed in order to locate those of them who remain,

meaning to take information from them and to record oral history, in order to record Palestinian memory through oral history, and to try in the future, if we are able to, what I told you about [earlier], which is to form a Palestinian narrative that can face Israeli memory.[22]

Thus, how activists envisioned the use of oral history sheds light on their understanding of memory, clearly conceived in its concrete and referential sense. Oral memory completes history because the latter is written and filtered, implying that the former is somehow pure, unmediated, and more faithful to the past. Thus, it is not history that activists were making available to the new generations; it was these referential memories on the verge of being lost to history, of being written and filtered, as a result of the death of the Palestine generation. The result is a division between memory and history, or a memory in realization of its sharp break with the past (Nora 1996b, 2001). "Palestinian memory" is constructed through this essentially antagonistic relationship between memory and history. There is also an attempt to turn the Nakba into Pierre Nora's *lieu de mémoire*, or site of memory. The primary purpose of a *lieu de mémoire* is to capture time and make the site of memory stand still, to act as a buffer from the loss of memory to history. It is therefore no surprise that the RoRM's site of memory is a "great event," what Nora (1996b, 18) also termed "spectacular" or "foundational" events.

These particular understandings of memory and of the Nakba were open to interpretation by members of the RoRM's target communities. Activists were, after all, mobilizing the resources available in their communities. Like the activists, the RoRM's target communities' members also have personal and emotional connections to their families' places of origin. This means that they participated in the RoRM's mobilization practices against the backdrop of their own understandings of their familial and Palestinian past. They also brought their own beliefs and perceptions of the RoRM's national arena of contention to bear on the movement's practices.

Two interviewees noted their participation in the RoRM's commemorative village day events when the village in question was that of their family. These events, known as Palestinian Village Day (*yawm al-qarya al-falastiniyya*), were organized by Wajeb but suspended during the first year of the uprising in 2011. The events were for the people of the village that was the subject of the commemoration and for their descendants (see, e.g., Wajeb 2010). The Wajeb activist explained his group's first event as follows:

We chose al-Tira [in the subdistrict of Haifa] as the first village. We decided to convene [the event] in al-Tira's square [in Yarmouk Camp], outside on the street. So we went to the square, and we pitched a tent, and we set up an exhibition, we put up pictures of al-Tira's martyrs, whatever we could find, we put up al-Tira's inhabitants' belongings in the exhibition. . . . Some one thousand people attended this activity. And we spoke about al-Tira . . . its name, the origin of the name, what happened in al-Tira, and its most important customs and traditions. After that, we showed a film about al-Tira, a new documentary film that has just been filmed. The people who were sitting, especially the elderly, began to cry. Many people cried. [They said,] "This is my land, this is the school in which I studied, and this is this, and this is that street," and so on and so forth. All these issues conversed with emotions. Afterward, four Nakba witnesses from al-Tira sat with a man who introduced them and led the questions and answers, and then the men started narrating. . . . [They] presented oral memory to the people, and after that, we honored the elderly, as well as the distinguished personalities from al-Tira.[23]

Much could be said about the al-Tira village day event from the point of view of the organizers. For example, their use of various materials to mobilize memories of the village, including the exhibition, the belongings of the people of al-Tira, the film screening, and the Palestine generation's memories. Together, these ironically speak to the copresence of memory and history, rather than the divergence between the two. In addition, these village day events are male centered, with the stage being occupied by men, and with the interviewees who related their participation to me being men as well. This gendered limitation has implications for the kinds of memories and histories that are mobilized in this particular public forum.[24] Finally, these village day events and the RoRM's mobilization efforts more generally also provide a space to realize community as practice. The idea of community as practice largely comes from the construction of collective identities and communities by activists in social movements (see, e.g., Melucci 1996, in Delanty 2010, 95). This kind of community arguably exists through Palestinian refugee activists' "communities of dissent" (Delanty 2010, 83–102). These village day events also clearly allow for the creation and realization of community for the participants (e.g., the descendants recognizing al-Tira as "our village"). Thus, such events allow for community as practice through providing spaces that allow for "the expansion in the community of reference and the attempt to make belonging a real possibility" (102).

With regard to community members' own participation, Muhammad, a young third-generation Palestinian refugee whose grandparents are from al-Tira, related to me his attendance of the al-Tira Palestinian Village Day.

Within the context of our discussion of the Palestine generation's memories, he said:

> They did the al-Tira tent, they invited four old men from al-Tira, and they began to narrate events. . . . The moderator asked one of the old men a question, he told him, "When was al-Yarmouk Camp established?" He told him, "During the 1960s." So there were [other] old men sitting with us, they weren't being interviewed, and one of them got upset and got up and left. I said to him, "Where are you going?" He said to me, "What nonsense is this man talking about?! He doesn't know anything, he has already spoken nonsense on four different occasions!" . . . Perhaps it stemmed from his [the first old man's] age or something like that, perhaps because he is old, he spoke a bit of nonsense or he was exaggerating and so forth. . . . So issues [of truth] come up through [reading] history, studying, knowledge. They [the Palestine generation] only gave us a piece of the string.[25]

Wajeb's creative use of memory was clearly effective if its purpose was to attract young refugees like Muhammad. In other words, to attract youths whose families were expelled from al-Tira in 1948 and to enable them to learn more about their families' place of origin in historic Palestine. However, for Muhammad, what is at stake in the al-Tira village day is not so much that he learned about al-Tira and his right to return to it. For Muhammad, what is at stake is the question of the truth and reliability of the Palestine generation's memories. Wajeb activists gave the stage to the Palestine generation and presented their memories as a source of authority on al-Tira, even honoring them in a closing ceremony. For Muhammad, however, this generation and their memories can never be the final authority on the past. Their memories are only partial, "a piece of the string," and within this generation there are disagreements over the past, as illustrated by the man who stormed off. Thus, if members of the Palestine generation and their memories are being given a central place in the RoRM's mobilization-derived memory discourses, this role is open to interpretation by community members. The same could be said for the centrality that activists are giving to the Nakba as well as to the notion that memories are guarantors of a future return. To extend Muhammad's metaphor, studying Palestinian history and understanding present realities, combined with his own political activism, which he also discussed in his interview, are for him the other pieces of the string.

Another village day event took place in al-Qabun, today a wartorn suburb of Damascus, where a small community of Palestinian refugees from the Haifa subdistrict village of Tantura and their descendants lived. Abu Muhammad, a second-generation Tanturan refugee, related the following about his attendance of this event:

> They were showing us that until this day, the generations that are like myself and younger, they care about these issues. Take this example, this paper which they printed: "On the occasion of the 60th anniversary of the occupation of Palestine, The Palestinian Return Community—Wajeb, al-Qabun Committee, invites you to attend the Palestinian Village Day event," and between three dots they have put "al-Tantura," which is our village, "and that is at 5:30 P.M. on Friday, June 6, 2008, in the tent that has been erected in al-Qabun Park that is to the east of the vegetable market. Your presence is support for the right of return." Look at how beautiful this sentence is: "Your presence is support for the right of return, and the invitation is public." I even have some Syrian friends who came with me and participated in this event, which made me so happy. . . . This paper, despite the fact that it has no value, it means so much to me and to my village, so I keep it with me in my pocket.[26]

Unlike Muhammad, Abu Muhammad ascribed the village day event's importance to its affirmation of his village, a community of Tanturans and their descendants, and of the right of return, despite the temporal distance to Tantura and the coming-of-age of new generations. From the organizers' point of view, the Wajeb activist related that 1,500 people attended this particular village day, despite the small size of the community in al-Qabun. He asserted that this was because "we carried out an event that perhaps in the end addresses [personal] concerns, emotions."[27] Thus, the RoRM provided spaces, whether concrete through village day events or discursive though oral history recordings and books, where memories and histories, their meanings and purposes, could be constructed, articulated, contested, and rearticulated. The RoRM's mobilization of memories as resources also provided spaces where communities could realize themselves. This realization of communities took place around members' shared cultural forms of memories as well as histories of specific cultural codifications, such as places of origin and the Nakba.

Communities as practice or as constructed and realized in the process of their achievement therefore need not be mutually exclusive or in opposition to communities understood through their members' shared yet interpretatively open symbolic cultural forms (Cohen 1985, in Delanty 2010, 33–35; Delanty 2010, 102). For example, in the Tantura Village Day, Tantura is constructed as defining the community of Tanturans and their descendants, with the commemorative events providing the space for the community's realization. At the same time, Tantura is a symbolic cultural form, the village of origin, relevant to those such as Muhammad, who chose to attend Tantura's commemoration because of his own imagination of belongings. Through creating spaces for the realization of communities, RoRM activists therefore also sought to influence the interpretation of these communities' forms and codifications in line with their overall political objectives. Ultimately, however, these forms, like the symbolic contours of the communities they mark, were open, fluid, and contingent.

CONCLUSION

On January 23, 2010, the Qatar-based Arabic- and English-language international news network Al Jazeera began publishing more than 1,600 confidential documents over a three-day period. Dubbed the "Palestine Papers," these documents were leaked from the PLO's Negotiations Support Unit (NSU) and spanned the last decade (1999–2010) of the Palestinian-Israeli negotiations (Hijab 2011; Swisher 2011). The leaked documents confirmed what many observers, including RoRM activists, had long feared.

One of the Al Jazeera analysts who pored over the documents noted that in a 2007 draft of proposals for a "Permanent Status Agreement," the Palestinian negotiators agreed to the return of only 10,000 refugees per year for a maximum of ten years (Abunimah 2011a). The papers documented how, two years later, Palestinian chief negotiator Saeb Erekat was even willing to waive this essentially symbolic number of returnees and "proposed accepting just one thousand refugees per year over ten years" (Abunimah 2011a; Swisher 2011, 48).

Whether 10,000 or 100,000, the documents therefore finally and conclusively confirmed that the Palestinian leadership had offered unprecedented concessions in its attempt to ensure its continued survival. This was clearly the case even if this survival had, within the framework of the Oslo Accords, become possible only in its role as a subcontractor of the Israeli occupation. These concessions included rescinding the right of return and any meaningful sovereignty. It also offered unprecedented security coordination with Israel following the second intifada and the victory of its political rival, Hamas, in local elections in the OPT (Swisher 2011, 25–71).

Following the leaks, the PLO and the PA went on an all-out media offensive. The strategy was to shoot the messenger rather than deal with the message. This approach was accompanied by a clumsy insistence that the documents were forgeries, even when some negotiators publicly confirmed their authenticity (Swisher 2011, 19). In an interview on Al Jazeera Arabic, Erekat went on a tirade in which he accused Al Jazeera's then Palestinian director general and British and American intelligence officers of being behind the politically motivated distortions in a bid to remove the PA president. The latter's mandate to govern had, in any case, expired two years earlier (AJA 2011).

Some two weeks after his interview, and following an internal investigation, Erekat announced his resignation as the PLO's chief negotiator. However, the premise on which he resigned was not so much the content of the leaked papers, for he retained his position on the PLO's Executive Committee. Rather, Erekat resigned because the investigation did indeed trace the leaked papers to the NSU that he led. The NSU, consisting of lawyers and policy experts, was itself dissolved. This move has been compared to "the US State Department firing its own legal advisors over the embarrassing WikiLeaks disclosures rather than addressing the causes of the leaks or the misguided policies exposed by them" (Swisher 2011, 19).

The leaked documents and the scandal surrounding their contents demonstrate the extent of the transformation of the Palestinian liberation movement post-Oslo, especially in terms of its subservience to US-Israeli dictates. They also expose the extent of its unaccountability and relinquishment of any pretenses to forwarding the cause of the majority of Palestinians, the refugees. Finally, the leaks and the scandal also demonstrate the nature of the Palestinian national arena of contention in which RoRM activists saw themselves operating and in which they were trying to exert influence. Clearly then, the RoRM's emergence may have heightened awareness of the threat posed to the right of return. The movement's ability to effect change, however, has been minimal, given the lack of accountability and political bankruptcy of the PLO and the PA in the wake of Oslo.

Whatever change RoRM activists have effected has been in their own communities. Through their mobilization-derived memory discourses, activists have constructed the Nakba as a marker of their communities' times and spaces. The Nakba has come to signify the singular extraordinary event that centers on a historical injustice that needs to be rectified through the return, no matter the position of the Palestinian leadership or the impossibility of return today. They have tied the Palestine generation's memories of the Nakba and pre-1948 Palestine more generally to the return and have used these cultural forms and codifications to mobilize in communities whose symbolic contours are marked by them.

While RoRM activists' discourses and practices essentially encapsulated one of the interpretively open meanings of the Palestinian Nakba today, other meanings of 1948 can also be found in community members' own memories of and narratives on the Nakba. In the subsequent chapters, I turn to these different meanings. I do this first through examining the narration and transmission of memories in Palestinian refugee families, then the Palestine generation's communities and their memories, and finally, the post-Palestine generations' postmemories and narratives on Nakba memory.

CHAPTER 4

NARRATING PALESTINE, TRANSMITTING ITS LOSS

I say [to my uncle] as though I were in front of a small pupil: "The English-man was right, but the mistake was neither yours nor that of Abu Durra nor the rest of the peasant farmers.[1] Your land was stolen from you as others bartered with the English and the Jews."

He didn't say anything . . . he who had reached seventy years with two torn and boneless shoulders, my mother asserts, as a result of the bullets that rained down on him in Umm al-Daraj. I felt shame as he fell silent and didn't respond. He was still over there, moving from one place to an-other as a young man with his rifle and belts of ammunition. I saw in his eyes something which no word that I write can describe. I was with an infinite harshness trying to steal from him what he once was. I who have come to have relatives made of words, and he whose relatives were the dew and the rocks.

MUHAMMAD AL-AS'AD, *ATFAL AL-NADA*

I open the map of the world
searching for a village I lost,
searching in the pockets of a grandfather I never got to know
for fragments of tales and rare fragrances.

ANTON SHAMMAS, "THEN HOW WILL THE POEM COME?"

ontemporary memory discourses in Palestinian refugee communities center on the idea of memory and its relationship to the return. These discourses have come about as a result of the work of Palestinian refugee activists, who have contested the Palestinian leadership's transformation in the wake of the Oslo Accords. These activists have in consequence constructed the Nakba as the one catastrophic site of memory that marks Palestinian refugees' times and spaces in the past and the present. As a result, the Nakba has become an important patriotic signifier that serves specific political objectives that challenge Oslo's institutionalization of the de facto separation of liberation from return. The activists' discourses and their related mobilization practices therefore advance one of the understandings of the Nakba today and are integral to the Nakba's contemporary Palestinian universe of meaning.

In these memory discourses, particular importance is ascribed to the generation of Palestine, given the centrality of their memories as guarantors of the future return. It was only some fifty years ago, however, that Arab nationalists, while articulating the Nakba as a catastrophe to pan-Arab national liberation, considered this generation "the generation of defeat" ('Allush 1964, 77). This importance is therefore newfound, and is also ascribed to the Palestine generation by its children and grandchildren, the second- and third-generation refugees (Ben-Ze'ev 2005; Mason 2007; R. Sayigh 2012). Unlike activists, however, members of the generation of Palestine are important to second- and third-generation refugees as they are elders esteemed in their own families and seen to have much experience and many memories (Halbwachs 1992b).

Given the different historically and politically contingent ways in which the generation of Palestine has been valued, I think of members of this generation as the "guardians of memory." This is because they are perceived by activists as repositories of memories that will ensure a return to the homeland. At the same time, as elders who have a wealth of experiences and memories, they are central to ordinary, everyday family occasions in which grandparents narrate their memories and histories to family members who care to listen (Fivush 2008a). What distinguishes their memories and histories from those that grandparents would ordinarily narrate is that they reflect a world ruptured through a collective uprooting that is yet to be acknowledged and resolved.

As a result, the generation of Palestine occupies varying and even competing roles. Similarly, their memories also have varying and even competing significations. Thus, in order to understand the Nakba in community members' memories and narratives, one must understand its meaning as impacted by different factors. These include what the generation of Palestine ought to do and their memories ought to signify in the post-Oslo memory discourses, how they perceive their own and their memories' purported roles, and what their memories have come to signify for their children and grandchildren. The generation of Palestine's memories of 1948 and their children's and grandchildren's narratives on Nakba memory therefore cannot be prized from the present social, political, and historical overarching context of their socialization. It follows that, to understand these memories and narratives, the subject of subsequent chapters, one must first consider several questions: How is the newfound centrality of the generation of Palestine understood, negotiated, or contested by them? How does it come to bear on their own memory-making? Finally, what is the generation of Palestine's and its memories' roles in every-day family occasions as perceived by the post-Palestine generations?

To answer these questions, I draw on three-generation interviews and recount my encounters in Damascus. I use these to examine what the generation of Palestine as the "guardians of memory" can critically tell us about their newfound roles as the narrators of memories to which the return has been appended. I also examine what the sharing of memories during ordinary family occasions can tell us about the meanings of the Nakba. The guardians, I argue, have an ambivalent relationship to their newfound central roles in their communities' memory discourses. Furthermore, the Nakba, understood in its patriotic signifier guise, is not the primary object of the narration and transmission of memories during everyday family occasions. Rather, the object of this narration and transmission is the generation of Palestine's memories of loss—their homes, lands, lives, and communities at large. What is transmitted to the children and grandchildren, in both narrative and nonnarrative forms, is the loss that has resulted from the Nakba as well as the generation of Palestine's own structures of attachments to this loss. This is primarily the refusal to accept it. These vivid imaginings of loss and its structures of attachments are powerful. When compared with how memory has been mobilized by activists post-Oslo, they are also more potent and meaningful to generations of Palestinians who grew up in Syria.

THE GENERATION OF PALESTINE, THE GUARDIANS OF MEMORY

Khan Eshieh Camp, March 28, 2008

I met the late Abu Khalil during the early days of my research because of his niece, who suggested I interview him. We sat in the family home's reception

room in the presence of several sons and the sounds of Abu Khalil's grand-
children or great-grandchildren playing outside. In between his tales about
life in Yaquq, Tiberias, the Nakba, and the early days of refuge in the Golan,
the sounds gradually faded as more and more of the children joined us. At
one stage, the sounds of children playing totally disappeared; the seven or so
children were sitting in a semicircle around us and intently listening to Abu
Khalil's stories. Or were they there because of this stranger that had come
to meet their grandfather and to hear his memories? One of Abu Khalil's
younger brothers as well as a daughter and a daughter-in-law had also
joined and began to take part in the conversation. In one of the moments of
silence in our encounter, Abu Khalil's daughter urged him to tell me a story
about Palestine. This spurred her father to narrate a story of a confrontation
that he had seen between two Salvation Army volunteers from Homs and
settlers from a nearby colony when he had taken the animals to graze in the
village's lands.[2]

Later, in my attempt to connect his patchwork of memories, I inferred
that the colony he referred to is probably Hukok, which took over the vil-
lage's lands, and ultimately, its memory. . . . Abu Khalil did not live to see
the community of Khan Eshieh torn apart and devastated by the arrival
of the war and the uprooting and scattering of his children who were lucky
to leave, while others remained, living under the mercy of the shells, barrel
bombs and snipers. . . . What future and memories for his grandchildren
and great-grandchildren now, those who survived their cousins' murder on
the Nakba Day March, disappearing at army checkpoints, and disabling by
the merciless weapons of war.

The sociologist Karl Mannheim ([1923] 2007, 292) argued that a generation is a "social location" or "a particular kind of identity of location,
embracing related 'age-groups' embedded in a historical-social process."
Building on this definition, Mannheim argued that one of the distinguishing
features of a generation is for members to take part in a temporally defined
section of the historical-social process. This process necessitates a continuous transmission of what Mannheim called "accumulated cultural heritage"
(292). Thus, for Mannheim, what he called "social remembering," is central
to his concept of a socially constructed and located generation. He defines
this as "all psychic and cultural data [which] only really exist in so far as they
are produced and reproduced in the present" (294).

Those who left Palestine in 1948 and who were cognizant of the unfolding
events constitute a generation. This generation's "social-location" is evident
in its name, the generation of Palestine. It has been argued that "Palestinian

memory is, by dint of its preservation and social production under the conditions of its silencing by the thundering story of Zionism, dissident memory, counter-memory. It contributes to counter-history" (Abu-Lughod and Sa'di 2007, 6). The idea that by virtue of the Palestinians' settler-colonized and stateless political reality, what Palestine's generation may choose to remember is dissident countermemory that can contribute to a counterhistory is integral to the Nakba's contemporary Palestinian universe of discourse. This is primarily why memories of pre-1948 Palestine in general and the Nakba in particular have been mobilized by community activists. "Palestinian memory" as a coherent, homogenous, and uncontested terrain that constitutes a "collective memory" is largely a construction of different activists' imaginings of memory. In these imaginings, "Palestinian" and "countermemory" are key elements of the notion that memories are guarantors of a future return. In addition, the countermemory aspect of the Palestine generation's memories, with the implication that these memories inherently constitute resistance, emerges through reading this generation's memories only against the backdrop of Zionist settler-colonization and erasure.

Rather than taking this generation's memories and purported role at face value, the challenge is to critically appreciate the ways in which these have become entangled in post-Oslo realities that accord them politically expedient value. The challenge is therefore to critically approach these multiple entanglements, examining the ways they may affect this generation's memories and these memories interpretation by the post-Palestine generations. What members of this generation have said, given their perceived or projected roles in the pervasive Palestinian imaginings of memory, provides a starting point for a critical examination of its various entanglements.

Toward the end of my interviews with members of Palestine's generation, many of whom have now passed away, I asked whether they narrated their memories to their children and grandchildren. This question was explicitly implicated in this generation's post-Oslo projected role in popular memory discourses. The responses to this loaded question therefore shed light on how the notion that this generation narrates memories meant to eventually reclaim Palestine or potentially resist Zionism is built on a common assumption. This is an assumption about the role and value of this generation and its memories, one that also takes their entanglements in dominant imaginings of memory for granted.

Abu Subhi of the 'Arab al-Shamalina tribe of the Safad subdistrict, who left Palestine in his early twenties, responded to my question by stating: "I don't tell them anything. They are going as *fida'iyyin* against our will."[3] Even though he did not narrate his memories of Palestine to his children, his children nevertheless joined the Palestinian national liberation movement, by becoming *fida'iyyin* (self-sacrificers), the name given to the Palestinian guerillas. Abu Subhi is alluding to what the role of his memories and his role as their narrator and transmitter ought to be: His willful narration of his memories is meant to instill patriotism in his children. He acknowledges this goal and turns these pervasive imaginings of the category of memory, with all their assumptions, on their head, since he had not shared his memories, yet his children nevertheless joined the struggle to liberate Palestine. "Against our will" is an allegorical statement that plays on the expectation that families ought to sacrifice their children for the greater Palestinian cause. This statement at once exonerates Abu Subhi for not having narrated his memories, albeit invoked allegorically (his children joined the armed struggle regardless), and venerates his children for their sacrifices.

Like Abu Subhi, but arriving at the same conclusion from a different angle, Umm 'Izz al-Din of Tantura, Haifa subdistrict, told me that she narrated memories to her children, grandchildren, and great-grandchildren "one hundred times." "They know everything, I have told them and they know everything . . . and my grandchildren . . . and my great-grandchildren, this son of Abdullah, the son of the son of Abu Abdullah, of 'Izz al-Din, when he was little, he was two years old, he would say: 'On the roundabout oh *fida'i*, on the roundabout oh *fida'i*, our president is Yasser Arafat, our president is Yasser Arafat ['ala al-duwar ya fida'i, 'ala al-duwar ya fida'i, ra'isna Yasir 'Arafat, ra'isna Yasir 'Arafat].'"[4]

Unlike Abu Subhi, Umm 'Izz al-Din asserts that she did indeed narrate and transmit memories and that her memories did fulfill their ascribed role: the politicization of her great-grandchild, related here through his recitation of a patriotic chant. Other members of the generation of Palestine rejected their own and their memories' purported roles. The late Umm Nimr, of the Akrad al-Baqqara tribe of the Safad subdistrict, who left Palestine during her second and final expulsion in 1956 after having given birth to six children, responded to my question with an unequivocal no. A friend who had brought me to meet her and her family then put it to her that in that case, how do her children know about Palestine? In response, Umm Nimr posed a counterquestion and poignantly asked: "Do you know al-Mazza [a southwestern suburb of Damascus]? Do you know al-Mazza well? . . . Stand there in Mazza, and turn toward Palestine."[5]

Umm Nimr's response clearly rejects the explicit implications of our questions about what her memories and her role in narrating these ought or ought not to do. The limitations of these assumptions were underscored through her counterquestion, whose answer was rhetorically self-evident to all present: How can we "forget," given that we were both third-generation Palestinian women living under the overarching context of the unresolved and ongoing nature of Palestinians' statelessness, literally visible from one of Damascus's suburbs? The limitations of our questions, and their underlying assumptions, were therefore grounded in an unresolved Palestinian present. Umm Nimr invoked this present through invoking our third-generation Palestinian subjectivities side by side with the visibility and physical proximity of the world that we had come to ask about.

Thus, as evident through their different answers to the same question, Abu Subhi, Umm 'Izz al-Din, and Umm Nimr all recognized the myriad assumptions implicated in the single question of whether they narrated their memories to their children and grandchildren. They did this through contesting, affirming, or rejecting the role ascribed to them in these assumptions. The late Abu Khalil, however, neither asserted nor rejected his role and the role of his memories. Instead, he told me: "I tell them about everything that happened to me . . . in this place, this happened, and in that place, that happened, in that place, our house, is like that, our land, is in that place, this is how I tell them. Palestine doesn't leave my mind at all. I make them know place by place. At night I sleep alone and I sit and remember everything that happened to me from when I was a child like them [his grandchildren sitting around us] and until now."[6]

Abu Khalil's answer complicates what his memories of Palestine are, what they do or ought to do, and by extension, what his own role in this is. Telling his children about his home and land can be interpreted as resistance within the context of his land's usurpation by a colony. However, Abu Khalil's memory-making sheds light on its familial context as well as its temporality. Narrating memories in Abu Khalil's answer is also the everyday act of a father or a grandfather whose thoughts in old age take him back to his childhood and early years. This takes place through memories that come back to him alone before he falls asleep or through reminiscing in the presence of his family members (Fivush 2008a).

What differentiates the content of Abu Khalil's memories from that of another grandfather reminiscing over his childhood is their evocation in an unresolved present. In this present, the overarching context is Abu Khalil's violent dispossession, the usurpation of his Yaquq, and his passing away without ever having been able to exercise his right of return to it. These memories are also socialized in a home in a refugee camp that sits on the road leading to the Israeli-occupied Syrian Golan Heights and historic Palestine. In short, the rupture with the past through Abu Khalil's uprooting and the ongoing statelessness of those listening as he narrates his memories coalesce to produce countermemories to ongoing Zionist colonialism in the Palestine of his memories and that of the present. This coalescing is neither deliberate nor exceptional. Rather, it is determined by the social, historical, and political context in which his memories are socialized.

Maurice Halbwachs (1992a, 48) has argued, "an old person is also esteemed because, having lived for a long time, he has much experience and is full of memories. Why should old people not then be passionately interested in the past, in the common treasure of which they are the guardians? Why should they not try quite consciously to fulfill the function which gives them the only prestige to which they can now lay claim?" Members of the generation of Palestine are in the final analysis therefore the guardians of memory as they are ordinary grandparents who happen to be the only generation that can narrate to their children and grandchildren the memories of all that was lost. This "common treasure" has taken on particularly important political implications post-Oslo and is a source of the post-Palestine generations' attachments. In view of this, I take a critical approach to the myriad entanglements of this generation's memories. I locate their narration and transmission of memories between their purported role and that of their memories in Palestinian memory discourses, as well as in those ordinary family occasions during which they share their memories of their past lives. It is from this in-between place that the post-Palestine generations related and negotiated the narration and transmission of memories in their families.

THE NARRATION OF MEMORIES

Qabr Essit Camp, June 4, 2008

I waited outside the beautiful gold- and turquoise-decorated mosque that is believed to hold the remains of Zaynab, the granddaughter of the Prophet Muhammad, brought over as a hostage after the Umayyads emerged as victors of the bloody power struggle that followed the Prophet's death. Although it was early in the morning, I silently observed the commercial hustle and bustle of the high street, which was already in full swing and packed with visitors to Zaynab's shrine, as I waited for an interviewee who had kindly offered to take me to the local camp. . . . When we entered the tight-knit camp community, all eyes were on me, the outsider, whose presence was visible to everyone who greeted us along the way, and to others whom I had caught looking down on us from their windows, as we made our way to our destination. . . . We reached a house and were welcomed in by a group of four men and a woman who were sitting in an outdoor guest-receiving space. Although the Salvation Army volunteer I was brought to meet was not at home, I was surrounded by five older men and a woman from the 'Arab al-Shamalina tribe of Safad, and realizing the opportunity, took out my recorder and asked the eldest, Abu Subhi, to tell me about the Nakba. As he began to make his memories public, the other present younger relatives intervened to agree or disagree and to offer their own memories and interpretations of past events in the process. In the next hour, I rushed from one narrator to the other in an attempt to record an unfolding discussion, even though it was impossible, as I would later come to realize . . . and to capture how one of the men walked out after he disagreed with what was said . . . or how I overlooked Abu Subhi being taken to task by the woman after she found what he said disagreeable. . . . What of everyone's fate, I wonder, now that the camp is under the army's control after the mosque's surroundings were engulfed by the flames of war, and the camp's people left, to other camps, Lebanon, and perhaps beyond.

THE GUARDIANS AND FAMILY OCCASIONS

In her discussion of family secrets and memories, the film studies scholar Annette Kuhn (2002) has argued that when thinking of ties within a family as given, rather than chosen, they share commonalities with our other attachments. Although we may bring these attachments into being through our imaginations (see, e.g., Anderson 2006), we nevertheless still have to negotiate their meanings in our daily lives (Kuhn 2002, 1). Families are also where children and grandchildren listen to members' memories and histories that are linked to larger communities (Bellah et al. 2007, 158). This is because the affiliations that construct the family as a group are created "through various relational, cultural and institutional processes" (Hirsch 1997, 10). The family is therefore an important site of given attachments where memories are narrated and histories constructed and instructed in relation to communities at large.

The post-Palestine generations related ordinary social processes and relationships, those common to all families, to have facilitated the sharing of memories in their own families. They did this while discussing their negotiation of the social meanings, attachments, and belongings to their families within the context of their wider communities. The ordinariness of these family-based practices and relationships and the stories of the family past that they facilitate have recently gained extraordinary and patriotic significations given Palestinians' political realities. As a result, the storied memories narrated in families also permit comparison with the "memories" that circulate in the memory discourses of Palestinian refugee communities.

Interviewees of different generations spoke of the family as an important, if not primary, site for the narration of memories. For example, when I asked Abu Nidal, a retired schoolteacher who left al-Ja'una, Safad subdistrict, at the age of three, what led him to comprehend the political issues regarding Palestine, he told me:

> As children, we didn't have this comprehension. The comprehension was formed, and it began to increase, after we grew up a bit and our teachers, they were Palestinians, so they would explain to us the truth and the reality . . . but also, at the same time, the parents, and the family. When those elderly would get together, during a late-night get-together—the social relationships used to be different to these days, in the 1950s. . . . People would stay up until late hours at each other's houses on a daily basis. Meaning, every day they would stay up at someone's house, they would gather, and they would sit and talk, they would discuss, and we the children would sit, because they didn't really have any other place to sit but in a room, and we as children, we would hear what they would say. They would talk about the homeland, how they went to other areas, this or that spring, and how they would hunt, and how they would set down traps, and so forth. They would talk about the life that they had there.[7]

Even though Abu Nidal asserts that his political awareness came later in life, he returns to his childhood and notes family gatherings as the inadvertent site that enabled him to develop his later political awareness. His family's inadvertent role is based on the fact that it constituted a site for sharing memories about the world the guardians once inhabited rather than a site of willful politicization. These memories were therefore transmitted to a young child who would later come to realize their meanings and understand his reality as a refugee unable to exercise his right of return to this world. Thus, though this narration may be portrayed and even mobilized for its political consciousness–forming potential by community activists, its potential political consequences are not deliberately enacted during ordinary family occasions. Indeed, how could they be, when the family occasions Abu Nidal recalls reflect the mundane reality of the daily social lives of families. In these occasions, older family members, as well as other generations in the home and neighbors and guests who may be refugees from the same or different destroyed places of origin, get together late at night and through their togetherness share their memories of the lives they once had. Thus, if "counter" and political consciousness–forming potential is to be found among the guardians and in their memories, then it is in the objects of these memories as well as in the overarching political context of these memories socialization in Palestinian refugee families. In other words, these memories are dissident memories when read as recalling worlds and lives in historic Palestine, now Israel, and as enabling political claims against the state.

The other entanglement of the guardians' memory making, as per Abu Nidal's interview, is in how it enables the construction of a personal narrative for the post-Palestine generations (Bruner 1991, 2004). It also enables the post-Palestine generations' construction of the "building blocks of a life story" (Fivush 2008a; 2008b, 51). Thus, the presence of children and grandchildren in family occasions where memories are narrated allow the post-Palestine generations to articulate a coherent understanding of their own, their families', and their communities' pasts and presents. These pasts and presents are constructed around the object of the guardians' memories which is their former lives.

Third-generation Palestinian refugee interviewees, or those born to parents who themselves were born or came of age in Syria, also emphasized the family and family occasions as important sites for the narration of memories. For example, while discussing the relationship between the narration of memories in her home and the realities of coming-of-age as a third-generation Palestinian refugee, Suzanne, a community volunteer whose grandparents are from Safad, told me:

> The family stories have a very big influence, do you see, along with the events that you see on the outside. But the foundation is that you are really somehow saturated by these stories at home. . . . Events consolidate [memory] when they take place outside, they further consolidate these stories. Because what happens is a kind of linking, or interrelationship, I don't know. My grandmother, when she used to talk about Palestine, and a martyr is driven in a funeral procession, we would tie the events to each other, and it conceives in us something on the inside. Now, this [something], it remains stored, because you can't express it until a later stage in your life.[8]

Like Abu Nidal, Suzanne is also constructing a personal narrative and a coherent life story by linking the basis of her later social and political comprehension to her grandmother's memories. She did this through interlinking what she heard in her family, or the memories of Safad and its loss, with making sense of what she later saw in life. This is the funeral procession of a Palestinian fighter who had presumably become one in trying to reclaim the world related to Suzanne through memories.

In the process of sharing how she came to comprehend the political implications of Palestine, Suzanne, like Abu Nidal, also noted the importance of her family. Unlike him, however, she mentioned a different family occasion as the site for the narration of memories. This occasion differs from others in that it brings together children and grandchildren with the women guardians in particular, or their mothers, grandmothers, and even other female relatives, but the main narrator is always the woman guardian. The importance of this particular kind of family occasion is derived from its striking reoccurrence in interviews with third-generation Palestinian refugees and, to a lesser extent, in interviews with the second generation. In what follows, I consider the role of the women guardians in particular in the narration of memories, before turning to the question of how and what memories are transmitted during family occasions.

WOMEN GUARDIANS

In her discussion of the narration and transmission of Nakba memories in her own family home, the sociologist Fatma Kassem (2011, 20) states that "as in other Palestinian homes, my family home was a site for telling and retelling stories related to events in 1948." Kassem grew up as a Palestinian citizen of Israel in the northern village of Buina to a mother who comes from the nearby destroyed and depopulated village of Sabalan. Kassem's family was a part of the 150,000 Palestinians who remained in their homes or became "internal refugees" in the wake of the Nakba. This segment of Palestinian society endured, among other things, "internal" Israeli military rule for the first two decades after 1948. Today, they constitute the 1.5 million second-class Palestinian citizens of Israel (Kanaaneh and Nusair 2010; Pappe 2011). In view of this, Kassem notes that her home was itself a site for the commemoration of Palestinian history through the narration of memories.

As this irredentist commemoration took place in her home, Kassem (2011) argues that the gendered spaces in which the telling and retelling of memories unfolded reproduced a gendered memory-telling hierarchy that devalued her mother's memories. She states that while her mother would sit with the family and listen to the stories that her father told, "she never contributed any of her personal experiences in the 'public space' of our family living room. . . . [It was] where my parents told their stories [that] have both a concrete and symbolic meaning." For Kassem, the "public" living room, where "a diverse group of people would visit, including neighbors, extended family members and other guests," was the domain of her father's narrations. Her mother felt more comfortable narrating in the "private" kitchen space, "with a much smaller audience of immediate family members" (26). Thus, a private/public dichotomy existed in her family home in ways that disadvantaged her mother's narration of her memories. Kassem attempts to move beyond the hierarchy that this dichotomy reproduced by arguing that although qualitatively different and given unequal importance, the memories of her mother and father were complementary.

That spaces are gendered in ways that can be reproduced within a family's home and that these spaces may hierarchize the guardians' memory-making in ways that disadvantage women are arguments worth examining further. This is particularly the case given the importance ascribed to women guardians by the post-Palestine generations. Some interviewees took Kassem's contention further and noted that the guardians' memory-making was also determined by a hierarchy of gendered roles within their families. For example, when discussing the differences between his mother's and father's narrations of their hometown of Safad, Abu Shadi, a second-generation retired UNRWA employee, said, "My mother, as any Palestinian woman, as long as her husband was talking, she wasn't going to talk, do you see?"[9] Later on in our conversation, as I pressed him on the differences between what his mother and father would narrate, he said:

Between my father and mother, the narratives were always complementary. . . . My father, because, we would be up having a late night, we would have a conversation, we would hear about an event on the radio, and my father would start commenting, my uncle would also be sitting, the women would either be working with wool, or preparing a meal, meaning there wasn't participation, apart from simple comments, in a family environment, so she [mother] didn't have this very big role.[10]

In addition to the hierarchies of gendered spaces and roles, Abu Shadi also notes a gendered division of labor within his family that contributed to the who, when, and what of the narrated memories. These factors combined can also reproduce a woman-disadvantaging memory-narrating hierarchy. However, I am interested in what Abu Shadi referred as his mother's and his uncle's wife's "simple comments." These were often made between working in the kitchen, carrying out the household chores, or letting the men talk among men or as those who occupy the living room. This is because these "simple comments" speak of the "interstices" (Leydesdorff, Passerini, and Thompson 1996, 8), or those moments in which women guardians nevertheless do narrate their memories despite the numerous gendered hierarchies of a family home.

These "simple comments" include the disapproving gesture and subtle interjection of the woman from 'Arab al-Shamalina in the very "public" outdoor guest-receiving space where I was welcomed. It is not coincidental that I never learned her name. Her interjection, like that of Abu Shadi's female relatives, complicates a simple reproduction of a public and private dichotomy within the family home and, by extension, in the guardians' narration of memories. Despite the numerous gendered hierarchies in his own family home, Abu Shadi nevertheless began our interview by referring to his mother's, rather than father's, memories of leaving Safad. When I asked him how his family left, he said:

> There was even a funny incident that my mother would tell me, you know I was some one year [old] and something when we left, that her wedding gold set and those things that she would hold dear as a newlywed, she put it in a cloth sack, and she tied it, and then she got on a horse, they had horses, she got on, and then my grandmother, her mother-in-law, came and told her: "Are you crazy? Return it, it will get lost on the way, we are going now, we are just going to leave for three or four days and we will return." So, my grandmother carried the gold and returned it to the house.[11]

That these memories are gendered, given the gender of their narrators, is self-evident (Humphries and Khalili 2007; R. Sayigh 2007a). What is important to consider, though, is that women guardians do narrate memories (R. Sayigh 1998, 2007b), even when operating within gendered hierarchies. Indeed, third-generation Palestinian refugees interviewed were nearly unanimous in highlighting their grandmothers as the primary narrators of memories in their lives. The question to consider therefore is how is it that women guardians have nonetheless come to narrate their memories and leave an important, even prioritized, imprint on those to whom these memories were narrated?

When I asked Umm Ghassan, a housewife and a second-generation refugee whose family were migrants to Haifa from Umm al-Fahm during the Nakba, about who would narrate memories in her home, she said that her mother

> would tell us, and my father, God have mercy on his soul, would tell us as well, but given that my father would work three different jobs. . . . it

was very rare that my father would sit around with the elderly, and they'd start talking and so forth, and we'd hear, but it was my mother who would talk. . . . When he would sit around and talk, him and the elderly who would come over to visit him, from his generation, yes, they would converse, about the memory of Palestine, and their trade, and my mother would sit and tell us how they used to live and so on and so forth. . . . She would tell us, or her friends would come and they would also talk, and no [not just us], it would become a family issue, and stretch over the years.[12]

When and if her father was around, he would indeed sit with the other members of the generation of Palestine and remember the days of Haifa. However, for Umm Ghassan, her father's role in narrating memories of Palestine was limited. This is primarily because, as she later put it, "he didn't really have the time for us, he didn't have the time, he had many other pressing concerns. The concerns of feeding the family, they were greater."[13] Thus, Umm Ghassan's mother had a more important role to play in narrating her memories within the home, and when she did, she would narrate her memories to her children or in the presence of guests. Most important, Umm Ghassan's mother's memories were not merely "kitchen talk;" they would turn into family issues and points of contention that could go on for years.

Thus, to do justice to the women guardians, it is important to discard the presupposition that rigid gender hierarchies in the home have had a correlation with the narration of memories. An adherence to the contours of these hierarchies runs the risk of overlooking the influence that women do indeed enjoy in their own homes, even if they occupy traditional roles. Through these roles, after all, women have been responsible for the day-to-day running of the household even when they worked outside the home, as many did, following the loss of everything in 1948. They have also been the primary caretakers who have as a result spent more time with their children and even grandchildren. These roles are therefore also a potential source of power and influence in families.

The gender hierarchies in the family home that may have influenced the ability of women guardians to narrate their memories were not referred to at all a generation later. Instead, all third-generation interviewees I conversed with, with the exception of one, conjured up the figure of the grandmother time and again as the narrator of memories par excellence. For this reason, I next examine the grandmother's role in the narration of memories, as told by third-generation interviewees, and what that relationship can tell us about memory and gender.

The central role third-generation interviewees ascribed to the grand-mother as the narrator of memories is striking. Most important was the grandmother during family occasions that brought her together with her grandchildren. With that said, interviewees mentioned other family occasions that facilitated the narration of memories and involved one or more guardian. These occasions, however, were never as important as the one where the grandmother and grandchildren spent time together, and they were never described in gender-determined language.

While this implies that family occasions in which the narration of memories took place included both men and women guardians, the question of memory and gender can be assessed through the one family occasion that was always described in gender-determined language. This is the aforementioned occasion that brought third-generation interviewees and their grandmothers together. Theoretically, this examination is an attempt to move beyond women guardians' memories "as counterhistory that restores forgotten stories to the historical record" (Hirsch and Smith 2002, 7). Although this is an important point (see, e.g., Kassem 2007, 2010), it is now well-established that women's memories constitute counterhistory. It is as a result more instructive to examine the centrality of women guardians in the narration of memories and how this centrality is deployed and constructed, despite the potential for gendered hierarchies, restrictions, and roles in the family home.

Khawla, a young mother and community volunteer whose grandparents are from Kafr Lam and 'Ayn Ghazal, Haifa subdistrict, related to me the following about her grandmother's storied memories:

> It was in detail, in details about how the house was, how the trees were, [what you are told] outside the house is that you are simply a Palestinian and you need to feel connected to Palestine because you have a cause, because your country is occupied and that is it. But [through grand-mother] you feel the emotions, because it is who you are: "Your grand-father was born here, this used to belong to you, and when you go back, it will belong to you." It ties you to it, it belongs to you, not just because it is an occupied country, like you learn outside. . . . [Outside] it is abstract, it is devoid of feelings or anything. Inside the home you really feel . . . [when] she talks, that, for example, or when an old person talks, that . . . that you went and lived, you lived there. But this is not the case [outside]. Outside the home they tell you we are being martyred, and people are dying and you feel depressed.[14]

It is interesting how Khawla contrasts her grandmother's memories with what is circulated outside the home, where memories are mobilized to build a political identity. These patriotic discourses that she alludes to and what they are meant to instill in third-generation Palestinians are ultimately not as valuable for Khawla as the storied memories of her grandmother. The value of her grandmother's memories is found in their content and the mode of narration. It is through simple stories, or "storied memories" (Abu-Lughod 2007, 79), about the trees, the land, and the house that Khawla locates the power and importance of her grandmother's memories. As equally important is the emotive force delivering these memories of the world of the Haifa villages. These factors that Khawla underscores move beyond women's memories as mere counterhistory. They shed light on the ways in which gender comes to shape "the technologies of memory, the frames of interpretation, and the acts of transfer they enable" (Hirsch and Smith 2002, 7).[15]

While discussing the narration of memories in his home, Bassam, a father and worker, whose grandparents are from Akrad al-Baqqara, Safad subdistrict, told me:

> What I know is through what the old folks said, my grandmother in particular. I didn't come of age to my grandfather, but know through what my grandmother said. . . . Sometimes you know, she would [reflect], what I won't forget, is that sometimes, I would, for example, sleep on her knee, and she would tell me how she'd go to the harvest, how she would reap, how they would sow, how they would go and fish from the Jordan River, how they would go out, how they would go and collect logs in order to heat themselves up in Palestine, how they would sing 'ataba and so forth.[15] We learnt about all these things through my grandmother.[16]

Bassam relates gendered "technologies of memory" such as being told storied memories while being lulled to sleep in his grandmother's lap. These technologies together with his gendered frame of interpretation, or his negotiation of the meanings of his grandmother's memories, enable the gendered transmission of Akrad al-Baqqara. Moreover, Bassam's grandmother narrated the storied memories of harvesting, fishing, and collecting logs through drawing on gendered cultural forms. These forms included women's fable- and storytelling, which are oral folk narrative genres with roots in historic Palestine (Kanaaneh 1995; Muhawi and Kanaana 1989), and singing 'ataba. These forms together allowed for the colorful details of the Hula Valley and the way of life and songs of those who once inhabited it to come to life for Bassam. Thus, it is through such family occasions and the ways in which they allow for the narration, interpretation, and transmission of memory, that the grandmother and women guardians more generally have come to occupy an important place in the narration and transmission of memories.

The interviewee who could compare his grandparents' narrations of Tantura because he had come of age to both was Muhammad-Khayr, a third-generation young father and drama studies graduate. When I asked him about his grandmother's memories, he told me:

> When she left Palestine she was young. She remembers, she would tell me about her mother and how they left. Because young women were different, a young man would come and go, and go out and see, whereas a girl in a Palestinian village, they lived in a state of backwardness, perhaps she couldn't [move freely]. But she'd tell me about how "we used to make bread, we'd go to the beach in the morning to collect the fish left on the sand by the ebbing of the waves, which would leave behind fish that used to get caught up in the sand, and I'd go there with a basket that I'd take and use when collecting the fish, and then I'd go back home and put the fish inside the kiln, and then we'd have the fish for lunch." Meaning she used to talk about things that have to do with housekeeping, preparing food, and washing up rather than the adventures and the kinds of stories that I'd hear from my grandfather. . . . I remember she used to sing songs that had to do with the village, there was a song that goes: "Loaded camels and camels that groan," you feel that it was like lamenting or weeping. Very sad songs, part of the folklore of the village, she would sing these songs to me as a child to make me sleep at night. I still have a hard time sleeping at night.[17]

Clearly, it is not that Muhammad-Khayr's grandmother's domain was restricted in a literal sense, as being able to narrate storied memories about preparing fish for lunch illustrates. Rather, it is Muhammad-Khayr's gendered frame of interpretation that leads him to prioritize his grandfather's gendered oral folk narrative genre of adventure stories over his grandmother's storied memories of daily household chores (Muhawi and Kanaana 1989). Despite this gendered hierarchization of his grandparents' memories, Muhammad-Khayr's grandmother's memories have nevertheless been clearly narrated to him. Like Bassam, he also links the narration (and transmission) of memories to his grandmother's putting him to sleep, along with yet another gendered cultural artifact that the women guardians use in telling their memories, which is singing.

The examination of the narration of memories through family occasions, the centrality of women, and the relationships between grandmothers and their grandchildren leaves the interrelated questions of what is narrated, why it is narrated, and what consequences follow open. Second- and third-generation interviewees all clearly underscored the fact that the memories narrated during their family occasions were about the worlds destroyed during the Nakba. That it was the worlds of Palestine that were narrated during family occasions, rather than the horrors the guardians lived through during 1947–1949 and afterward, speaks to the ways survivors of catastrophes do not necessarily cling to the memories of these catastrophes. Rather, they hold on to the unquantifiable loss of worlds and communities that results from catastrophes.

In the case of Palestinians in Syria, it is not that second- and third-generation refugees did not know or could not talk about the Nakba, given that it is what led to the loss of the lives narrated in the guardians' memories. The Nakba of course also remains unresolved, and has a central place in popular memory discourses in their communities. Rather, the Nakba is simply not what they chose to emphasize in detailing the guardians' narration, and thus transmission, of memories. Instead, they emphasized memories of loss that resulted from the Nakba. The objects of these memories are imagined as "Palestine" by the post-Palestine generations (see also Farah 1997). Their only lived connection to this imagined past, as well as the structures of attachment to it, or the refusal of its loss, is through the quickly disappearing guardians of memory. These intimate imaginings, I contend, are also particularly potent and more meaningful to interviewees than the memories mobilized in their communities as part of the memory/return matrix.

THE TRANSMISSION OF LOSS

Yarmouk Camp, May 25, 2008

Umm 'Izz al-Din says that she is a hundred years old, although her official birth date, arbitrarily estimated by a state official some sixty years ago at the time of our interview, deems her a hundred and ten. . . . She could be my own grandmother, with her familiar dialect and expressions, which a hundred years later, subtly imply a belonging to the world of the Haifa villages that continue to exist through her. . . . She moves with ease in the world of Mount Carmel in the present tense and tells me about the Balata spring in Ijzim, which, with a play on words, is mockingly deemed the source of the

notorious obstinacy of its people. . . . And of Umm al-Zinat's austere villag-
ers. . . . When I move to conclude the encounter after two long and engaging
hours, I ask her for her opinion on my research. . . . "What you are doing is
for your own benefit, I am neither ashamed nor fearful of anyone but God
and say the truth... If it wasn't so, would you go through all the hassle and
go around peoples' homes? And ask all these questions? Look, I am illiterate,
but I know everything. . . ." But what about the importance of remember-
ing? . . . "Remember, it is a memory, remember if this memory serves any-
thing." . . . Undeterred by her dismissal, I try once again, and ask her about
the prospect of publishing peoples' memories. . . . "So what if you publish
it in a book? So many books have been buried by time and disappeared,
my daughter." . . . A few weeks later, I find myself in the Tanturans' part
of the camp again, today a war-torn ghost of its previous bustling self, and
I see Umm 'Izz al-Din sitting on a chair outside her home. . . . As I greet
her, I wonder where her thoughts take her as she sits in that chair where she
spends her long summer evenings. . . . And her words on the ephemerality of
memories and the futility of my endeavor come back to me. . . . I ask myself
whether she is still with us today, if she lived to see the Tanturans' quarter
shelled, bombed, and subjected to a siege that has made life impossible for
the poor, destitute, and trapped who could not leave Yarmouk.

Cultural memory, it has been argued, is memory "understood as a cultural phenomenon as well as an individual or social one" (Bal 1999, vii,
see also Erll, Nünning, and Young 2008). The cultural studies and literary
theory scholar Mieke Bal (1999, vii) has argued that "cultural recall is not
something of which you happen to be a bearer but something you actually
perform, even if, in many instances, such acts are not consciously or willfully
contrived [emphasis in original]." According to Bal, those who choose to
share their memory in an act she denotes as "memorizing," or memory-
making, and the others who constitute the second-personhood necessary
for the facilitation of memory are together engaged in what she terms "acts
of memory." This is "an exchange between first and second person that sets
in motion the emergence of memory" (x). Bal theorizes acts of memory's
co-constitutive "memorizing" and "second-personhood" in relation to traumatic recall, which is distinct from narrative memory. However, this co-
constitutive necessity is also equally important for memories related through
narratives, as memory narratives or storied memories. This is because it
comes about within a cultural context that facilitates the remembering,
whether through ratifying the memory or through enabling the presence of
others who can relate to it (x).

It could be argued that the different family occasions examined are the cultural context that facilitates and enables the narration of memories in families. This context provides the guardians with the second-personhood necessary for their memory-making and acts of memory. This second-personhood can be other guardians or different generations present while the guardians remember their pasts, as examined earlier. 'Ammar, a lawyer whose grandparents are from Nasir al-Din, Tiberias subdistrict, related the following as we discussed the narration of memories during family occasions in his home: "It happened normally, perhaps in most gatherings or get-togethers [when they would say], 'Remember the times when this or that happened,' and so forth. . . . I don't personally remember [one of them telling me], 'Come my son, this and that happened to us.' But, no, it was brought up as part of a conversation."[18]

'Ammar is invoking spontaneous family occasions that involved guardians getting together and through their togetherness providing the second-personhood necessary to remembering what they once had. Thus, the guardians who can remember this or that time, or this or that event, together ratify and enable the socialization of each other's memories. Given the presence of different generations during these occasions that bring them together, these occasions also enable the transmission of the guardians' memories.

Second-generation Palestinian refugees, like the third-generation, also pointed to these family occasions as sites that facilitated the guardians' acts of memory. The primary difference between second- and third-generation interviewees is that for the second generation, these family occasions involved their own parents. For several interviewees, it also involved their grandparents who lived in the same family home during the early post-1948 years. For example, Abu Shadi told me:

When we left Palestine and lived here [in the same house], it was us and my paternal uncle's family . . . [and when] the radio [was] on, and we would hear about an event, it would be the beginning of a conversation, a discussion between my father and my uncle, [and they would say,] "Listen children, tomorrow when you go back to Palestine, you have this and that" [or] "we have this and we have that." . . . It wouldn't be out of nowhere, [it would result from] an event [on the radio], or a guest would come over [and say], "What do you remember from the days of Palestine?" They'd talk and they'd tell the children to come and listen, right? So they would always insist that we ought to listen, we ought to know, we should know what we have and what we owe.[19]

Despite the generational differences, Abu Shadi, like 'Ammar, also describes the frameworks of different family occasions in his home as having enabled his father's and uncle's acts of memory. The co-constitutive narration of memories and second-personhood needed for these acts could be triggered by diverse sources. These include a news item on the radio, a discussion between his father and uncle or a guest who would come and remember the days of Palestine with them and listen to their memories. Within such family occasions as an enabling framework, these acts of memory are informed by the loss that resulted from the forced collective expulsion of 1948. In remembering what was lost and invoking it over and over, the guardians also enact their refusal to accept this loss. Abu Shadi, for example, pointed to his father's and uncle's memories as revolving around what they once had. Their narrating memories in the present tense or insisting that the children should listen and know of the world that belongs to them are acts that refuse the loss related through their memories.

This emphasis on the narration of memories of loss has important implications for the post-Palestine generations postmemories and narratives on Nakba memory, a point to which I return in chapter 6. For now, the question is, how do the family occasions' cultural frameworks that enable the narration of memories of loss also enable the intergenerational transmission of these memories beyond the literal act of narration? While discussing the narration of memories, Ahlam, a worker whose grandparents are from al-Shuna, Safad subdistrict, told me: "They didn't tell me [personally], they used to talk among themselves: do you remember [this] and do you remember [that]? I was unlike the other girls, I used to go there and sit in the middle. . . . 'Do you remember the day of this and the day of that? Or this and that and how we would spend our days?' They used to talk and laugh, but I used to feel a sorrowful regret in their laughter, a sorrow for everything they lost."[20]

While underscoring family occasions as the framework that enables the guardians' narration of loss, Ahlam also points to a transmission beyond the content of the guardians' memories. This is not to downplay the importance of the transmission of these memories or the narration of the worlds and lives of al-Shuna. Rather, it is to highlight that something else is at stake for Ahlam beyond the memory of this or that day or this and that event that the guardians together shared and affirmed. Through her invocation of the guardians' sorrowful regret (*hasra*), she is also alluding to the transmission of loss itself.

Thus, beyond the worlds destroyed in Palestine, it is loss that is transmitted to the generations of Palestinian refugees who came of age or were born in Syria. This loss "continues as an animating absence in the presence, one that makes itself known precisely in and through the survival of anachronism itself" (Butler 2003, 468). This painful absence is transmitted through affects that structure the guardians' attachments to the objects of their memories of loss. It is therefore not just an inventory of material losses that the guardians transmit to the post-Palestine generations but also powerful affects that structure their own attachments to the lives, communities, and worlds of their memories and that translate into their refusal to accept their loss.

AFFECTS OF GRIEF

The question of historical loss and its resultant bodily, spatial, and ideal remains is the subject of an edited collection by literary and cultural theory scholars David Eng and David Kazanjian (2003b). In their introduction, Eng and Kazanjian (2003a) revisit Sigmund Freud's thesis in *Mourning and Melancholia* ([1915] 1917, 2001) and cast doubt on Freud's separation between the two psychic states. Through reading Freud's ([1923] 2001) later work, they also argue that melancholia need not be inevitably pathological. They draw on the philosopher Judith Butler's (1997) argument that the "incorporative logic of melancholia founds the very possibility of the ego and its psychic topography" (Eng and Kazanjian 2003a, 4). They contend that melancholia is in fact necessary for both the ego and the work of mourning. They argue that the ego's melancholic attachments to loss "might be said to contribute not only [to] psychic life and subjectivity but also [to] the domain of remains" (5).

The most compelling aspect of what Eng and Kazanjian (2003a, 4) term their "counter-intuitive" reading of mourning and melancholia is to allow for an understanding of melancholic attachments that highlights "their creative, unpredictable, political aspects." In her astute critique of what she calls "the melancholy turn," the cultural studies and critical theory scholar Rey Chow (2008, 572–573) notes that this turn has been compelling because of the theoretical potential it carries, or the "twin rhetorical move of essentializing-cum-deconstruction, asserting paradoxically both the existence of an original and its irrevocable loss, both a lost object and its continued spectral presence, [which] leads to an inexhaustible theoretical productiveness." It is this theoretical potential, rather than what Chow argues is essentially this body of work's engagement in a "second-order mourning" (573), that provides an opening through which to understand the affects that enabled the transmission of loss in the families of the post-Palestine generations (see also Tabar 2007).

I employ "affect" to mean "an impingement or extrusion of a momentary or sometimes more sustained state of relation *as well as* the passage (and the duration of passage) of forces or intensities . . . that pass body to body . . . [and are] resonances that circulate about, between, and sometimes stick to bodies and worlds, *and* in the very passages or variations between these intensities and resonances themselves [emphasis in original]" (Gregg and Seigworth 2010, 1). Sorrowful regret and yearning, the two affects described by interviewees as structuring the guardians' attachments to their memories of loss, belong to the domain of mourning and melancholia insofar as they are responses to loss that at their very core also encapsulate its refusal.

Interviewees related sorrowful regret as the unspeakable force hovering over and realized through these family occasions. Yearning, in contrast, was the force propelling the guardians' narration of their memories. I refer to sorrowful regret and yearning as affects of grief within the context of psychic and material practices of loss and its remains being potentially productive, "full of volatile potentiality and future militancies rather than as pathologically bereft and politically reactive" (Eng and Kazanjian's 2003a, 5). These affects are an experience of an emotive event during ordinary family occasions. They also, as noted, structure the guardians' attachment to the loss narrated through their memories (see, e.g., Berlant 2008).

In what follows, I examine the potentiality of these affects through their transmission of loss itself, and with it, the guardians' structures of attachments to the objects of their memories of loss.

SORROWFUL REGRET

The Arabic word *hasra* and its verb *tahasara* entail both sorrow and regret. I therefore translate *hasra* as "sorrowful regret." Later in the interview with Ahlam, I probed her further about what she described as the guardians' sorrowful regret. She said:

In their conversations, they would talk a little and then they would stop. You feel that this silence, it has something strange about it. They would look at each other and then stop talking. Like they are still talking but . . . among themselves, alone. . . . What I mean is that they would say, "Do you remember?" And then they would look at each other and fall silent and then [eventually] start talking again. You feel that there was something strange in the matter. . . . I think it was sorrowful regret [*hasra*].[21]

For Ahlam, the impingement of sorrowful regret is through the guardians' silence in the face of the painful question "Do you remember?" The pain is derived from the question's rhetorical power to invoke all that was lost. The silence that follows is therefore a response, but one audible only to the guardians, who communicate by looking into each other's eyes or simply through saying nothing. It is in and through these silences that Ahlam locates sorrowful regret as the force of the guardians' encounter.

Other interviewees also noted silence as the moments in which sorrowful regret and other affects of grief make themselves present. When I asked Muhammad-Khayr about silences in the guardians' memories, he said: "Silence is an expression. . . . You feel like they'd fall silent and the atmosphere would turn gloomy, you feel that they dwell silently on their memories, they dive into them, and they ache and shed tears, this happens a lot. You feel that there is something heavy that hovers over the gathering, something foggy."[22]

It is through silences that Muhammad-Khayr feels the guardians' grief, the gloominess of their encounter, and even their dwelling on and diving into their memories or their holding onto their loss. It is also through silences that the guardians' aching and shedding of tears, the heaviness that hovers over their gathering, are realized. The sorrowful regret described by Ahlam and Muhammad-Khayr therefore circulates among those present and dominates their understanding of the family occasion. It also structures the guardians' attachments to the loss of the world of their memories, their holding onto this world, and the refusal of its loss.

When I asked Ayman, a third-generation interviewee and a graphic designer whose grandparents are from al-Kabri, Acre subdistrict, whether his grandmother openly expressed her sorrowful regret as she told him about al-Kabri, he said: "No, she wouldn't say it. But she would fall silent, it was a silence, she would become quiet for a while, and then she would begin responding, and she would respond very slowly, she would take her time, and you would feel that, meaning, the problem is I can't describe it to you unless you see it with your own eyes, it is a feeling, you feel that she is really sad, that perhaps if she could roll back time she wouldn't have left Palestine."[23]

Ayman describes silence as the state through which his grandmother's sorrowful regret is realized and tells how this affect transmits the enormity of the guardians' loss to generations who have come of age in the shadow of its consequences. He also moves from describing his grandmother's sorrowful regret as she narrates her memories to pointing out how this affect in fact structures her attachment to the worlds she narrates. In other words, this same affect that she herself feels for the world she describes makes itself felt as she narrates her memories, so much so, her grandson concludes, that if she could roll back time she would not leave Palestine. Thus, the potential of the guardians' attachments to loss is found not only in the narration but also through the transmission itself.

A very similar description of sorrowful regret, imposed through silence, and its implications was related by Suzanne in relation to her late grandmother's narration of Safad:

> When she used to sigh or for example she would stop at a certain event [of her memories], or if her throat would dry up, we would feel it. . . . She would sigh, or she would wipe her face, or [pause and] ask God for forgiveness, do you see? . . . What would make me feel that she feels sorrowful regret over the situation [that she narrates] would be when her throat runs dry, or when she would wipe her face, I'd feel that she wanted to shed a tear, but in order for us, to continue the story with us, she wouldn't be able to tear or cry.[24]

Suzanne, like Ahlam, Muhammad-Khayr, and Ayman, is relating events whose affects—sadness, regret, sorrow, pain—are coherent only in terms of her grandmother's attachments to the worlds of the memories she narrates. It is through sorrowful regret circulating in the guardians' silences and pauses that interviewees also locate the affects that structure the guardians' relationship to the world of their memories and that the loss is transmitted to them. These are the moments when Suzanne's grandmother would sigh, her throat would dry out, or she would wipe her face and ask for God's forgiveness, and even instances of weeping. Similar to Ayman, Suzanne too later affirmed that her grandmother's sorrowful regret was related to her leaving Palestine.

YEARNING

Another affect of grief that the post-Palestine generations described while relating the guardians' transmission of loss is yearning (*hanīn*). Unlike sorrowful regret, however, yearning was related as the force propelling the guardians' narration of their memories rather than the force of the guardians' encounter. For example, when I asked Abu Nidal why he thought the guardians would narrate their memories, he replied: "To remember, to remember. And some of them, when they would remember, they would cry. . . . Sadness, meaning they would yearn."[25] To yearn is therefore to invoke memories of loss just as this remembering is also an expression of sadness.

Interviewees also described yearning as the force through which guardians enacted a certain refusal of loss. While describing her family's late nights around the heater in winter, Maha, a third-generation refugee and community volunteer whose family is from Kafr Sabt, Tiberias subdistrict, told me: "They would remember the old days, they would yearn for the past. . . . [You'd sense this] from what they would say, from the way that they'd talk. . . . Sometimes they would say, 'If only the old days would come back,' if they could go back to Palestine, but no, they won't go back."[26]

Like sorrowful regret, yearning is also a force and an intensity that circulates among those present during family occasions, one that is not necessarily articulated but is nonetheless felt. For Maha, the guardians' yearning is in what they would say and in the ways they would recollect their memories. Yearning, like sorrowful regret, also structures the guardians' attachment to the objects of their memories of loss. This manifests through their desire to turn back time and their hope to return. These desires are fundamentally tied to yearning and at their core encapsulate a refusal to accept the unquantifiable loss that resulted from the Nakba.

When I asked Buthayna, another second-generation refugee and a housewife whose family is from Tantura, why she thought the guardians narrate their memories, she noted: "They'd remember because it is something— they'd remember something painful, but something you feel that also has a hope for the return in it. Meaning, you feel that they would say things, about the simplicity that was there, the riches and the agriculture, meaning, you feel yearning when they would talk, do you see?"[27]

Like Abu Nidal, Buthayna also describes the act of remembering all that was lost as the result of the guardians' pain and yearning. Once again, these affects of grief structure the guardians' attachments and transmit loss and its refusal to their children. This is what Buthayna describes as the guardians' hope and desire for return.

CONCLUSION

The foregoing examination of the narration and transmission of memories in Palestinian refugee families demonstrates why the worlds that were destroyed as a result of the Nakba, rather than the Nakba per se, are the objects of the guardians' memories. As argued, it is not the Nakba that is prioritized by the post-Palestine generations as having been central to their family occasions and the guardians' memory-making more generally. This is, of course, not to imply that Palestinian refugee families do not remember or discuss 1948. The narration of memories of lost worlds and lives are clearly implicated in the reasons for their loss, just as the transmission of loss and the structures of attachments to it are implicated in catastrophes and their human, material, and psychic remains.

However, as survivors of catastrophic events, the guardians hold on to the memories of what these catastrophes deprived them of, rather than the memories of the catastrophes themselves. Thus, the Nakba is the extraordinary event to which community activists have, since Oslo, given coherence and form as the one event that encapsulates the rupture from Palestine. It is also an event to which they have appended their political claims and aspirations through making it central to the memory/return matrix. These significations of the Nakba do not necessarily correspond with its place in memories narrated and transmitted in Palestinian refugee families.

Furthermore, in Palestinian refugee families, the guardians are the willful narrators of neither the homeland nor the Nakba. Nevertheless, the guardians are clearly aware of the roles ascribed to them in discourses that place prime political importance on them and their memories for the future return. Thus, Palestinian refugees more broadly make meaning of the Nakba by taking into account their families' memories and histories and the meanings of these memories as defined, articulated, and deployed in their wider communities. This had implications for how the guardians articulated their memories of the Nakba on its sixtieth anniversary and how their children and grandchildren negotiated and articulated their narratives on Nakba memories, the subject of the next chapters.

CHAPTER 5

THE GUARDIANS' COMMUNITIES AND MEMORIES OF CATASTROPHES

We got off there in al-Lajjun, we crossed the water and the pigeons saw us. . . . Those pigeons saw us, and they started flying all around us; these pigeons, they flew around us and started fluttering their wings around us.

UMM HASAN, FROM 'AYN GHAZAL, HAIFA

By God, I remember everything, I remember that we—it was 2 A.M.— on the fifteenth of April, Haifa fell, you see? So the Jews began to send us—meaning, in order for us to reconcile and not leave, I wish they had reconciled and we didn't leave, the people of the village didn't agree. And then, my love, on the twenty-first of May, this month, the Jews came to us at night, at 2 A.M., and I swear to God, I stuck my head out of the door and it started to pour down with rain . . . at 2 A.M., before dawn.

UMM 'IZZ AL-DIN, FROM TANTURA, HAIFA

As the last remaining individuals with memories of Palestine, members of the generation of Palestine have central and competing roles. While right of return activists and second- and third-generation refugees may agree on this generation's centrality to memories of the lost Palestine or the 1948 Nakba, they nevertheless, as demonstrated, underline different facets of their centrality. The guardians are aware of the important yet different roles ascribed to them in activists' memory discourses and in their own families. It is in relation to the value of the roles ascribed to them and their memories that they recollected the Nakba to the researcher who arrived to invoke their memories after six decades. Against these overarching realities, in this chapter I examine the meanings of this generation's Nakba memories through their circulation in the communities I encountered while in Damascus.

Throughout this book, I have demonstrated how community is about certain modes of social relations, experiences, discourses, and institutions that individuals share within socially, historically, and politically constituted parameters. I have also demonstrated how community is also about individuals' fluid and contingent interpretation and meaning-making of symbolic forms, boundaries, and belongings that result from the aforementioned modes and their structures (Delanty 2010, 18–36). In what follows, I explore the second facet of community further. I do this through thinking the guardians as constituting communities based on shared memories, and I examine the meanings of these memories as understood through their circulation in these very communities.

This approach allows for the thematic analysis of different meanings of the Nakba as encapsulated in the memories of these communities. It also allows for the appreciation of another meaning of the Nakba today. This meaning lies in the spatial and temporal realities that resulted from the Zionist-inflicted catastrophes of 1948 and afterward. It has resulted from how these realities gave way to shared memories and histories around which the symbolic contours of the guardians' communities would crystallize despite the devastation and destruction. The very existence of these communities therefore itself embodies a meaning of the Nakba today that sometimes overlaps and at other times contradicts and even contests 1948 as the urgent patriotic signifier that is at once meant to commemorate, mobilize, and ensure the return.

THE GUARDIANS' COMMUNITIES

Damascus, June 11, 2008; June 21, 2008; Quneitira, April 17, 2008

I met Abu Ahmad for an interview he had kindly agreed to give me in downtown Damascus. His sharp irony and dry wit, like that of other Safadi interviewees and acquaintances, was ubiquitous during our interview, and charming. . . . These characteristics that I had come to associate with Safadis have their roots in Safad's tough mountainous terrain, I was told time and again by Safadis and their children, a geographical reality that the people of Safad tried to replicate on the slopes of Mount Qasioun when they first came to Damascus, inhabiting heights that, as the story goes, no one but the Kurds dared to inhabit . . . "My father would tell me . . . we used to have dinner in Damascus, they would come here for dinner, and go back [to Safad]" . . . this geographical and material proximity of the two towns, related by the nephew of Fu'ad Hijazi,[1] was also articulated by others through reminders of the insignificant distance between Safad and Damascus . . . a proximity I could only imagine through the unmistakable Damascene dialect of Safadis, blurring the contours of the past proximity and present place of exile, collapsing the boundaries between time and space, a then in the now. . . . "There, behind Tal Abu al-Nada is the way to Safad," . . . I was told by a Safadi, no longer with us, who left his birthplace as a four-year-old, after I recounted my trip to the ruins and rubble of Quneitira, and that hill and its menacing watchtowers looking down on us, standing between Safad and its people.

I first learned of the massacre at Kafr 'Inan, Acre subdistrict, during my interview with the late Abu Khalil. His maternal uncle had heard news of the surrender of the village in nearby Yaquq and headed there, as they had relatives residing in the now occupied village. Upon his uncle's arrival, he watched from a safe distance as fourteen men were selected from those who had surrendered and were executed by a four-man Zionist firing squad. After hearing the news of the massacre and the fate of her son, the mother of one of the murdered men returned to the site of the massacre after some six days. There, she loaded her son onto a donkey and took him back to the Syrian Golan with her. Despite being riddled with up to fifty bullets, Abu Khalil told me, the man became the sole survivor of that massacre. He recovered, married, and had children in Khan Eshieh Camp, where he would eventually die without ever returning to Kafr 'Inan.

Later during my stay in Damascus, Umm Abdul 'Aziz, who as a child fled Jubb Yusuf, Safad subdistrict, with her family following the Zionist onslaught against that village, narrated the same story. She too mentioned the man from the Mawasi tribe of Kafr 'Inan who had survived despite being riddled with bullets. I asked her how she knew of the man's survival. She told me they became neighbors in Jaramaya, a village in the Golan where her family had also sought refuge until it was occupied, depopulated, and destroyed by Israel in 1967 (U. Davis 1983). Later still, the same story was narrated by Abu 'Ammar, who as a child had fled to the Golan with his family from Nasir al-Din, Tiberias subdistrict, after the Zionist attack on his village and yet another massacre (Abbasi 2008). He emphasized the same miraculous survival, the multiple bullet wounds, and the mother's insistence on bringing her son to Syria.

The internal constants of this one storied memory within the larger memory of the Nakba are striking: the fifty bullets, the bullet to the mouth, the return of the mother on the donkey, and the miraculous survival. These details were also remembered and narrated by interviewees who hailed from adjacent subdistricts in historic Palestine, survived different Zionist onslaughts against their communities, had initially sought refuge in the Golan in Syria and had been uprooted for the second time during the Israeli occupation of the Golan in 1967. They were, at the time of these interviews, living in the Palestinian camps or communities that are in or surround Damascus. Today, some of the interviewees have passed away and others have been uprooted yet again as a result of the war.

There are two overlapping constants in this storied memory, which is precisely what makes it compelling. One is internal, within the storied memory itself. The other is external, across different shared times and spaces, in both historic Palestine and Syria, turning on the key dates of 1948 and 1967. How does one begin to understand the constants of these fantastical memories of what are essentially a series of catastrophic events? How does one understand these memories when these events are today collectively invoked as the one catastrophic and extraordinary event of "the Nakba" that is meant at once to commemorate, mark time and space, mobilize, and demand the return? To begin with, what is constant about these memories, the fantastical, makes impossible an absolute and fixed understanding of the series of catastrophic events of 1948 as the singular, extraordinary event of the Nakba. This is because the fantastical in this storied memory diminishes its "truth value" for those seeking to construct a positivist history and, indeed, the Nakba as counterhistory to the ongoing project of Zionist settler-colonization and erasure of Arab Palestine.

Yet it is precisely the fantastical and its internal and external constants that encapsulate the "truth value," if one must be found, of the meaning of the survival of the man from the Mawasi tribe. To appreciate this, this one storied memory must be understood within the context of the physical destruction and death of Palestinian communities wrought in 1948, rather than the needs of positivist history and, indeed, law (Esmeir 2007). The witnessing of the massacre, the miraculous survival, and the mother's implicit heroism also tell of the wanton destruction and killing that the Nakba as a series of catastrophic events brought upon different communities. They also tell of survival's possibility only over the borders redrawn during 1948, and of women's central role in reconstituting the uprooted and dispersed families and communities in exile. Thus, the miraculous survival speaks to the 1948 catastrophes as well as their enormity. These can be comprehended only through speaking of the fantastical and understanding survival itself as therefore fantastical.

Moreover, what is externally constant in this one storied memory is the possibility that despite the destruction of 1948, members of the generation of Palestine constitute communities whose symbolic contours are expressed through shared memories and a shared loss (Bellah et al. 2007; Butler 2003). This possibility can be read in these shared storied memories that revolve around 1948 and afterward as realized and narrated from within and despite uprooted and fractured temporalities and spatialities. The fantastical therefore also speaks to the shattering of the guardians' times and spaces across historic Palestine, and the constitution of their communities' fractured times and spaces in Syria. It also speaks to the survival of the guardians in communities in which the past and the present, survival and death, Palestine and Syria, coexist in nonlinear temporal and spatial realities. Against this, the guardians' shared memories provide another meaning to the Nakba today. This is the Nakba understood not just as a singular, extraordinary event, but as a series of catastrophes visited upon their communities in 1948 and beyond. This meaning is embodied in their living communities and marks them as such.

I encountered the guardians' communities through their shared memories, as with the storied memory of the miraculous survival, while probing their Nakba memories. On other occasions, I also encountered the guardians' communities through the immediacy of the social, that is, through expressing belongings and constructing or imagining relationships (Delanty 2010, 35). For example, during my interview with Abu Ahmad from Safad, another man, whom I call Abu Karim as he never intended to be a part of this story and who like Abu Ahmad was also eighteen at the time of the Nakba, was present in the same building. He occasionally entered the room where Abu Ahmad and I were recording the interview. At one point in the interview, Abu Karim, whose natal village of al-Ja'una, Safad subdistrict, lay five kilometers east of Safad, intervened.

ANAHEED: Uncle, you were telling me that you left Safad, and you ended up in a village—

ABU AHMAD: We came, we walked from Safad to Wadi al-Tawahin, we have, over there, a valley [wadi] called Wadi al-Tawahin, from there to al-Rama, and from al-Rama we took cars and went out to the Syrian borders—

ANAHEED: Meaning, did you spend the night in al-Rama?

ABU AHMAD: Yes, we stayed for a night.

ANAHEED: And did you sleep in Wadi al-Tawahin?

ABU AHMAD: No, we didn't sleep there, we kept on walking.

ANAHEED: So how long did it take you to walk from Safad to al-Rama?

ABU AHMAD: Perhaps some ten kilometers, or more, perhaps twelve kilometers—

ANAHEED: So how long did it take you, a day's walking?

ABU KARIM: No, it's an hour, or three-quarters of an hour walk from Safad to Wadi al-Tawahin.

ABU AHMAD: Yes, but from Wadi al-Tawahin to al-Rama or—there is about—

ABU KARIM: An hour—

ABU AHMAD: [A total of] some two hours approximately, on foot.[2]

Toward the end of our interview, Umm Ya'rub, whom I had interviewed some three months earlier, also joined us in the room. Umm Ya'rub was born in al-Rama in the Acre subdistrict in 1922, and during the 1920s she went to primary school in Safad, where her father worked as a teacher. Upon completing her education in Jerusalem's Teacher's Training College, she returned to her primary school, where she began working as a teacher, and helped set up a women's cooperative in Safad. During our interview, she told me that "on a surface level, [the cooperative] was to help improve women's conditions, but it was really set up to help the revolutionaries."[3] This was a reference to the Palestinian uprising against British colonial rule (1936–1939) that was brutally suppressed on the eve of World War II (Swedenburg 2003, 2004).

After my interview with Abu Ahmad came to an end, all three began a conversation that centered on their joint recollections of Safad. Notwithstanding that my interview may have triggered their conversation, the co-constitutive memory-making and second-personhood that allowed for their acts of memory were possible for several reasons. First, they had all lived in or near Safad, a concrete space that informed their memories, regardless of whether they had known each other there. Furthermore, they had all shared their later lives as refugees in Syria, regardless of when they came to know each other in that country. This commonality further enriched their acts of memory, given the acquaintance and familiarity that manifested itself during that memorable early afternoon in which we were all present in that room.

During their conversation, Umm Ya'rub recalled the name of the street where her family had lived in Safad, where their house was on that street, and where it stood in relation to what neighborhood and which neighbors. She evoked these particulars in the presence of others who could affirm the Safad of her memories by relating their own stories and adding to the details of the town. Indeed, this was also the case during Abu Karim's intervention on the distance between Safad, Wadi al-Tawahin, and al-Rama. Like other guardians who recount memories of places in Palestine, Umm Ya'rub spoke in the present tense of the streets and neighborhoods of Safad that she had not seen in sixty years. Through this tense and the presence of others who knew that Safad, she brought the town to life as she conarrated her memories with the others. Their memory-making together temporally stretched past Safad by also encompassing their shared lives in Syria. Abu Ahmad asked after Umm Ya'rub's late father, her brother, and other relatives and friends, collapsing the past as lived in Palestine and the past as lived in Syria in a shared present in Damascus. The conversation gradually moved to this present, and there followed a heated discussion about the treachery of Palestinian Authority president Mahmoud Abbas. Abbas is a Safadi who, like the majority of people from the town, also became a refugee in Syria after the Nakba.

This encounter that brought Safad to life sixty years later was possible only because Abu Ahmad, Abu Karim, and Umm Ya'rub shared uprooted and fractured times and spaces in the past and the present. Their encounter and the sharing of their memories in the present tense therefore underscores their and their memories' common temporal and spatial referents. These referents, as Maurice Halbwachs (1980) has argued, are central to shared memories. Members of the generation of Palestine whom I met that afternoon ultimately shared a commonality based on their constituting a community. This community was expressed through their shared memories—its members' shared symbolic cultural forms —that also symbolically demarcate their community's boundaries (Cohen 1985, in Delanty 2010).

In their study of individualism and solidarity in American society, the sociologist Robert Bellah et al. (2007) discussed the possibility of a community in relation to its members' shared memories (and commitments). According to them, "Communities . . . have a history—in an important sense they are constituted by their past—and for this reason we can speak of a real community as a 'community of memory,' one that does not forget its past. In order not to forget that past, a community is involved in retelling its story, its constitutive narratives" (Bellah et al. 2007, 153; see also Delanty 2010, 65–66; Zureik 2003). As evident in these encounters as well as the ways memories are shared in Palestinian refugee families, the guardians clearly form not one single and coherent community of memory but various communities with shared memories. The plurality derives from the guardians' communities in Palestine whose uprooting meant that they later intersected and overlapped in Syria with other uprooted Palestinian communities, thereby creating Syrian Palestinian refugee communities with new shared histories and memories.

The shared yet fractured past and present times and spaces set the guardians' communities apart from Bellah et al.'s (2007) "community of memory" in yet another way. It is not so much that tradition and stories of exemplarity, as per Bellah et al. (2007), are so central to their shared memories. Rather, according to the guardians' children and grandchildren, as previously examined, it is their memories of unfathomable loss that ultimately mark their communities. Judith Butler (2003, 468) has argued that belonging can take place "in and through a common sense of loss . . . [and that] loss becomes condition and necessity for a certain sense of community, where community does not overcome the loss, where community *cannot* overcome the loss without losing the very sense of itself as community [emphasis in original]." The interrelated questions that this raises, and to which I now turn, is what kinds of memories circulate in communities defined in this way and what could these memories say about the meanings of the Nakba today?

MEMORIES OF DEATH IN THE VALLEY: WADI AL-RAQQAD, WADI AL-T'IN

Death was an important theme in the guardians' memories of the events surrounding 1948. This death took place as the Zionists began their onslaught against Palestinian communities in 1947 and continued after the expulsion from Palestine. The Nakba, in its pervasive imaginings in memory and patriotic discourses, revolves around the critical year of 1948. The guardians' memories in general, and memories of death in particular, make the case for extending the temporal framework of the Nakba beyond that crucial year. They also make the case for thinking about the catastrophe that engulfed their communities in the plural. For the series of catastrophes that were visited upon Palestinians did not simply end with the expulsion but extended to their post-1948 realities.

Memories of death were related to me through a colloquial expression literally meaning the "world died" in Wadi al-Raqqad during what historians have noted was a particularly harsh winter, the freezing winter of 1948–49 (Pappe 2006b, 137). During that winter, the Palestinians dispossessed during the Zionist onslaught had been made refugees overnight. Those who made it to the Golan on foot also became homeless in a colder environment, without adequate food, clothing, or shelter. The world died in Wadi al-Raqqad, I was told by three different guardians, who all hailed from the adjacent sub-districts of Safad and Tiberias. There, all three had lived in settled Bedouin communities, would seek refuge in the Golan in 1948, and with the exception of 'Arab al-Shamalina who were expelled for the second time in 1951, were uprooted for the second time after the Israeli occupation of Syria in 1967 (see also Al-Mawed 1999). At the time of the interviews, they were living in three different areas adjacent to camps or in the camps that surround Damascus, some of which continue to be war zones today.

Like the memory of the survival of the man from the Mawasi tribe, the guardians' memories of death in the valley also share temporal and spatial referents. In telling their memories, the three guardians also used the same language and expressions to refer to the death that overtook their communities during that particularly harsh first winter as refugees. The colloquial expression used by all three interviewees to describe the catastrophe that unfolded was "*el-dinya matat*" or "*matat el-dinya.*" Here, the world's death refers to a world made up of people (*el-nas*), human relationships, and the environment, of a living community as one knows and inhabits it. In what follows, I lay out these memories of the death of the world as told by its survivors and as I chronologically encountered them.

Umm 'Abdul 'Aziz fled the Golan a widow after the invading Israeli army killed her husband in 1967. She would eventually settle in al-Hajar al-Aswad, an informal neighborhood that borders Yarmouk and that was home to mostly Syrians displaced from the Golan. Today, al-Hajar al-Aswad has been depopulated and is the site of intense clashes between government forces and ISIS fighters. As she related her early days in the Golan, she told me her memories of the transition from living in the emergency tents to living in tents made of camel hair that her family eventually bought in the Golan.[4] She said the following about the early years in Syria:

> They later took us out [of the valley], UNRWA took us out, and everyone had to take care of himself, you see? . . . They took us out because the people died [*matat el-dinya*], every day they would go out on a funeral procession, ten funeral processions, [or] eight, the elderly and the young were dying . . . The climate changed for people [*el-dinya*], the environment changed for them. The people began to die [*sarat etmut el-dinya*], and then there was overcrowding in the valley. UNRWA took us out, you see, and the day it took us out, we sat for, you can say three or four months in the Golan, everyone went wherever he wanted to. Later UNRWA informed us—we used to go and get relief, right?—they said those who want to get relief have to go to Khan Eshieh, this Khan Eshieh that is here [now], they said we want to take you to Khan Eshieh, you see? The people

[el-nas] left, they went to Khan Eshieh, yes by God. God have mercy on her soul, my mother, and my two sisters, they went to Khan Eshieh. And my father, God have mercy on his soul, he made us stay, we had cows, we remained with the cows in a village called Jaramaya.[5]

About a week later, I was in Khan Eshieh interviewing Abu Kamal, who as a child with his family had fled al-Wa'ra al-Sawda', Tiberias subdistrict, the site of yet another massacre (W. Khalidi 1992, 545–546). He made Khan Eshieh his home after his displacement for the second time, when Israel occupied the Golan in 1967. During our discussion of where the tents were initially set up for the refugees in the Golan after the expulsion from Palestine, Abu Kamal said: "[There were tents] in al-Jokhdar [village], what is it called, and in al-Korsi [village], and al-Jokhdar, and Wadi al-Raqqad, Wadi al-Raqqad, they lived, in a camp. Then a lot of people [el-nas] started dying. From the cold and the humiliation. The state gathered them and brought them here [to Khan Eshieh]. They took them in cars, and I don't know what, and brought them, and housed them in this area, on the A'waj River."[6] When I pressed him on why people died, he added: "In the Golan the people got sick from the cold, and the humiliation. And for your information, they lived in the camps, and the tents don't keep one warm during winter."[7]

About two weeks later, the most vivid memories of that first winter and the death of the world were related to me by Abu Subhi in yet another camp that has been his home since the 1967 Israeli invasion and occupation of the Golan. He related his memories to me, in the presence of other relatives in Qabr Essit Camp, when I asked about his multiple uprootings after 1948. Abu Fu'ad, a second-generation refugee and a relative of Abu Subhi whose family had left the Golan to Khan Eshieh shortly after the establishment of the camp in 1949 (UNRWA n/a-b), also related what he knew of the death of the world in Wadi al-Raqqad.

ABU SUBHI: Abu Fu'ad, the gathering, first of all, in 1948, [it was] in Kafr Alma [village], from Kafr Alma to al-Razanniyya [village], from al-Razanniyya to Wadi al-Samak, and then they took them out again from Wadi al-Samak to al-Razanniya, do you understand me? In, at the end of 1949, in 1950, they deported them all and put them in Khan Eshieh, they deported them three times.

[*Someone interjects to disagree about number of times, Abu Subhi, the only man present who lived through 1948 as a young adult, makes his point again.*]

ANAHEED: And where is Kafr Alma?

ABU FU'AD: . . . It is called Kafr al-Ma' [*sic*]. And it is located on—

ABU SUBHI: Wadi al-Raqqad.

ABU FU'AD: No, no, it overlooks Wadi al-Raqqad, they call it . . . what is the valley's original name according to the Hawranis? . . . [*Several interjections on the name, someone suggests al-T'in*] Wadi al-T'in, in Wadi al-T'in, the village—the valley is like this [*gestures with his hand*], the valley is like this [*gestures with his hand again*], and the village is here [*gestures to note that the village overlooks the valley*]. Where did they put us? They put us at the bottom of the valley. Most of the people died at the bottom of the valley. Of course there was no hygiene, or food.

[*Discussion continues among all present on names of villages and valleys in the Golan and how many times they were moved. I eventually ask about the nature of the diseases that plagued the refugees in the Golan.*]

ABU FU'AD: The disease was in the valley . . . during the winter and the summer, many people died in the valley. There was no hygiene, no soap, no food, even clothes, there was none. Meaning, most people were naked.

ABU SUBHI: By God, the lice ate people's hair, the lice, the lice. . . . When we first fled, in 1948, they put us in Wadi al-T'in, many people died. . . . From the severe weather and the dirt and cold and hunger, and dirt, and cold, do you understand me? And hunger, do you understand me? There were no health services at all, none at all. . . . Old and young [died], by God, yes. . . . This is in 1948. At the beginning of 1949, a [harsh] winter [came]—in this valley that I am telling you about, there was no water, no firewood. . . . There were no services at all, even [no] food and water too—you see? The people died [*el-dinya matat*]. . . . I swear to you, look, they couldn't keep up with burying the dead during the day, given how many people died.[8]

Whereas Abu Subhi referred to the death of the world during that first winter in the Golan, Abu Kamal spoke of people dying, and Umm 'Abdul 'Aziz used "world" and "people" interchangeably. Thus, while the expression "*el-dinya matat*" or "*matat el-dinya*" as used by all three can be translated as the "the people died," it is an expression that refers to the death of people inhabiting a community composing a lived world in its human relations manifestation. This common language is used to relate common memories of death in Wadi al-Raqqad that revolve around the fatal cold, hunger, and homelessness, the succumbing of the young and the old to death, and the daily funerals. There is also a common loss spoken through and beyond the guardians' memories. This is the loss of the death of the world itself in Wadi al-Raqqad and the continued loss expressed in these memories. This is therefore also the loss encapsulated in the guardians' continued "presence in an absence" (Butler 2003, 468). In other words, this is their presence despite and because of the absence created by the death of their communities in Palestine and these communities succumbing to that first winter in the valley.

Thus, the use of the same language, the circulation of common memories of death in Wadi al-Raqqad, and the sharing of a common loss together outline the symbolic contours of this particular community of guardians in the present. This community, as encountered through its common memories and loss, embodies one of the meanings of the Nakba today. This is the meaning to be found in the possibility that the guardians' memories of death in the valley are contours of a living community. Although marked and defined by the death, destruction, and uprooting of 1948, this community has also been constituted anew, for life and death, the past and the present, and even memories and histories, continue to coexist within it. Thus, this is one of the Nakba's meaning today, as embodied in the survivors' shared memories of catastrophes. It is a meaning which also moves beyond the Nakba's significations in the post-Oslo popular memory discourses.

Other meanings of the Nakba can be found in the content of the memories that circulate in these communities. All three memories of death in the valley have an actor, both visible and invisible, given that the actor's visibility is expressed only indirectly through the actor's power over the refugees during that cruel first winter in the Golan. This actor appears in these memories in order to express the helplessness in face of the unstoppable death that overtook the refugees in the valley. In Umm 'Abdul 'Aziz's memories, this actor is UNRWA, which "took them out" of the valley. In Abu Kamal's memories, this is the state, which "gathered" the refugees and took them to Khan Eshieh. For Abu Subhi, when I later probed him about this invisible actor, "it was the Red Cross that was responsible for us. . . . And after the Red Cross came UNRWA."[9]

Whether UNRWA, the state, or the Red Cross, the official body is described through passive language, in a literal rather than grammatical sense. This language speaks of the guardians' loss of control over their lives. Thus, the meaning of their memories, when read through the possibility of the guardians' communities as embodying the meaning of the Nakba, is of helplessness in the face of unrelenting death. This sentiment is evoked in all three memories through the refugees' surrendering their fate and agency over their lives to an external power. This power nevertheless failed the Palestinians in Wadi al-Raqqad, adding another catastrophic dimension to the fate of those whose lives, homes, families, communities, and worlds were brutally destroyed in 1948.

As the researcher who was listening, recording, and on many occasions also arguing with the guardians after sixty years, I did not always have the opportunity of encountering their Nakba memories' circulation within their communities. This possibility is even more remote today, given the passing of the generation of Palestine, the death and destruction of the war in Syria, and the extent of its resultant human, social, and communal devastation. Consequently, in what follows, I examine the guardians' memories of catastrophes thematically and analyze their content against the overarching context of their communities. The themes include the mythic and heroic, memories of survival and shaming, and ambivalent memories. These themes do not exhaust the guardians' memories. Rather, they provide a cross-section of the most frequently repeated themes conveyed to me when I asked members of the generation of Palestine to relate their memories of the Nakba. The Nakba in these memories can also be compared with the meanings of the Nakba that circulate in its Palestinian universe of discourse today.

MEMORIES OF CATASTROPHES

al-Hajar al-Aswad, April 25, 2008

Umm Hasan began her story with the fall of Haifa on the first of Rajab, the day when the father of her children, as she called him, was killed in Balad al-Shaykh. The attack on her village of 'Ayn Ghazal began on the first of Ramadan, two lunar months later, but it was on the eleventh day of the month of fasting that three warplanes began the aerial bombardment of 'Ayn Ghazal and its two neighbors, Jaba' and Ijzim, those three Mount Carmel villages that historians note withheld the onslaught until the middle of the summer. . . . On that day, Umm Hasan's house was hit, her head was struck by a stone from her destroyed house, and she couldn't remember whether she was conscious, but she recalled that two of her children were inside, buried underneath the rubble. . . . The story continued, and she began to talk about herself in the third person, about what others were doing while she lay unconscious.

They did eventually find her third child, a five-year-old son, on the fifth day of the search, when her aunt told her brother to lift the door of the destroyed house, where Uthman was, his back broken. . . . Umm Hasan paused, visibly moved to dry tears six decades after the death of her first-born son, whose name she no longer carries, but the tears did not flow. . . . She continued, and her storied memories overlapped and blurred with the storied memories that had been narrated to her and that had become a part of her own memories. . . . She moved back and forth between the times of Palestine, the Nakba, the early days of refuge in the east of Palestine and then Syria. . . . She was still arguing with the past, a past she had not forgiven after all these years, despite the passage of time. . . . And she narrated to all present as though they too are a part of this past. . . . As though I knew the persons involved in the quarrel that happened between this and that family or that bridge in Haifa from where she had collected firewood on the day they brought King Faysal to town. . . .[10]

I wonder about her fate now, and the fate of her family, whether she lived to see al-Hajar al-Aswad transformed into a battleground, and the killing, death, destruction, and uprooting that enveloped the Golani people of al-Hajar, to displace them yet again.

MYTHIC MEMORIES

Every member of the generation of Palestine had his or her own storied memories of death, destruction, and expulsion. Some survived massacres, lost children, husbands, brothers, sisters, and other family members. Others, especially those from the tribes of the Galilee, saw their communities burned to the ground. Some men I interviewed had been shot and injured; others narrated memories of gruesome massacres and indiscriminate murder during the occupation of their villages and towns. Others were stripped of all their belongings and plundered by the invading Zionist militia in the process of being rounded up for expulsion. There were those who survived aerial bombardments of their villages or witnessed the aerial bombardment of other villages. Many endured separation from their families; some were reunited, others were not.

One memory of death, destruction, and expulsion that I encountered repeatedly was that of a woman who left behind her child as a result of the catastrophic events that unfolded during the Nakba. Other researchers have also encountered this memory. Indeed, the story of the child left behind is also inspiration for an important short story, "Returning to Haifa" ([1969] 2000), written in the wake of the June War by the late writer and Popular Front for the Liberation of Palestine activist Ghassan Kanafani. I encountered this memory mostly through its gender-defined woman narrator and woman protagonist. Sometimes, the protagonist was indefinite, a woman who can be interpreted as any woman. This indefinite woman's story was related by the guardians as well as the post-Palestine generations. In other instances, this figure was definite, a specific person, remembered concretely and referentially by women guardians. This women in her definite guise also appeared in the post-Palestine generations' narratives on Nakba memory as they recounted the guardians' memories.

This particular storied memory of death, destruction, and expulsion has therefore taken on mythic qualities. This is not to imply that this storied memory, especially when recounted in definite mode, is not of a real woman who was seen or recalled as having left her child. Neither is it to imply that it may not have been narrated by the woman who herself left her child behind in the midst of the overwhelming horrors of the Zionist onslaught. Rather, its mythic qualities result from this memory's circulation in both modes: definite in being real memories of real women, and indefinite in reflecting a female figure that is also part of popular memory discourses and even modern literature on the Nakba.

I first encountered this mythic memory in the definite form that makes it more than mere myth during my interview with Umm Hasan. Twenty-five at the time of the Nakba, Umm Hasan came from the peasant farming community of 'Ayn Ghazal in the Haifa subdistrict and had no formal education. As she narrated her storied memories of the series of catastrophes visited upon her, which for her began with the death of her husband in 1948, she said:

> One woman came [to 'Ayn Ghazal], my mother's relative, her son had gone to Haifa and he had fallen on his hand, he had cut his hand. The wretched woman didn't bring him with her, he was her only son, this wretched woman didn't bring him with her, she left him there. "Why didn't you bring him with you?" [we asked.] She began to weep and wail, to weep and wail, and she lost her mind over her son. She died underneath the rubble, on the day in which I was hit, the day I was hit she was also hit. Her son started going from one village to another spending his days [in] one [village] after the other, until after some fifteen years, yes, perhaps some fifteen years, no, not fifteen years, perhaps it was, let us say seven or eight years. Yes, they said that there is a boy who they want to

bring to his family—the Red Cross—to his maternal aunts, his maternal aunt had asked for him and they came and handed him over. The boy was his mother's only child, and then, there, he sat and ate well, and you know, they had left [Palestine] and there was no work or anything, so this boy didn't like the food at his aunt's house. So then his aunt died, his aunt died, and who took the boy? He was taken by his relatives, the husband of his aunt or the relatives of his father. They took him and the child grew up a little bit and they sent for his family in Iraq, and they took him to Iraq, yes, his father, his father was in Iraq. His father was my mother's maternal cousin. They called his family and told him that his father was alive and so they took him.[11]

The woman in Umm Hasan's storied memory is the wife of her mother's maternal cousin; she is, therefore, or was until her death during the Zionist bombardment of 'Ayn Ghazal, real. The memory does not end with the child being left behind; the woman's realization that she had left her son in Haifa amid the panic of her flight and horror of the bombardment leads her to lose her mind. Umm Hasan offers no explanation to her relative leaving her son behind, only the weeping and wailing. Perhaps the woman's loss of her mind, her weeping and wailing, and her death underneath the rubble of her home during the bombardment of 'Ayn Ghazal are what make explainable that which cannot otherwise be explained. This is a mother leaving behind her child in the midst of the horror of the full-scale military onslaught that Haifa witnessed from the Zionist quarters that overlooked the town. This onslaught against one of the biggest towns of historic Palestine saw the indiscriminate bombardment of the elderly, men, women, and children and corpses piling on the streets as mass panic gripped the townspeople. They were collectively pushed into the harbor by the indiscriminate bullets and shelling of total war, their only escape the boats that were barely able to carry them (W. Khalidi 2008).

This definite storied memory of death, destruction, and expulsion continues, however, after the mother dies beneath the rubble. Umm Hasan relates the son's wanderings, looking for his family, which was not only uprooted but also scattered and torn. When he did eventually find those who survived the bombardment of 'Ayn Ghazal, Umm Hasan notes, and despite eating well— well, at least, according to their changed circumstances—the son disliked the food. This implicit reference to their changed standards of living, to the poverty they had to endure after the loss of everything, was echoed throughout Umm Hasan's memories. She often described the catastrophes visited upon her life through food associations. Such associations included hunger, loss of appetite, being given food, begging for food, trying to feed her children and the seventy-year-old man she had been married off to before her family went to Iraq, and working on a farm in exchange for fruit and vegetables.

The catastrophes in the definite storied memory of Umm Hasan's relative revolve around the destruction of one of the most important and basic bonds in a family, that between mother and child. Umm Hasan's memories of this woman also recollected death itself as having entered people's lives and their homes as having been turned into graves. The subsequent tearing apart and scattering of families, and the poverty are also remembered as no less catastrophic. In short, Umm Hasan's memories revolve around a series of catastrophes that resulted from the Nakba. There is clearly nothing mythic about the woman or the catastrophes figured in Umm Hasan's memories. In view of this, what could the transformation of these definite memories into an indefinite and thus mythical "memory" of a woman leaving behind her child tell us about memories of the Nakba today?

To begin with, the memories that circulate within the guardians' communities defy the patriotic tropes associated with them in pervasive memory discourses on 1948. In these discourses, the dominant significations of 1948 trump the woman-child core of the "memory." That "memory" is in quotes is because in its indefinite form, it is far removed from Umm Hasan's maternal cousin's wife and perhaps memories of other women like her. In the process of becoming part of popular memory discourses on the Nakba, it also no longer becomes a memory in a referential sense. Rather, the indefinite woman becomes a mere signifier of the Nakba-as-death, the Nakba-as-destruction, and the Nakba-as-expulsion of the people.

The memories of the guardians' communities therefore signify these essentially hypersignified "memories," or supposed memories, that circulate in memory discourses on the Nakba. They are hypersignified because the woman who leaves her child behind comes to stand for 1948 as the singular catastrophic event of the Nakba. Hence, this woman can be any woman, not just the definite woman of Umm Hasan's or other guardian's memories. At the same time, the "memories" about a woman who leaves her child behind circulate under the guise of being referential memories, and herein lies their "mythic" facet. There is therefore a relationship between the guardians' memories that circulate in their communities and the patriotic signifiers found in popular memory discourses based on the content of their memories. However, this relationship is not a direct correlation; rather, the memories that do circulate are transformed by becoming common tropes or indefinite "memories."

Some memories can be categorized under the broad label "heroic memories." One particular storied memory, that of the men of the village who buy rifles to defend themselves against all odds, was a heroic memory of the Nakba that was repeated by various male interviewees. As I probed Abu Samih about what he had seen during the Nakba in and around Lubya, he told me:

> What I saw with my own eyes is that the people frantically ran looking for weapons . . . and the people of my village, meaning, perhaps some three thousand or thirty-five hundred, something like that, the people of the village managed to buy from outside of Palestine, from Jordan and Syria and Lebanon, perhaps some one thousand rifles. . . . The people of my village, [they did so] with their private monies. One would sell his cows and sheep and so forth and buy, so we began to resist the Jews, we began to, meaning, to prepare for defense. Because the Jews, we know that they wouldn't have accepted partition, we had a conviction that they were greedy.[12]

Like Abu Samih, the late Abu Khalil also repeated the story of buying rifles when I asked him to recount what he remembers of the Nakba.

> The English, their mandate finished. They were supposed to leave on this [set] day and in this [set] hour. They handed over to the Jews the[ir] tanks and the artillery and the airplanes and everything. We the Arabs in Palestine, we didn't have anything at all. . . . The English when they would find a rifle with someone, they would execute him—execution—they would hang him from the noose. We couldn't buy rifles. . . . When the English left, though, we then began to buy from traders, from the black market; they would come, for example, from Syria and bring us ten rifles, from Lebanon, from Egypt. From, traders, meaning traders. I am telling you there was a man who said, "Take my two [unclear] for a rifle." I swear to you there was one man who sold, he had, work, work, he didn't have [work], but that one, he sold it for ninety Palestinians liras, ninety, and he bought a rifle for one hundred ten."[13]

The late Abu Hind was fifteen at the time of the Nakba and from Mi'ilya, a village that was not destroyed, though some of its people were rounded up and expelled. This was a policy adopted by the new Israeli state to decrease the number of Palestinian under its jurisdiction as it began to register them during its first census (S. Robinson 2013, 68–112). When narrating his memory, he said:

> There were several Jewish settlements around us, so we were guarding our village from them, lest they come and carry out attacks at night, because we had information that they were attacking some of the villages, like in Sa'sa', Fassuta, al-Bassa and al-Mazra'a, so for this reason there [we] were on guard [duty]. But insofar as the weapon [issue] was concerned, it was a hidden weapon, because it was still, the mandate was there, and those who were caught with a rifle, meaning, they wouldn't be able to leave jail, if not executed that is. So the rifles, the several rifles, they were hidden, and at night, in the darkness, they would go out and they would lean against [inaudible]. The rifles were bought from Syria. They were poor people who sold their marriage gold and bought rifles, and then the rifles increased [in numbers].[14]

Although all three interviewees were young men during 1948, and all related the same memories around buying rifles in 1948 for self-defense, they were nevertheless also three men with very different life experiences and different origins as well. The late Abu Khalil had no formal education and came from a settled Bedouin community in Yaquq. Abu Samih had formal education at the primary level, had taken up arms with local volunteers in 1948, and came from the peasant farming community of Lubya. The late Abu Hind, though also from the peasant farming community of Mi'ilya, had formal and higher education and would come to Syria via the Palestinian liberation movement, of which he was one of its prominent intellectual figures.

Despite these differences in origins, life experiences, and education, all three interviewees related common storied memories by and about men, the heroic memories of the locals buying rifles despite all odds. The risks the villagers and settled Bedouin communities of the Galilee faced are commonly foregrounded through "official" historical actors and terms. These include the "English", the (British) "Mandate," and the "partition," the latter in reference to UN Partition Resolution 181 of 1947. All three men invoked the English and their role in disarming the Palestinians. This was at least a decade-old policy that followed the defeat of the Palestinian uprising of 1936–1939 and played a critical role in the total defeat of the Palestinians during the Nakba (R. Khalidi 2007). Thus, all three memories are also in dialogue with historical accounts of these events, or the Nakba's Arab universe of discourse, the place from which the heroism in these accounts, the "despite all odds," is iterated.

For example, only after I repeatedly asked Abu Samih to recollect what he personally saw and remembered did he finally note how the people frantically ran to buy weapons. The adjective he used implies that he had seen and therefore remembers the people buying weapons, while his overall mode of recollection nevertheless lapsed into repeating patriotic tropes. This was a typical response to the Zionist-supporting Western audiences that I was seen to encapsulate (Al-Hardan 2014). This is not to imply that Abu Samih's memories are any less truthful or worthy. Rather, the main point is that the symbolic forms that circulate in the guardians' communities consist of common memories and also engage historical accounts of the Nakba as examined through its Arab and Palestinian universes of discourse. In other words, Abu Samih's memories of the people of Lubya buying rifles coexist with, and in many ways cannot be prized apart from, the now seventy-year retrospective need to remember the people of Lubya as having bought rifles.

As noted in the introduction, the historian Patrick Hutton (1993) has argued that history is in fact an "art of memory" precisely because it provides an opening between two moments of memory that makes historical thinking possible. This is recollection, or active memory-making, and repetition, the bringing forward of images of the past in present. Hutton's thesis complicates the simplistic reproduction of arguments on orality (memory) and literacy (history) in accounts of "Palestinian memory," as does the fact of the coexistence of memories and histories in the guardians' memory-making. Having seen the people of Lubya buying rifles, the "we did our best against all odds" of Abu Samih implicitly absolves his generation of responsibility for the final defeat and departure. He even retrospectively affirms the past in the present when he says that despite their acts of heroism, despite selling their cows for rifles, the men of Lubya ultimately knew that the Zionist leadership would not accept partition. This is a retrospective judgment possible only in the present. Thus, this coexistence of memory and history, especially when narrating memories that are in part informed by different discourses on the Nakba, should put the idea of "pure" memories of 1948 to rest.

This coexistence also demonstrates the ways in which the guardians, even when affirming pervasive discourses on 1948, are aware of these discourses and seek to carve a space for their roles within them. The late Abu Khalil's memories, like those of Abu Samih, also centered on the heroic, of men having tried to defend themselves at all costs and against all odds. He also narrated how the people of Yaquq tried to buy rifles despite the British. The same could be said of the late Abu Hind's memories of the preparation for the Zionist attack against Mi'ilya. The heroism in these memories makes itself present when understood within the context of the Nakba's Palestinian universe of discourse, or 1948 invoked to commemorate, remember, and return. Against this universe of discourse, the guardians' actions in 1948 could easily (and are easily, as evident in the next chapter) be interpreted as treachery, ignorance, or cowardice for having fled. Thus, these memories circulating within the guardians' communities do so in dialogue with these different Nakba significations and carve a heroic space in which the past can be absolved in the present. This is the clearest example of Hutton's memory in dialogue with history. It is also a clear example of the ways in which the guardians' memories of 1948 do not simply affirm the Nakba's different pervasive meanings.

MEMORIES OF SURVIVAL, SURVIVAL MEMORIES

All the guardians had to rebuild their lives, and the overwhelming majority had to do so from nothing. Even those who were relatively well off in Palestine had to start from scratch. While the latter may not have faced the same hardships as those who were in the camps during that first freezing winter, they nevertheless had to face a new life as refugees who had lost everything in Palestine. Some guardians had to rebuild their lives more than once, given the multiple expulsions. Women had a central role, since they had to work in and outside the home, rebuild their own and their families' lives, and in the process constitute their decimated communities anew. The guardians' survival of the series of catastrophes visited upon their communities in 1948 is therefore not merely a question of their surviving the Zionist military onslaught. It is also survival in the aftermath of an all-encompassing catastrophe that destroyed and uprooted communities, the death of their world as it was known and inhabited in Palestine.

Survival in these different guises is a central theme of the memories commonly shared in the guardians' communities when discussing the 1948 and later catastrophes. While recalling the fate of Tantura's prisoners of war who survived the massacre and were held captives by Israel, Umm 'Izz al-Din, had this to say about the early days in al-Mu'alaq mosque in Damascus:

[They came] after a year. After a year where were they to go? There was no money or work. The young man would go and clean carpets in Suq al-Hariqa, and in 'Ayn Karsh, he had [*unclear*] all day. Those who would bring a paper from the landowner and work in the company, they'd give them one and half lira per day, he would be considered well off, every Thursday he would get nine liras. We, my daughter, we lived through bitter times, by God, we lived through bitter times, it was only when the children were older that we [unclear], and the people, what else could they do, other than this, there was nothing else. . . . We got milk and wheat and rice and sugar [from the Red Cross] . . . and then UNRWA took over. They formalized it, they gave us booklets, and they began to give every single person ten kilograms of wheat, sugar, soap, and oil or animal fat, the people began to take relief, one family would take some one hundred kilograms of wheat. We used to get, my children and I, some fifty kilograms of wheat. People began to make dough and bake it in the bakeries, and the people worked. We worked in the chickpeas [trade]. I was pregnant with a child. . . . I worked, I sorted chickpeas for a trader. For one lira all day. . . . I would sort the chickpeas, from the dirt and its straw, and pick the red pea.[15]

Umm 'Izz al-Din's memories tell of the hardship of survival in the face of the loss of everything. Her continuous invocation of having lived through hard and bitter times reflects the hardship of becoming a refugee, of starting over and resorting to any kind of work in order to survive, given that the relief they received was insufficient for their most basic physical needs. Someone able to work all day would be considered well off or, to use Umm 'Izz al-Din's expression, a "Sultan of his time." Those lucky enough to find menial jobs would be paid a pittance, for example, to clean carpets all day in Suq al-Hariqa in Damascus or, as in the case of Umm 'Izz al-Din, to sort chickpeas. That she would do such work even though she was pregnant stands in stark contrast to her former life. This is because she came from a well-off family in Tantura, was the daughter of one of the village's former heads, and was married to a man who had worked in the British Palestine police force. Her labor also needs to be understood in terms of the double burden shouldered by women in light of 1948, of working outside as well as inside the home. Umm 'Izz al-Din temporalizes these bitter times with child rearing. It was only when the children grew older, relieving their families from the burdens of providing, or perhaps working and providing as well, were families' lives finally slightly improved, a whole generation later.

Like Umm 'Izz al-Din's, Abu Samih's memories also center on survival. When I asked him about his late wife and whether she would narrate memories of the Nakba during the early years, he said:

I no longer remember, because we remained, my daughter, from 1948 and until the sixties, we were in a miserable state. We remained for twenty years, nearly, in Syria, in a state of misery . . . [where] by God, [we] worked as laborers, worked in whatever, and I did, meaning, we didn't eat from a spoon of gold. By God, I left Palestine, by God, I was wounded and in my pocket I had two Palestinian piasters, only. By God, I reached the Syrian border [where] I bought a newspaper with them. . . . The Nakba wasn't simple, it was a disaster. . . . Some of us lived in tents, we, the people of Damascus, they put us in mosques. There was a big mosque, and they separated us with blankets and sheets, and we sat . . . here in Damascus, in al-'Amara quarter [in the Old City].[16]

As with Umm 'Izz al-Din, the catastrophes visited upon Abu Samih did not end on his reaching the border; in fact, there they took on a whole different dimension. Like Umm 'Izz al-Din, he also temporalizes his experiences as total misery and poverty that lasted twenty years, or a generation. He uses the expression "we didn't eat from a spoon of gold" to describe the memories of those who lost everything—family, relatives, communities, homes, entire worlds—and had to start from scratch. In fact, the generation of Palestine often used this expression to describe the differences between their lives and the lives of their grandchildren's generation. They emphasized the extent to which their own generation had to build lives, homes, and communities anew whereas the new generations, at least prior to the war in Syria, simply benefited from their families' hard work. These memories of survival underscore the ways in which the guardians would come to build and constitute their communities anew—constitute, rather than reconstitute, since the world as lived in Palestine was irrevocably destroyed and lost.

Thus, these memories also point to these new communities through their common experiences grounded in uprooted and fractured temporalities and spatialities in both Palestine and Syria. In view of this, they are memories of survival as well as survival memories. They tell of the survival of the guardians and of their post-1948 communities and the nature of this survival in communities built anew. In these communities, life and death coexist and times and spaces in the Palestine of the past and the Syria of the present are nonlinear, uprooted, and fractured.

Like both Umm 'Izz al-Din and Abu Subhi, Umm Ya'rub hails from a peasant farming community in the Galilee, one, however, that was not destroyed. She differs from her generational peers in having a formal education and work experience as a teacher in Safad and later Syria, where she also became a writer and a public figure. Despite these differences, she too narrated memories of survival that are also survival memories. When narrating how she left Palestine and then stayed in her mother's village of origin in Syria, Umm Ya'rub said that she went

> from the south of Lebanon to Damascus and from Damascus, [where] I sat . . . for four days in a hotel, and then I went to Hina. In Hina, I got news that my father had arrived, because I had informed those around me [that I was there] and the children of my brother had followed me. . . . Then I left to Damascus and took them with me, and we stayed there for the whole summer, there, in my mother's house. My mother wasn't there, but her brother was there. We stayed there for a while, for the rest of the summer. And I immediately was thinking about where I could work, how we were going to live. So they said that the nearest place for you is Qatana. So I went to Qatana and I asked about their schools. There was a school there for the Greek Orthodox, it was a boys' school. . . . I went there and the head teacher told me to come in and I told him I want to teach and he said you are welcome here. I told him that I am Palestinian and I come from Palestine. At that time, my father was in Hina and he came, he knew that I was in Qatana and he came to Qatana and also taught in the same school, he and I.[17]

Despite the educational and economic class differences between the three interviewees, their storied memories of survival share a striking commonality of theme. Whether sorting chickpeas, working as a laborer, or working as a teacher, all three interviewees had to work to provide for their families. Although living with relatives cannot compare with living in a mosque where hanging sheets separated different families, their memories all speak to their uprooting and the ways in which they rebuilt their lives. Further, despite the uprooted and fractured times and spaces of their lives, their memories circulate within and encapsulate the possibility of communities that embody one meaning of the Nakba and the guardians' ongoing survival.

SHAMING MEMORIES

Whether as states or peoples, Arabs formed an important part of the guardians' memories. The guardians were unequivocal about whom to blame for the loss of Palestine, for their memories repeatedly pointed to Arab states' treacheries and collusions with the Zionists. More concretely, several common storied memories make this accusation. The ones I examine in this section relate to the reception of the guardians and their communities and to the stigmatization of the guardians' newfound refugee status and homelessness. When I asked Abu Hind about the early years, he related the following about his brief time in Beirut in the wake of 1948:

I was on a train, every day I would get a few piasters to spend, so I would spend a frank, and I would take the train, the tram, from the door of the American University of Beirut, and I would remain on the train until the [unclear], the tram would turn around and go back, and I would go back to al-Zaytuna. In al-Zaytuna I would go down and walk on the seaside promenade; there was no seaside promenade, it was rocks and so forth, and I would return home, in Ras Beirut, in the Jeanne d'Arc Street, the neighborhood. . . . So one day on the tram someone told me, "Your face is like the face of a refugee." I was either going to hit him or—and I was someone who was [unclear] and I was still strong, not like today. So, I left. Now the Lebanese, there were dirty attitudes, if you want the truth.[18]

Umm 'Izz al-Din also narrated a similar memory of the stigmatization associated with being a refugee when she said:

They used to call us refugees, those Hawranis, they used to tell the donkey . . . they would tell him: "Hey, you! You have a face like a face of a refugee." Unity happened between Egypt and Syria, Nasser came here and said those Palestinians, no one go near them, and anyone that calls them a refugee [unclear]. Then we gained value. And they began to employ them.[19]

Abu Hind's and Umm 'Izz al-Din's memories of the petty prejudice they encountered, despite the differences in the location and nature of their refugee lives, show the ways in which the figure of the Palestinian refugee had become common as early as 1949. That the expression "You have a face like a face of a refugee " was used as an insult meant that the Palestinians' destitution as refugees must have become well known. In addition, for that destitution to become an insult and even a source of shaming means that petty prejudice against the Palestinians was, in the best-case scenario, spread and, in the worst-case scenario, widespread. Being called a refugee was also clearly ascriptive—as Umm 'Izz al-Din put it, "They used to call us refugees"—and also highly stigmatizing and shameful. Abu 'Imad, who as a young adolescent had survived the

Tantura village massacre, explained what being called a refugee meant to him: "[It was] the worst feeling. . . . Just like that, from this label, 'refugee,' 'refugees.' 'Refugees,' [meaning] beggars, Gypsies, meaning. . . . Is their anything worse than this word?"[20]

The insults and prejudice described by the guardians made it shameful to be a refugee. This shame derived from the realities of what it meant to be a refugee—a beggar—and as told by many guardians, including Abu 'Imad, many refugees were indeed forced to beg for survival. The shaming lay precisely in the conditions that made the guardians' survival possible in those early years, especially begging. Abu 'Imad also refers to the shaming of their homelessness by being equated with Gypsies (invoked through the derogatory Arabic *nawar* rather than *ghajar*). The label refugees in those early years was therefore a shaming as well as a shameful ascriptive label.

Other guardians more directly associated the stigma of being a refugee with what they noted was the commonly held Arab perception that the Palestinians really did sell their lands to the Zionist movement. When I asked Umm Ahmad, at the time of the Nakba a newly wed eighteen-year-old from a well-off Safadi family, about her memories of the early years and whether she had encountered prejudices, she said:

> The Syrians would say you sold your homeland and left. . . . Yes, when we first came, they would say you sold your homeland and came. . . . And when 1967 happened, I told them one word in the school [where she worked], to the Syrian teachers, I told them, now your turn has come and much worse than ours. [A teacher asked,] "Are you being spiteful?" I said to her, "We didn't leave out of our own will, but you, the army . . . came to the school and you fled and left one hundred girls in al-Baq'a alone." They left one hundred girls in al-Baq'a alone, I was the one who took them down to Jisr al-Abyad, put them on buses and sent them to their homes. They all ran away and went to their homes, the teachers. . . . Here, in Damascus, in Jisr al-Abyad. . . . They would blame us and say you sold your countries. . . . I would say it's you who sold us, not us. . . . Because it was Syrians' land that was sold to the Jews in Palestine, not ours.[21]

The idea that Palestinians sold their lands and left in order to leech off other Arab countries is a prejudice that continues to be held by Arabs of different nationalities. As examined through Muhammad Amin al-Husayni's attempts to refute these assumptions in his book, it is also a notion that was in circulation as early as 1954. That the Zionist movement bought land, especially from Beirut- and Damascus-based large-scale landowners, and proceeded to dispossess the tenant peasant farmers and communities living on that land is not a historically contentious claim. The sale of Palestinian land, however, whether through large- or small-scale landowners, is a much more divisive issue among Palestinians. To put this into perspective, however, it is worth noting that even though the large-scale landowners sold the overwhelming majority of the land, on the eve of the Nakba the Zionist movement had nevertheless managed to buy only less than a tenth of the land of historic Palestine, regardless of the selling party (Wolfe 2012).

The memories of how the guardians were shamed and stigmatized are therefore also contentious. They are memories that contest the role of the Arab states in 1948, and they also contest the Arabs' allegedly "brotherly" reception of the refugees. Shaming the Palestinian refugees for what they had become and blaming them for allegedly selling their lands has been much easier than reckoning with the past and present role of Arab states in relation to Palestine. Thus, shaming memories that circulate in the guardians' communities contest and destabilize Arab popular perceptions by underscoring the Arab states' failures in relation to Palestine and its loss. They also highlight the prejudices held against Palestinian refugees to this day.

AMBIVALENT MEMORIES

The guardians related the series of catastrophes visited upon individuals, families, and whole communities in Palestine through both what was done to them, in memories that relate passivity, and what they did, in memories that relate agency. In Umm 'Izz al-Din's interview, and her memories of Tantura's prisoners of war, she said:

Yes, they took them [the prisoners of war] and locked them up in, what is it called, in Umm Khalid, in Khdira, Khdira is close to Tulkarm. They took them and locked them up and they remained in prison for about a year. We were taken out by King Abdullah through an exchange. They had Jewesses who had fought, they put them in the castle and they brought them everything; we, on the other hand, we tasted bitter times. They took us to Tulkarm, and they didn't feed us. So we began to beg for bread from the bakeries. They'd give one or two pieces of bread that were this big [gestures], like this, and one would eat them plain, so the people began to beg. By God, the people began to beg. And then they took us to Hebron, we stayed in Hebron for six months. . . . In Hebron, there was a monastery there, that the Russians had built, we used to call it al-Muskubiyya, and it had a cleric and a housekeeper who worked for the cleric, his name was Ya'qub. They took us to the monastery, it was far.[22]

The passivity in Umm 'Izz al-Din's memories is also the mode through which she relates her early days in the east of Palestine: they took the men and locked them up; they were taken out by King Abdullah; they were taken to Tulkarm; they were not fed. These storied memories of the early years are therefore memories of powerlessness and helplessness. Umm 'Izz al-Din nevertheless figures memories of survival that occasionally puncture the passivity related through her memories. In addition to telling of the survival of the Zionist occupation of Tantura, the gruesome massacre, and the killing of members of her immediate family, she also narrates memories of surviving the deportation to the east and of begging for survival. Indeed, begging, as one of the conditions that ensures survival, punctuates Umm 'Izz al-Din's memories of powerlessness, even if only for fleeting moments. In the quoted interview segment, begging is immediately followed by how the refugees were given bread that they would nevertheless eat in order to survive.

In a similar way, Abu 'Imad also conjured up the past through memories that relate passivity and agency:

We left in May, we remained in Hebron until November. At the end of November, we were in Hebron. On the first of January [1949], we moved from Hebron to Syria. On the first of January we entered Syria. The first of January 1949 . . . we entered Syria, where did they put us? In Busra al-Sham, in the citadel. We remained in the citadel for five or six months, for seven months. Summer came, we couldn't bear life, poverty, and no work, and nothing, a miserable state. We moved— "Move us to Damascus," they wouldn't take us to Damascus, they took us to Suwayda, to the Druze. . . . In Busra, we would beg, we would walk barefoot on the snow and beg, from the houses, [they'd] feed us. Meaning, [it was like] a dead person who carried a dead person. They [Hawranis] are a people who had five or six or seven years of drought, they are poor, and we came, meaning, poverty on top of poverty, meaning. . . . From Suwayda, we moved to Damascus at our own expense, we didn't [remain until] the state moved us, I mean. We came and we rented and lived in Jubar. We lived in Jubar for fifteen or sixteen years, and then we came to the camp.[23]

Like Umm 'Izz al-Din's, Abu 'Imad's memories of powerlessness are punctured by memories of survival. This mode of recollecting the Nakba and its consequences, through passivity and active agency, points to what are ultimately ambivalent memories that circulate in the guardians' communities. In this instance, it is the ambivalence of being shamed, yet having to survive; of being one dead person atop another, yet having no choice but to beg Hawranis for their meager scraps.

In other instances, memories that relate both passivity and agency were recalled to describe one particularly important subject of the guardians' ambivalent memories. This is the thorny question of the guardians' departure in 1948 and the choices they were compelled to make. For example, many interviewees invoked the omnipresent and omnipotent phrase "Leave and you will return" while relating their memories of their departure from Palestine. When I spoke to the late Umm Rim about her feelings in the wake of 1948, she said, "During that time we were very shocked, very shocked about what happened in Palestine, and then shocked by the Arabs . . . because they are the ones who even encouraged, also, that 'leave and we [will sort things] and after two weeks [you'll return].'"[24]

The phrase "Leave and you will return" in its different guises and its attribution to some omnipresent and omnipotent force, in this case the Arabs, made its similar sudden appearance in interviews with other members of the generation of Palestine. For example, when I asked Umm 'Izz al-Din whether she knew she would not be going back to Tantura, she said: "No, seven days and we are returning. . . . We thought they will return us. . . . Yes, [even] after they slaughtered the people of Tantura, because we were supposed to go back within the next seven days. One Jew told a woman—she [the woman] said to him: 'Oh foreigner, when are we going back?' He told her: 'When you see your own ear.' He was a Jew. He told her, 'When you see your ear.' It was supposed to be seven days."[25]

Later, when I pressed her on whom she was invoking—in the passive "We thought they will return us"—she said, "The states." Clearly, Umm 'Izz al-Din is alluding to the idea that the generation of Palestine were instructed to leave and were promised an eventual return once the fighting is over. The significance of the continued circulation of these memories in the guardians' communities underscores ambivalent memories regarding the generation of Palestine's departure in 1948. The onslaught they were subjected to notwithstanding, "Leave and you will return" ultimately absolves the generation of Palestine from their collective and final departure.

Thus, the ambivalence around the 1948 departure speaks to a charged topic. At times, the guardians proudly shared memories of having put up a fight—hence the expulsion. This also suggested that those who did not fight were able to remain in Palestine, implying a certain treachery. At other times, however, as the guardians recounted their memories, they related their regret for not having surrendered and not having remained. These contradictions exemplify the ambivalence relating to the most difficult decision confronting Palestinian communities in 1948. In addition, these ambivalent memories circulate in a present in which these decisions, as evident in the following chapter, have been deemed incomprehensible by the post-Palestine generations. It is now a tragic historical irony that the same post-Palestine generations who made an overwhelmingly harsh judgment regarding the guardians' decision to leave in 1948 are making the same choices that their parents and grandparents were compelled to make in 1948.

While describing the journey from the river near al-Lajjun across to the east of Palestine, Umm Hasan recalled the Zionists expelling them: "So what did they tell us, they said, 'Go on, move it, go to King Abdullah, to King Abdullah, run to King Abdullah,' I swear this is what he told us. 'Go on, move it, to King Abdullah, to King Abdullah.' My mother then said, 'No we are—long live Sharon!'[26] I don't know what, this was my mother. And my maternal aunt told her—['What are you saying']. And she [my mother] said, 'What do you think, we want to live here? Abdullah is the biggest bastard.'"[27]

Similarly, Umm 'Izz al-Din said: "Yes, I wish we had remained, those who surrendered remained. Now Nazareth is full, its people are in it. Fureidis, its people are in it. They are harvesting and sowing and doing—but they have no say, all of them work as servants for the Jews."[28]

The ambivalence in Umm Hasan's and Umm 'Izz al-Din's memories is striking. Umm Hasan's memories reveal her mother's willingness to live in the Zionist state rather than go to Transjordan, even her willingness to sing the praises of Zionist leaders, against the reluctance and dismay of her aunt. Umm 'Izz al-Din wishes that the people of Tantura had remained, like the people of Nazareth and Fureidis, Haifa subdistrict, the latter who nevertheless ended up working as servants for the nearby Jewish colony. Thus, it is through this ambivalence around leaving or remaining, revealed in the guardians' memories that circulate in their communities, that one meaning of the catastrophes that befell these communities is figured. This is the catastrophe of the impossible decisions that members of the generation of Palestine were compelled to make in 1948. It is also the price they continue to pay as stateless refugees now seven decades later.

CONCLUSION

The guardians' memories of catastrophes' shared yet uprooted and fractured temporal and spatial referents, in both the lost Palestine of the past and the present in Syria, are symbolic cultural forms. These forms point to the possibility of the symbolic contours of the guardians as constituting communities. As argued, these guardians' communities embody a meaning of the Nakba today. This meaning is found in the very nature of these communities, both as marked by the destruction of 1948 and as constituted anew as a result. The Nakba is therefore a catastrophe that marks them as communities.

The memories that circulate in these communities can be read in relation to multiple references. They at times affirm the meanings of the 1948 Nakba as the one catastrophe meant to commemorate, mobilize, and ensure the return. At other times, they contest the singularity ascribed to 1948 Nakba in popular memory discourses through its pluralization and through extending its temporal framework. They also signify memories of 1948 that have otherwise gained mythic qualities as they have turned into patriotic tropes in post-Oslo imaginings and mobilization of memories for the return. Finally, these memories also carve acceptable spaces for the guardians in these popular imagining of memory by deeming their actions in 1948 as heroic or indeed comprehensible.

The various memories that circulate in these communities are therefore ultimately in dialogue with different significations and understandings of the Nakba examined in this book. These include the Nakba's Arab and Palestinian universes of discourse, the Nakba in post-Oslo activists' memory discourses and mobilization practices, and Palestinian refugee family members' own understanding, negotiation, and interpretation of the guardians' memories. I now turn to one final way in which the meanings of the Nakba can be understood today. This is the meaning of 1948 as negotiated and interpreted by the post-Palestine generation of refugees.

CHAPTER 6

SECOND- AND THIRD-GENERATION POSTMEMORIES OF PALESTINE AND NARRATIVES ON NAKBA MEMORY

The sources [of memory] that formed the complete picture, the most important sources were the stories that I heard inside the house. But coming of age is what clarified the meaning of the picture. You have this frame which was imparted to you from the family, but there is still—to simplify the metaphor—something foggy about it. [The clarification took place] from the outside, from the surrounding [environment], from school, from the relationships that I had in terms of my own experiences, or [through the relationships I] was compelled to form. . . . In this way the picture was further clarified, but the picture was already there in the first place, do you get the idea?

MUHAMMAD-KHAYR, THIRD-GENERATION PALESTINIAN REFUGEE FATHER
FROM TANTURA, HAIFA

If I take a paper and a pen, and I start drawing, I will draw actual parts of Safad. I might draw the bakery of the town, the shops, the lands, the lands of Safad, the deserted lot they talk about where children used to play, the citadel where the children used to play . . . because of the extent to which I've heard about them. And then also, she [grandmother] used to say "to the north of the citadel," "to the west of the citadel," "facing the citadel," you see. So our house was like—she'd give clear landmarks, she used to say if you go there, there is so-and-so's shop, and this and that lane, in the back of this and that, there you'll find our house.

MANAL, THIRD-GENERATION PALESTINIAN REFUGEE MOTHER FROM SAFAD

The memories of catastrophes that circulate in the guardians' communities are only intelligible within the context of the different meanings and significations of the Nakba. These include the popular, patriotic, nationalist and the meaning embodied in the very possibility of their own communities. Similarly, second- and third-generation Palestinian refugees' Nakba postmemories, or imagined rather than referential memories (Hirsch 1997, 2012), and narratives are also only intelligible when read as resulting from their negotiation of these different Nakba meanings. In addition, they articulate their postmemories and narratives in reference to the guardians' own memories of catastrophes, even if this is not what they emphasized as having been the most important aspect of the memories narrated and transmitted in their homes.

The ongoing war in Syria means that the meanings of the Nakba for these generations are today articulated in drastically different ways. For the first time since 1948, the lives of generations of Palestinians who were born or came of age in Syria have been affected by unprecedented displacement, devastation, and closed borders that cut off all possible legal and safe exits from the war. As a friend unable to leave Syria put it toward the end of 2013, should I come back to war-torn Syria, I would record a Nakba that the post-Palestine generations in Syria lived through rather than one they were told about.

In this chapter, I examine second- and third-generation interviewees' prewar postmemories and narratives, made possible by a world that is today being violently transformed beyond recognition. I draw on the notion of postmemory to argue that the objects of these generations' postmemories are also the objects of the guardians' memories of loss as narrated in their own families. These postmemories are of the guardians' former lives, homes, and worlds imagined as Palestine by the post-Palestine generations. Where the Nakba does figure for second- and third-generation Palestinian refugees is in their negotiation of the guardians' own memories of the Nakba as well as the pervasive popular significations and understandings of 1948 in their communities.

Thus, second- and third-generation Palestinian refugees are cognizant of and engage the place of the Nakba in the post-Oslo memory discourses, as well as the event's myriad patriotic and nationalist significations. However, unlike their parents' or grandparents' generations, these younger generations have no referential memories to invoke, no lived memories of 1948 with which to engage the different meanings of the Nakba in these various discourses. As a result, second- and third-generation refugees articulate their understanding of 1948 through what I call "narratives on (Nakba) memory." These take up the different meanings of the Nakba as articulated in the memories that circulate in the guardians' communities as well as in the various discourses this book has explored. It is important to distinguish these narratives from memories, understood in a concrete and referential sense, because they are essentially an engagement with what is seen to constitute the meaning of the Nakba as well as its memory. Thus, in engaging these discourses and the guardians' memories in generationally dependent ways, the post-Palestine generations articulate their own understandings and ultimately provide yet more possible meanings of the Nakba today. It is also within this context that the post-Palestine generations are today referring to the calamity that has struck their communities in Syria as the new Nakba.

POSTMEMORIES OF PALESTINE

Jaramana Camp, February 9, 2008; al-Husayniyya, April 22, 2008

It was on the first day of our arrival in Damascus that I first saw Jaramana Camp; the highway that connects the airport to the city cuts right through it. The closely built brick and unpainted house structures line both sides of the broad highway, some zinc roofs and the alleyways clearly visible, even to those speeding by. A couple of months earlier, a family friend from Jaramana, the neighborhood adjacent to the camp, today the site of inter-mittent booby-trapped car explosions and mortar attacks, told us he never knew that there was a camp on the edges of his neighborhood. . . . Three months after seeing Jaramana for the first time, I was in al-Husayniyya, an urban sprawl that houses purpose-built apartment blocks for those whose homes were in the way, I would learn, of the construction of that highway. Husayniyya was the site of fierce battles, and its people have been selectively allowed to return to their homes, now that the area is under the army's con-trol. . . . I was in al-Husayniyya with a friend on an unusually hot spring day, five years prior to the dislocation of its people yet again, in order to meet one of her own friends, another third-generation Palestinian refugee woman. She seemed quite hesitant and reluctant to talk at first, insisting that she knew nothing. . . . At one stage in our interview, after she shares the ways in which memories of Palestine were narrated to her, I remind her of her initial unfounded self-effacement: "How can you not know, you do know what your grandmother narrated to you. . . ." She laughs and I can't hear what she says in her defense as our three voices cross over in the recorded interview that I listen to now, after all these years that have elapsed since the encounter, and the intrusion of war into her life and the life of her family in the cruelest of ways. . . . "It is imperative that one knows these things," my friend says "[because] it is about knowing your origins, where you are from."... Little did we all know that five years later, she would be yearning for her devastated camp and her family that has now been torn between the barrel bombs of Khan Eshieh, safer neighborhoods of Damascus, the camps of Lebanon and even the processing camps of northern Europe.

The English and comparative literature scholar Marianne Hirsch (1997) first coined her notion of "postmemory" in her study of the visual representation of European Jewish family life before and after the annihilation of European Jewry. She noted that her focus on the European Jewish Holocaust is not to assert the event's exceptional status but, rather, to explore a personally devastating episode in her family history (Hirsch 1997, 14). Understanding the Holocaust as an unexceptional historical atrocity in relation to other historical atrocities has become an important part of the so-called "colonial turn" in Holocaust studies. In this new literature, rather than considering the Holocaust as a unique and therefore ahistorical, unrepresentable, and anomalous episode of modern history, the Holocaust has been historicized. This has taken place within the context of European imperialism, colonialism, the project of modernity, and certain racist ideals of the Enlightenment (Langbehn and Salama 2011; Zimmerer 2004). This new body of work makes possible solidarity between peoples whose communities have historically been invariably colonized, enslaved, and exterminated (Rothberg 2009). It also allows for the decolonization of the Zionist appropriation of the Holocaust for its settler-colonial project in Palestine (Grosfoguel 2012).

Hirsch (1997, 22) makes important theoretical gestures that consequently make engaging her notion of postmemory possible. These include her emphasis on the autobiographical rather than the exceptional in her choice of research subject and the applicability of her postmemory to the children of Holocaust survivors as well as to "other second-generation memories of cultural or collective traumatic events and experiences." She argues that "postmemory is a powerful and very particular form of memory precisely because its connection to its object or source is mediated not through recollection but through an imaginative investment and creation.... [Postmemory is] the experience of those who grow up dominated by narratives that preceded their birth, whose own belated stories are evacuated by the stories of the previous generation shaped by traumatic events that can be neither understood nor recreated" (22).

In her later work, Hirsch aligns her notion of postmemory with other attempts to theorize the relationship of the generation that came of age in the aftermath of the annihilation of Europe's Jewry to its parental past.

She acknowledges the contradictions inherent in the phenomenon she theorizes as postmemory. She also argues that postmemory is a structure, the process of its generation, resulting from being "shaped, however indirectly, by traumatic fragments of events that still defy narrative reconstruction and exceed comprehension. . . . [These are] events [that] happened in the past, but their effects continue into the present" (Hirsch 2012, 5). Critics of Hirsch have argued that there is essentially no purely referential memory, that memory is always postmemory after the event, hence post/memory rather than postmemory (Stanley and Dampier 2005, 94). Clearly, however, this de-emphasizes the central generational component of Hirsch's theorization of postmemory.

Second- and third-generation Palestinian refugees' postmemories and their structures of attachment and generation can be considered through the relationship these postmemories have to the objects of the guardians' memories of loss. These are, after all, the only remaining memory fragments of the worlds, communities, and lives that were lost for those expelled beyond Palestine in 1948. Here, my first departure from Hirsch is in extending the possibility of postmemories beyond the second generation. I also use the notion of postmemories to examine memories of loss, the defining feature of the intergenerational narration and transmission for the post-Palestine generations. This use is, of course, to imply neither that the Nakba has defied narrative construction nor that it has exceeded comprehension insofar as the guardians' memories of catastrophes are concerned. Indeed, the post-Palestine generations partly engage the guardians' memories of the Nakba when they articulate their own narratives on what they understand to constitute Nakba memory. The point is that there is a correlation between what the post-Palestine generations emphasized as having been the most important aspect of the memories narrated in their homes and what they also articulated as their own postmemories.

For example, Manal's postmemories of Safad, as quoted in the opening of the chapter, are so powerful that she can use her postmemories to literally draw the town of her family. She related the following when I probed her about the context in which her late grandmother would narrate her memories of Safad:

When guests came and the gathering grew in numbers, my grandmother would talk, I would then at this stage become eager to sit with the people and to listen. . . . When she sat with the elderly, she'd ask them to affirm her story because some of them were there, sort of . . . like "So do you remember when a certain event happened," "Remember the quarrel between the family of so and so and the family of so and so," and so forth, or "No, you were too young to remember." If a particular person challenged her story, for example, [she'd say,] "Your brother was there." During these conversations my mother would ask me to prepare her a cup of tea or coffee, I would get upset because I wanted to listen, the whole conversation became more interesting. . . . You feel that the small things become bigger, the intensity increases, you see. The scenes become more interesting, the stories become nicer, a discussion takes place, and so it's not only the voice of my grandmother narrating. . . . There is more of a spark, there is more of "Those were the days, remember this and that, remember Umm so and so." As I told you, our house was the meeting place of the elderly, more than one old woman would meet in our house, and when they started to affirm or comment on each other's stories, you feel as if you had been there. . . . When they spoke you'd feel that they go around and around trying to evade the subject of leaving, they want to feel that they still live there. They'd start talking about their cooking, their meals, their family, and so on, you see; that is, they would go around trying to ignore the fact that we have left. . . . The point of the departure in the story was very limited, why? Because it was something of a shock.[1]

In this interview excerpt, Manal underscores several issues, all of which have been visited at great length. First, she affirms that the primary narrators of memory were the guardians, and in this instance, her grandmother. She points to how the narration of memories would occur during ordinary family occasions, in this case, receiving guests who could remember Safad together with her grandmother. She recollects how these guests happened to be fellow women guardians, making her grandmother's narration more exciting for her. She underscores how these women and guests in fact constituted a community with common memories, who would affirm their memories of Safad and through this affirmation and memory-making bring it to life in the present tense. Finally, she points to how the object of these women's memories of loss were the worlds they had lost in Safad, that they would recollect what they would cook, what they would eat, their families, lives, in other words, everything but the Nakba. The issue of the Nakba and of leaving, Manal says, was something that was evaded in their memory-making. This evasion ensured that they could continue to remember Safad in the present tense and hold on to all that it encapsulated in terms of their unfathomable loss.

Manal also relates how these family occasions and the guardians' memory-making enabled her own postmemories of her family's town. The presence of the guardians' communities during the family occasions meant that for her as a child, the smaller things that were remembered became bigger, the intensity increased, the scenes become more interesting, the guardians' stories nicer. This presence also meant that it was not only the voice of her grandmother narrating, but several voices, making her feel as though she had lived there.

This feeling that Manal alludes to, the intensity of the guardians' stories, and her imagination of these scenes and lost places of her grandmother's and other Safadis' memories are her postmemories and the structure of their generation. They are postmemories, rather than lived memories of Safad, because they are informed by her "imaginative investment, projection, and creation" (Hirsch 2012, 5). This distinction between postmemories and memories is not to suggest that there exist unmediated and mediated memories. Rather, it is to emphasize two different processes. The social process of articulating memories by those who have a referentiality to draw on differs from the imagination of places in Palestine by those who never lived in Safad and other towns and worlds of historic Palestine.

That Manal's postmemories are informed by Safad, rather than the Nakba, is the result of the ways in which survivors of catastrophes, as argued, together recollect and affirm that which was lost in the wake of catastrophic events rather than catastrophe itself. Thus, Manal argues that the departure from Safad was limited in the guardians' memories, a point that underscores that it is loss, rather than that which led to loss, that informs the post-Palestine generations' postmemories. Similarly, Tahani, a third-generation refugee young mother and teacher, whose family from Akrad al-Baqqara, Safad subdistrict, was expelled for the second and final time to Syria in 1956, echoed Manal's assertion. She did this with regards to what did and did not constitute her postmemories. When I asked her about the memories that she heard during her family get-togethers, she said: "They would talk about their life there, how they lived there, and then they would talk about how they left. . . . It was stories, it was simply stories. . . . For example, my grandmother would say that we used to go and harvest, or something along those lines, and then the ogre would come out . . . or that so and so was killed here, and his blood was shed, these were the stories that they would tell us."[3]

When asked whether memories of leaving or memories of Palestine had greater impact on her, Tahani said: "Look, she [her grandmother] wouldn't talk more about how they left, do you see? She would tell us about the days that they had lived through there and so on, so perhaps because of this, what was implanted in our minds was about the days that they lived in Palestine, more so than them having left Palestine."[3] Thus, like Manal, Tahani notes that her grandmother would talk about her past life, how they lived in Palestine, and relate simple storied memories of this lost life. Also like with Manal's grandmother, the departure and the Nakba as leaving was not the focus of Tahani's grandmother's memories. As a result, it is Akrad al-Baqqara, rather than the Nakba, that is the object of Tahani's own postmemories. These postmemories are based on the stories of the times of harvest, and even folk narratives of the ogre that were "implanted" in the grandchildren. In view of this, Tahani's postmemories are also imagined as Palestine rather than as simply the world of Akrad al-Baqqara.

Like his generational peers, Muhammad-Khayr also emphasized the relationship between the guardians' narration of memories of all that was lost, rather than the Nakba, to his imagination of his postmemories of Palestine. He said:

> They narrated to each other; they'd narrate and re-narrate the same things. They'd sit together, two or three of them, and they'd repeat the same things they'd discussed before, and then on another day they'd repeat the same kind of discussions, they'd repeat it over and over . . . how their life was and so forth. This was the kind of talk that used to be very influential during my childhood, not the Nakba stage as such. The talk was about what the Nakba had deprived them of, more than the Nakba per se. This is what had a lot of influence during my childhood, during the early beginnings, since the first or second grade, as a seven-year old child. This is what I remember, the kiln, fishing, the small islands that face the village, how they used to swim to the island to play there, to fish, the caves under the island, how wasps stung my grandfather on his way to bring back a donkey from I don't know whom, perhaps a neighbor from whom he had borrowed it. These were the stories that made you feel that there was another world, they spoke of something you wish to see but you can't.[4]

Muhammad-Khayr, like Tahani and Manal, points to the guardians' memory-making during ordinary family occasions as having enabled him to "remember" the lost world of Tantura: the kiln, the fishing, the islands, the fish, the caves under the island, the wasps, and the donkey. Hirsch (2012, 5) notes that one defining feature of postmemories is that they constitute "stories, images and behaviors . . . transmitted so deeply and affectively as to *seem* to constitute memories in their own right [emphasis in original]." This "remembering" is therefore a reference to Muhammad-Khayr's postmemories of Tantura, of this other world he could only and also very clearly imagine, a world he has always wished to see.

Third-generation interviewees were thus adamant that the Nakba was secondary to their grandparents' sharing of memories and that their own postmemories were informed by their grandparents' memories of all that was lost. Second-generation interviewees, however, did not exclude the Nakba altogether. When I asked Abu Muhammad about his parents' generation's narration of memories, he said:

> They would narrate about everything, you can say. They first and foremost used to narrate the story [of the life] which they used to live, the simple life of course, the village, the agriculture, the water well, the car of so and so, the family of so and so, the coffee shop of so and so. They would go and hear the news in the coffee shop because there was one radio in the village, there wasn't any other. They would talk about the Nakba, about the massacres. Meaning, they would talk about more than one issue.[5]

Abu Muhammad, like his children's generation, notes that the objects of the guardians' memories, in the first instance, are the objects of their loss. Although he does not articulate these details of village life in Tantura as his own postmemories, he nonetheless concretely lists them as the guardians' memories. These are their former lives, what he imagines as the simple lives of peasant farming communities, the village, the agriculture, water wells, the odd car in Tantura, the families of the village, and even the communal radio in the village's coffee shop. In a departure from the third generation, however, Abu Muhammad does not dismiss the question of the Nakba altogether. He does note the Nakba through massacres, presumably referring to the massacre of Tantura, his family's village of origin.

Although Abu Muhammad gives the Nakba a secondary place, it does nevertheless have a place. This was common to second-generation interviewees and is what primarily distinguishes them from their children's generation. Thus, the second generation's postmemories, like those of the third generation, are based on the imagination of what their parents had and what they lost. Nevertheless, unlike the third generation, they emphasized the guardians as having shared memories of the Nakba. For example, Umm Muhammad (unrelated to Abu Muhammad), another second-generation interviewee and a mother whose family also comes from Tantura, told me that her grandmother "would talk, one story leads to another, you know the elderly, when they want to talk. They can talk about one topic and then switch to another one. . . . She [her grandmother] would talk generally, about the life they lived, Nakba and without a Nakba."[6]

Umm Muhammad, who grew up with a stepmother and attributed the narration of memories of Palestine to her paternal relatives, including her father, aunts, and grandmother, underscores that her grandmother's memories were simply about the life they had. Thus, in this she shares generational commonalities with Abu Muhammad in terms of the emphasis on the guardians' memories of loss, as well as the presence, rather than complete dismissal of, memories of the departure.

When I asked Buthayna about the memories that were shared in her own family, she echoed both Abu Muhammad and Umm Muhammad:

> It was, meaning, father would talk to us about everything—about the Nakba and about Palestine, how beautiful it is, about Tantura, our village, how it was on the sea, and how it is one of the most beautiful places on earth, meaning, it is even more beautiful than Europe. Meaning Tantura was a valley, and a mountain and the sea, do you see? There is even a picture at my parents' house, did you see [it]? . . . It is so beautiful. And they'd talk to us about those that were martyred, about, meaning, the massacres that happened there.[7]

Buthayna, like the other second-generation interviewees, notes that both Palestine and the Nakba informed the guardians' narration of their memories of loss. It is her father's, rather than mother's or grandmother's, memories of all that was lost that inform her postmemories of Tantura. These are an imaginative investment in the sea, the valley, and the mountains that surround Tantura. She also points to the picture of Tantura that hangs in her parents' living room, the same post-1948 picture I saw in the living rooms and workplaces of other Palestinian refugees whose families were expelled from Tantura during the Nakba.

In Hirsch's (1997, 23) study of postmemory, which centers on photographs, she argues that photographs are "the leftover, the fragmentary sources and building blocks, shot through with holes, of the work of postmemory." They affirm the existence of all that was lost while at the same time signal the unbridgeable distance to it (23). However, private family photographs were the privilege of the wealthy few in historic Palestine (W. Khalidi 2010), and several interviewees referred to photographs of their families' places of origin after rather than before their destruction. Thus Hirsch's proposition that photographs are the "umbilical" medium that connects the generations after to postmemories of the parental past is in fact reversed by what Buthayna had to say. It is the post-Palestine generations' postmemories that make these photographs legible. In other words, it is postmemory that forms the building blocks of these photos. This is because they allow the post-Palestine generations to imagine and inscribe the guardians' lost lives onto photographs of places that no longer bear any traces of their parents' and grandparents' former lives and communities.

In addition, while relating her postmemories of the sea and the valley of Tantura, Buthayna, like Abu Muhammad before her, also notes that her parents narrated the Nakba-as-massacres. Given that all three second-generation interviewees' families hail from Tantura, the site of a notorious 1948 massacre, this is unsurprising. However, this association of the guardians' Nakba memories with massacres also shows that both Buthayna and Abu Muhammad filter the Nakba through some of its important patriotic significations circulated in popular memory discourses. This is the Nakba-as-death, the Nakba-as-massacres, the Nakba-as-destruction. Thus, while second-generation interviewees did not dismiss the question of the narration of the Nakba altogether, they nevertheless invoked the Nakba as it circulates in discourses in their communities, rather than as a postmemory.

These generational convergences and divergences demonstrate that the Nakba, as the imperative to remember for the return, does not figure through postmemories for the post-Palestine generations. Rather, the question of 1948 is either made secondary, as is the case with third-generation refugees, or figures as a narrative on what is understood to constitute Nakba memory, as is the case with second-generation interviewees. These narratives take up the guardians' communities' memories of catastrophes. They also take up these "memories" as they circulate through the activists' created memory discourses. It is therefore through these narratives on what constitutes the Nakba and its memory, rather than through postmemories of all that was lost and imagined as Palestine, that the post-Palestine generations shared their different understandings of the Nakba.

NARRATIVES ON NAKBA MEMORY

al-Mazarib, Dar'a, April 17, 2008

After the ruins and rubble of the destruction of Qunaitira, we continued our day trip south and drove through Dar'a, the town where the Syrian uprising would begin three years later. . . . We picnicked in a beautiful green area by a lake outside of the town of al-Mazarib, another site of war, death, and destruction today. . . . I wonder how history will come to remember Dar'a, and the fire that it ignited, the one that has now engulfed

the whole of Syria. . . . We found a spot among the many picnicking fami-
lies, and spent the rest of the afternoon eating, chatting, laughing, and sing-
ing. . . . In between tea and chatter, one of the young women in our company
asked about my research, the raison d'être of my presence, clearly always
in the foreground. . . . As I explained my interest in memories of 1948, the
third-generation Palestinian refugee woman from Khan Eshieh remarked
that "yes, we learned about the Nakba in schoolbooks. . . ." The same Ba'thist
schoolbooks, I would later learn as I browsed through the sixth grade Arab
nationalism class textbook, which taught all students about the Nakba
of Palestine. . . . "Yes, it is important," another one of the young women in
the group, interjected to tell us. . . . I wonder what has happened to these
third-generation Palestinian refugee women from Khan Eshieh who learned
about the Nakba through schoolbooks, and who nonetheless chose to wear
the kufiyya that day . . .[8] those who have left their camp, and the others who
have seen their families torn apart and scattered by war yet again, some
even arriving at the shores of the Ionian and Baltic Seas, to tell of the minute
details of the horrors of war.

Shared second- and third-generation narratives on what constitutes
Nakba memory are negotiated through the Nakba's consequences as remembered by the guardians. The main intergenerational differences in narratives
on Nakba memory therefore lie in the temporal demarcation that has led to
different generational experiences (Day Sclater 2003; Scott 1992). Thus, the
second generation came of age to the Nakba's aftereffects, especially materially, while the third generation came of age to rebuilt shattered lives and
communities. The latter's narratives on what constitutes Nakba memory are
primarily understood in terms of the Nakba's impact on their own life experiences. Before the Syrian war, this impact was mainly expressed through
their refugee status and a belonging to an elsewhere that complicated their
belonging to Syria. Against this, I first examine the shared narratives of what
interviewees understood to constitute Nakba memory before moving to the
main intergenerational differences.

SHARED NARRATIVES ON NAKBA MEMORY

Shared narratives on what constitutes Nakba memory mainly center on
an understanding of the Nakba as the aftereffects of the guardians' dispossession from their homes and lands. These narratives are negotiated and
understood in reference to the guardians' memories of their former lives

and their loss. For example, at one point during our interview, I asked Muhammad-Khayr whether there were contradictions in the guardians' storied memories. He replied:

It's not a matter of contradictions; rather, they try to attribute every-thing to the Nakba. . . . I mean, for example, if they'd buy oranges, they'd say, "If only you could see the oranges of Palestine." If they'd buy apples, they'd say, "If only you could see the apples of Palestine." . . . [It is a] n exaggeration that you feel has become a disease for the person who lived the Nakba. It's like he wants the world to feel the greatness of his loss. My grandfather didn't say these kinds of things, but I once heard a man named B. say, "The orange in Palestine is this big" [gestures with his hand]. [I thought] this big?! Is it a watermelon or what?![9]

In Muhammad-Khayr's narrative, what constitutes Nakba memory made itself evident through its psychic impact on the guardians. Thus, what con-stitutes Nakba memory is understood as being a "disease," one that contin-uously plagues the guardians through their unrelenting need to express or make felt the greatness of their loss. This "disease" is therefore also grief, the lifelong impact of 1948 made present in the guardians' day-to-day lives. In this instance, this grief made itself present in reference to the loss of the fruits of Palestine.

Similarly, while explaining her understanding of the Nakba as expressed through its effects on the guardians' lives, Mayada, an engineer whose grand-parents are from Safad, put forth her narrative on Nakba memory this way:

It is like they awoke from a shock. It is like they suffered from a shock. For example, imagine if your house is burnt down, ok? The first thing that you ask is not about your house or the furniture, you ask about the peo-ple in the house. If they have all left unharmed then there is no problem, later, when things calm down, they put out the fire, and you go back to the house and you see that you have no furniture left, only then do you begin to realize that you have a problem, or if the house was burnt down totally, your problem is even greater and bigger, ok? And from there your second suffering begins. But the first concerned what? It concerned the people who were with you. So I think that this is what happened to them.[10]

"Shock" like "disease" points to an all-encompassing catastrophe that the guardians lived through and survived, and its afterlife is also expressed through the psychic impact it had on them. For Mayada, the meaning of the Nakba can be understood through this very shock, realized only once they awoke from it. Given the burned house metaphor, at first it was the immediate survival of their families that was the most pressing concern. It was only later, once they realized that the entire house had burned down, that the awakening from the shock began. The extent of the loss itself became even greater, with its own aftereffects revolving around suffering and grief. Thus, the Nakba for Mayada is not only the shock itself but also the awakening from it.

Other interviewees, like Khawla, shared a similar narrative on what constitutes Nakba memory. When I asked Khawla whether the Nakba was an important part of her grandmother's memories, her answer was an unequivocal no. For her,

> the most important aspect, what she used to repeat over and over was that, how after they left, how they sat in the tents, this is the most important aspect, that she would really bring up a lot. How she was hurt, and how no one took care of her and her wound was dangerous, in her head, and how she gave up [one of] her children, in the middle of the way [out], in order to [be able to] continue, and the way [itself], how they were subjected to disease along the way, to the lack of health attention, to hunger, to thirst, to the difficulties of the way, it was all, of course, walking, and they were carrying things. She was talking a lot about some who left and left their children on the way, and they kept on going. She is one of them, she left her daughter for a distance. . . . Then she came back for her, she couldn't continue on the way.[11]

Khawla's assertion that the Nakba was not the most important part of her grandmother's memories, followed by an emphasis on its repercussions as more important, means that she is deprioritizing the Nakba understood strictly as 1948. Instead, she highlights its consequences and gives them greater importantance. Thus, Khawla's narrative on Nakba memory is what Khawla's grandmother would repeat over and over. This is the Nakba of the tents, of injuries she sustained during the bombardment of the village, of the hunger and thirst after the departure, of leaving behind one of her children. What constitutes Nakba memory here, as with the memories of other interviewees, is negotiated through the unfolding of the story of the departure itself rather than the cause of the departure.

Second-generation interviewees' narratives on Nakba memory are also negotiated in a similar way. For example, Fatima, a second-generation refugee whose family hails from Yaquq, Tiberias subdistrict, told me the following about her mother:

> She told us, as you can say, that they actually fled twice, twice. They fled to an area called Wadi al-Samak, we fled. This is the tragedy, their departure from Palestine, they would say was fatigue, humiliation, and agony, but the tragedy was actually in Wadi al-Samak . . . in the Golan. They stayed there for maybe a few months, a few months. They were eaten up by, what can I tell you, humiliation, anguish, dirt. They would say it was an area that, as we would say, even monkeys won't inhabit, but our grandmother was there for months. My mother would say we used to walk like from here to Qatana. Where is Qatana? We can reach Qatana in half an hour or an hour by car, by a minibus, but they used to walk for firewood and water so they can wash and drink. . . . So they can drink, so they can wash. One of them would only have one dress, imagine you left with one dress, the dress on you, how is a woman, you know [how it is] with one dress, to leave with one dress. So [there were] many tragedies.[12]

Once again, for Fatima, understanding what Nakba memories are is not so much about the guardians having to leave Palestine as about the consequences of this departure. Referring to the guardians' memories of death in the valley, she underscores the twice uprootedness of the guardians as the real tragedy, as the Nakba itself. The consequences of the loss of everything, of being engulfed by humiliation, anguish, and dirt, are what constitute Nakba memory for Fatima. This is therefore a Nakba that unfolded through its aftereffects, which lasted for months if not years.

Similarly, when I asked Buthayna about the Nakba in her family's memories, she said:

> When they would say, eat this meal, for example, why are you, why are you being picky over this meal? We were hungry, when we left Palestine, during the days of cold, we used to wish for bread. Meaning, mother would have cooked a meal that isn't very nice, yes, like green plants, like cheeseweed mallow or dandelion greens and so forth, [we'd say], "What is this," meaning, "Does someone cook grass?!" "One can go and eat grass, no need for cooking, Mother" . . . . So my mother would say, "Thank God that you have this blessing, we lived through days in which we had nothing to eat, not even a piece of bread."[13]

Buthayna, like Fatima, articulates her narrative of what constitutes Nakba memory primarily through negotiating its consequences as recollected by her mother. In the example she uses, memories of the Nakba made themselves present around food in particular. Her mother's cooking, as well as the kind of food she would cook and her and her siblings' reactions, facilitated her mother's memory-making. This revolved around the days of hunger and cold to which she and the family were subjected following their expulsion from Tantura.

Abu Shadi emphasized the same facets of shared narratives mentioned by other second- and third-generation interviewees when he said:

> The Nakba for my family, they didn't live the Nakba that others lived. Like I told you, they left spoiled. When they left Safad, with horses for my mother and grandmother to ride, to take them to Bint Jbeil, where they remained as guests of leaders of the Shia in the south [of Lebanon], to remain there living in luxury, meaning, as guests, until my uncle got in touch with my father from Damascus and told him [to] come to Damascus, and we came here, do you see? Meaning, I don't remember all these days."[14]

Abu Shadi here conveys a clear narrative on Nakba memory that takes its meaning to be, a priori, about the departure, the departure with nothing, and this departure with nothing's consequences. He does this by underscoring how his family, unlike most Palestinian refugee families, did not in fact live through this particular trajectory that commonly constitutes understandings of Nakba memory. The women of his family left on horses and were received as guests; they were "spoiled," to use his words. Thus, by discussing how his family's Nakba experience was contrary to that of the average Palestinian refugee family, Abu Shadi is also clearly aware that Nakba memory is understood as being all about leaving with nothing. That it is about destitution and the immeasurable suffering as a consequence.

SECOND-GENERATION NARRATIVES ON NAKBA MEMORY

Second-generation Palestinian refugees in Syria came of age to the immediate and material aftereffects of the Nakba. This explains the main intergenerational divergences in narratives on Nakba memory. The second-generation's narratives relate how their families were still struggling to rebuild their lives from nothing. Most third-generation interviewees, in contrast, were born into families that had already established themselves anew in Syria. As noted, this generation's experiences and that of the fourth in particular are as a result now undergoing radical transformations in light of the war in Syria.

During my interview with Fatima, she told me that her second generation is in fact the generation of the Nakba:

> Should I tell you why we are the people of the Nakba? . . . We lived, we lived a difficult life, we lived a difficult life, very, very difficult. No matter how much Ahlam [her present third-generation niece] tells you that we lived a difficult life, our life was more difficult. Why do I say this? First of all, our parents couldn't dress an entire family. An entire family, they couldn't. Imagine, for example, the son would be dressed as the first[born], and his clothes the second[born] would wear, and then the third. No one had his own personal belongings, there were always people sharing with you.[15]

Fatima is no longer only relating a narrative on Nakba memory that encapsulates the aftereffects of 1948 on the guardians' lives. She is, like other second-generation interviewees, also extending these repercussions into her own life. Third-generation interviewees also insisted that the Nakba extends to their own lives because of their ongoing statelessness. Nevertheless, for the third generation, their narratives on Nakba memory did not materially extend the Nakba to their own lives in the same way as their parents' second generation. In other words, the poverty that Fatima stresses she was born into, one of the most concrete material consequences of the Nakba as it affected her own life, was not echoed by third-generation interviewees.

Even those second-generation interviewees whose parents could afford to rent private homes in Damascus, rather than live in the camps, underscored 1948 as extending into their own lives. While relating his father's narration of memories of Safad as well as the Nakba, Abu Shadi said:

> We lived a life, meaning, let me tell you, it was a difficult life. It is true that we came to a house that wasn't available to other Palestinians, but I didn't see my father until nighttime, he was working the whole time, in order to secure a living for the family members. My grandmother was here, and my mother, and my uncle's wife, my uncle, as I told you, he was in Lebanon and he was a pharmacist, but we didn't have the money to start a pharmacy, for example. . . . So most of his [father's] time, he was preoccupied with securing a source of income for our living and for our education. You know the schools here are expensive, it is true that it is

part of the state [education system], but the costs of books and the costs of uniform, and the costs of clothes, and the costs of this and that, and there was nothing with them in the first place, meaning when we came from Palestine they had nothing at all . . . and if it wasn't for his reception in Lebanon as a guest, and we came here to people who also received us as guests, we would have perhaps lived in a tent for a very long time.[16]

Abu Shadi, like Fatima, narrates the aftereffects of the Nakba as extending into his own life, even though he acknowledges his family's relative fortune of having had acquaintances to host them in Lebanon and later in Syria. He links the consequences of the Nakba to his own life by highlighting what would have happened had his family not had the contacts who ensured that they did not stay in the tent camps. Nevertheless, he mentions the difficulties of not seeing his father, who had to work long hours in order to secure a decent living for his family and an education for his children. Thus, the difficulties that Abu Shadi's family experienced, albeit alleviated in comparison to those of others, were a direct outcome of the Nakba, extending well beyond 1948 and into his own life.

Another important reason for the divergences in second- and third-generation narratives on Nakba memory stems from the second-generation's relationship to the guardians of memory, who were mostly their parents rather than grandparents. This means that when and how they came of age is an important factor that distinguishes what constitutes their Nakba narratives from those of the third generation. As a result, the narratives of second-generation interviewees are by far less contentious than those of their children's generation, and they more directly take up, and converse with, the memories that circulate in the guardians' communities. These include the guardians' mythic, heroic, survival, and ambivalent memories.

For example, while discussing whether his family would narrate how they left Palestine, Abu Bassam, a retired schoolteacher from Akrad al-Baqqara, said: "Yes, yes, they would tell us how we left, and how so and so forgot his son, and how another one forgot her daughter, and another person so and so, and another person went back and got some things for him and so forth. All the Palestinian people know the truth."[17]

Abu Bassam's narrative on Nakba memory touches on the guardians' mythic memories of the father leaving behind his son or the mother leaving behind her daughter. At the same time, Abu Bassam is clearly engaging something other than the guardians' memory when he affirms that all the Palestinian people know the truth. His is therefore a narrative on Nakba memory that is in dialogue with the guardians' memories of 1948, and the meaning of the Nakba in popular memory discourses. In other words, the parent forgetting his or her child is the quintessential memory of the Nakba, the truth that all Palestinians know.

Another common second-generation narrative on Nakba memory revolves around the role of the Arabs in 1948 and also partly engages the guardians' heroic memories. These narratives almost always center on the Arabs' treachery and machinations against Palestine and the Palestinians. The Nakba-as-Arab-betrayal was also an important part of the Nakba's Arab universe of discourse following the demise of the ancien régimes that presided over the loss of Palestine. Umm Shadi, a pharmacist and second-generation refugee mother who left Haifa at the age of seven, said the following when I asked her about the place of the Nakba in her father's memories:

> For example, in the story he said, when in 1948 they went to the harbor, in the middle of Suq al-Shwam [Damascene Market], where his shop is, the harbor is close to them, he saw an armed Arab man, he had grabbed a rifle and he was breaking it, and he [father] then told him: "Are you crazy, man? Why are you trying to break the rifle?" The man said: "God curse their fathers, they have given us faulty weapons, you have no idea, and you are giving me lessons?! Those Arabs are dogs!" And he told him you shouldn't say things like this, why do you say this when all the Arab armies are coming within the next seven days, all the Arab armies, they have already reached I don't know where. Perhaps the Iraqi army during that time, it was the first army [to reach Palestine]. So those are things that he would say, and he would say, "Can you imagine, the Arabs have been betraying us since that time."[18]

Umm Shadi's narrative is distinguished from third-generation narratives by her ability to recall her father's own storied memories with vivid details. She locates the story at the Damascene Market by the harbor, where the encounter unfolds, and she also relates the conversation that took place between her father and the man who was breaking the rifle. The meaning of her narrative on Nakba memory as Arab betrayal is in its rhetorical force and moralizing impulse. This is found in her father's cluelessness as the bombardment of Haifa was going on, followed by his later bitter realization that the Arabs not only had betrayed and let down the Palestinians in 1948 but also have been betraying the Palestinians ever since. In addition, Umm Shadi's narrative is also about heroic Nakba memory, one in which a people betrayed nevertheless did not hesitate to take up arms. She also clearly engages the Nakba's Arab universe of discourse, as the reference to the faulty weapons and Arab betrayal demonstrate.

Second-generation narratives on Nakba memory also take up the themes of survival memories and memories of survival that circulate in the guardians' communities. They do this in relation to engaging what constitutes Nakba memory as centering on death, destruction, expulsion, massacres, the annihilation of communities, and the dispersal and shattering of families through their uprooting. These meanings of the Nakba, as noted earlier, are important in popular memory discourses on 1948, leveraged to mobilize memory for the return. This once again underscores how narratives on what constitutes Nakba memory converse with the Nakba's myriad significations in Palestinian communities.

An example of this narrative was related by Abu 'Ammar, a retired schoolteacher born in Nasir al-Din, Tiberias subdistrict, who left his village as a three year old child. While discussing the guardians' departure as a result of the massacre that occurred in Nasir al-Din, which was critical to the Zionist conquest of the first town in historic Palestine, Tiberias, and the expulsion of its people (Abbasi 2008), he said:

No, no, there is no excuse for them [having left]. Death is more honorable in one's homeland. Yes, death is more honorable. In our village, there was a massacre. They killed all the residents who were there. . . . My mother told me about it. They gathered the people and they killed them. . . . There was a massacre, but it wasn't spread on a media level like Dayr Yasin and Qibya and these other places.[19]

In Nasir al-Din, they destroyed it, they burnt it down completely. . . . The Jews came and they destroyed the village, they burnt it. My mother then went out to a place outside of the village, so after the destruction, they passed near where my mother was, she was telling me [this] and I was with her, she told me they passed by this area, there was just a little distance between us and them, and my mother saw them, when they entered [Nasir al-Din] and destroyed, and killed, and they destroyed the village, they burnt it. The village of Nasir al-Din, it is known to have had a massacre like the massacre of Dayr Yasin, but no one heard about it like they heard about Dayr Yasin, meaning.[20]

Abu 'Ammar begins his narrative by contesting the guardians' decision to leave, because as he put it, "death is more honorable in one's homeland." In the moment in which Abu 'Ammar constructs his narrative on Nakba memory as a moral claim about the guardians' departure, he is also therefore making his narrative and its claim within the context of Palestinian patriotism. This is death as more honorable in one's homeland, those who remained as the example. He is also articulating his narrative in dialogue with and in contestation of popular memory discourses, especially which massacres they seem to have emphasized and popularized and which massacres they did not. The third layer of his narrative on what constitutes Nakba memory engages his mother's own survival memories, despite its being shrouded with heavy patriotic rhetoric that condemns the people's decision to leave Nasir al-Din.

Thus, while his rhetoric condemns the people for leaving, by including his mother's memories of the massacre Abu 'Ammar simultaneously and thereby implicitly absolves the villagers from the decisions they were compelled to make. Although he gives a nod to Palestinian patriotism by stressing what would have constituted honorable behavior, he implicitly qualifies this by conjuring up an understanding of the Nakba as mobilized for the return (the massacre in Dayr Yasin). Thus, though partly based on his mother's memories, this understanding nevertheless also revolves around Nakba-as-massacres.

Finally, second-generation interviewees' narratives also took up the thorny question of leaving, this time through engaging the guardians' ambivalent memories. For example, when I asked Abu Nidal what he had heard from his family about the Nakba, he told me:

> My father in particular, he told me that when the Salvation Army entered, they asked us to leave the village because the village was within the area of their artillery. So it began, and of course, in the nearby villages, the Jewish gangs began to kill and to spread propaganda of killing, it was a very big propaganda, in order to scare people, so we left, my grandfather and grandmother left in one direction, and my father and with my mother and with my sister and me—we were only two—my sister and I, they left in the direction of Syria. So, the end of the road was in the village of al-Harra, which is within Syria. We remained there for some five or six years, and there I came of age, and I remember the threshing floors of al-Harra.[21]

This narrative on what constitutes Nakba memory centers on the departure, one for which the Salvation Army is to blame (see, e.g., Abassi 2004). Abu Nidal's narrative engages his father's memories in several ways. He does this through relating the ambivalence around the Palestine's generation loss of agency over their lives in 1948, the sudden appearance of "Leave and you will return," and the largely destructive role of the Arabs in general and the Salvation Army in particular. Abu Nidal's narrative movement from his father's memories to massacres in other villages blurs the boundaries between his father's memories and popular memory discourses on the Nakba-as-massacres.

Thus, a defining aspect of second-generation narratives on Nakba memory is that they involve the memories that circulate in the guardians' communities, the popular memory discourses on the Nakba, and the Nakba's various patriotic and nationalist significations. Another defining aspect is how these narratives portray the Nakba as having found its way into the very lives of this generation's members, especially in terms of their having come of age to 1948's immediate material consequences. I now turn to a brief examination of the third generation's narratives on Nakba memory. The distinguishing feature of this generation's memories is that they contest the guardians' abdication of responsibility for the departure during the Nakba and blame them for leaving Palestine.

"WHY DID YOU LEAVE?" THIRD-GENERATION CONTENTIOUS NARRATIVES ON NAKBA MEMORY

All seventeen third-generation interviewees, without exception, related having asked their grandparents or having pondered, "Why did you leave?" Some second-generation interviewees also noted having the same question, but the extent of the blame and contention this one query engendered was not comparable to that of their children's generation. Neither was this question as conspicuous in second-generation narratives on Nakba memory. After I asked Suzanne whether there were issues left unanswered by her grandmother's memories when compared with what she would hear about the Nakba outside her home, she said: "The question that I would always ask myself was why did they leave? This is really the [heart of the] issue, why did they leave? They should have remained like those who are still there now. Why did they leave, why did they leave [everything] behind?"[22]

Sarab, a factory worker whose family is from al-Wa'ra al-Sawda' in the Tiberias subdistrict, made a similar association between questioning why the guardians left and blaming them for leaving. She uses the example of those who remained as a possible alternative to the guardians' fate in 1948. When I asked her whether she blamed the guardians for leaving, she said: "[You mean] that they should have remained and held on? Yes, they should have remained and held on because there are people who until now, since

1948, who are still in Palestine. How come they never left? Meaning there is a difference, they left and those didn't leave, and because my cousins are there until now [as well]."[23]

These third-generation narratives on Nakba memory blame the guardians by mentioning those who could, for whatever reason, remain in Palestine. One possible explanation for the universal occurrence of this question among third-generation interviewees, and the blame it encapsulates, is in the temporal distance of this generation's narratives from the memories of the guardians. Thus, while third-generation interviewees could relate vivid postmemories of their grandparents' loss, they could not recollect the guardians' memories of the series of catastrophes around 1948 as vividly or in the same way as members of the second generation. As a result, while third-generation interviewees' narratives on Nakba memory included certain facets of the memories that circulate in the guardians' communities, they nonetheless prioritized the Nakba's meaning as furthered in popular memory discourses. They also prioritized the Nakba's patriotic and nationalist significations.

Niyazi, a third-generation student whose family hails from Yaquq, Tiberias subdistrict, was perhaps one of the most unequivocal in blaming the guardians for leaving. His narrative on Nakba memory also most clearly included the Nakba's myriad patriotic and nationalist significations in order to lay this blame. When I asked him on what basis he blamed the guardians for leaving, he said:

What is happening now. The people who are inside are not really manlier than those who left. What is the difference between those who left and those who remained inside? I wish one of the people who left can answer this question. Why did you leave and those inside, why did they stay inside? You, who talks to me about memory and that we fought and that we led wars, and so forth, answer me, why? Why are the ones on the inside [there], are they manlier than you? Are they better than you? Do they have abilities to withstand the killings, slaughters, and massacres and you don't? You feared for your children and they don't fear for their children? I want one of them to answer me.[24]

Niyazi is referring to the guardians' various responses to the question of why they left. These can be summarized as follows: "We thought it was a matter of days and we will return," "killings," "slaughters," "massacres," "fear for children," or "We fought" (but ultimately lost because the Arabs sold us out). These possible responses to the thorny question of leaving have been examined in relation to the mythic, heroic, survival, shaming, and ambivalent memories that circulate in the guardians' communities. Niyazi's narrative, however, clearly prioritizes the Nakba's patriotic and nationalist significations. He talks about those who held on and remained, the Palestinian citizens of Israel and the Palestinians living under occupation in the Occupied Palestinian Territories. He uses anticolonial patriotic and nationalist values associated with masculinities and manhood with which to admonish the male guardians for leaving (see, e.g., Massad 1995). He also cites these same "manly" values to challenge the justification for having left as a result of the purported betrayal of the Arab states. He does this through juxtaposing the "truly manly" endurance of sixty years of Israeli settler-colonialism in contradistinction to the allegedly "manly" endurance of a singular Nakba in 1948 by the generation that fled to Syria. This juxtaposition therefore also nullifies the male guardians' use of patriotic values in order to justify what Niyazi sees as unjustifiable: leaving one's home and land behind, regardless of the circumstances.

Thus, third-generation narratives on Nakba memory contest the role that the guardians ascribe to themselves in their memories of the Nakba, especially around the question of leaving and remaining. This contestation does not necessarily mean that the guardians are accused of lies, hypocrisy, or contradictions. To the contrary, in order for this contestation to take place, the guardians must be more than just the narrators of storied memories; they must also be regarded as repositories of history. In other words, it is only when the guardians' memories are held to historical scrutiny, because these memories are regarded, a priori, as history, does the process of contestation emerge. This historical scrutiny is greatly indebted to the Nakba's Arab and Palestinian universes of discourse.

These contentious narratives lead to different understandings of what the Nakba actually is. In this particular example, the Nakba gains meaning through a retrospective and cumulative view of Palestinian history. This is one in which 1948 is only one catastrophe in a series of catastrophes that have taught people how to persevere and hold on to the land since (see, e.g., Jayyusi 2007). This understanding also demonstrates how the Nakba's patriotic or nationalist significations are integral to Palestinian refugees' narratives on what constitutes Nakba memories. The guardians, as previously argued, carve themselves an acceptable heroic role in these discourses or resort to a certain ambivalence when relating their memories in order to vindicate their departure. Members of the third generation, in contrast, draw on the different Nakba meanings in these discourses as they seek to understand the departure.

Thus, seeking an acceptable answer is important to those who pose the question. As a result, third-generation interviewees often relegate the guardians' departure to a matter of the guardians having had a limited worldview grounded in their "parochialism" at the time. Given this parochialism, the guardians are, in the third-generation's contentious narratives simultaneously blamed and vindicated for leaving (albeit pejoratively). Later during my interview with Niyazi, I told him that he was being unnecessarily harsh in his judgment of the generation of Palestine. This question needs to be revisited today in light of the war in Syria, given that he along with most of the people of Khan Eshieh has now left the camp and many have left the country. At the time, I put it to him that he had neither lived through nor survived the atrocities of 1948. His response nevertheless remained unequivocal:

> There is no awareness [among the generation of Palestine]. I told you there is an aspect of it that is related to a lack of awareness. You want me to justify them leaving. I am telling you, let us say that half of it is a lack of awareness, another aspect is fear, like I told you, "This happened in this area," "We better leave, we are next in line," and there is an aspect that is stupidity, [such as] "Leave and you will return in a few days." Meaning, stupidity and lack of awareness, a part of it is fear but another part is a lack of awareness, this is what I think.[25]

The guardians' departure from Palestine as being the result of a "lack of awareness," ignorance, and even stupidity is also Niyazi's answer to why they left, the question so central to his narrative on what constitutes Nakba memory. This answer, however, also serves to ultimately vindicate the actions of the guardians during 1948. This is because if the patriotic values that lay blame on the guardians for the departure are taken to their logical conclusion, then the guardians could also be accused of treachery. Thus, in the third generation's narratives, the guardians are not "traitors" but illiterate local peasant or tribal people who simply did not understand the bigger picture or the unfolding Zionist (and Arab) master plan. 'Ammar related the following when I asked him about how his understanding of the Nakba differed from that of the generation of Palestine:

> When they simply tell you, they tell you about—first of all, they left illiterate, they didn't know what schools meant, what awareness meant, this is in contradistinction to the cities, some people left the cities and they were educated and they knew what the Nakba meant and—when they simply

tell you that "we were expelled" or "we were hosted in nearby countries" so that we could go back as soon as the problem with the Israelis ends. This is a naive people's talk, and a lack of comprehension and a lack of in-depth thinking. Now we, what do we think of the Nakba? It is a conspiring between various entities, Zionists, states, in order to expel a people from their land, and to take over their country.[26]

The third generation's contentious narratives are constructed in terms of a cumulative understanding of the events leading up to and unfolding during the conquest of Palestine, as well the conspiring of the Zionists and Arab regimes that made the conquest possible. In this narrative, it is the guardians' parochialism that did not allow them to see the bigger, master plan. Had the guardians seen what was in store for them, they may have held on to their land at all costs, as those Palestinians who remained have been doing since 1948. Another interviewee, Ayman, summed this up as follows:

Now, look, those [survivors] of 1948 don't have difficulties because they lived through it, they lived through the suffering, they lived through the suffering, meaning that they have the excuse that allows them to say why they left. But, this new generation, this generation is becoming aware, you can no longer tell a child, or a young man, at the beginning of his [adult] life, that they killed us. He will tell you—we are in fact having this conversation now [between the generations]—okay, they killed us, and then we went and fled because they were going to kill us. So why do you leave in the first place? Die in your own countries. This is the kind of conversation that happens between the different generations, the discussion between our generation and the generation of the grandparents, why did you leave and make us refugees, and stamped this name on our identity [cards], this word. Why didn't you stay and die in the homeland, you would have at least died as martyrs, and at least we would have either stayed in Palestine or not have come to this life. Rather than having come—and [then] this word "refugee." The old person [usually] says, "Well, we fought as much as we could but no one supported us." . . . This is how the discussion and the conversation unfolds between [the two generations]: "No, you should have remained in Palestine." The Nakba generation says, "No, we suffered and we saw unspeakable horrors and that is why we fled, that is why we left, on the basis that we are going back," and of course there were Arab promises, external promises, guaranteeing the return, but no promises were fulfilled.[27]

Ayman's narrative is an eloquent summary of the third generation's understanding of what constitutes Nakba memory. Blaming the guardians for fleeing in 1948 is possible only as the cumulative catastrophes of Israeli settler-colonialism in Palestine demonstrate that they could have stayed no matter what. Further, their decision to flee in part resulted from their parochial view of the events that engulfed Palestine in 1948, a "lack of awareness" of the overall plan to rid Palestine of its inhabitants. Had they known, they would have remained regardless of the massacres that they were subjected to. What is contentious is therefore not so much the details around the Nakba-as-war but the actions that were or were not taken by the guardians, articulated as the lingering effects of these decisions on third-generation lives. The guardians are therefore simultaneously blamed for leaving yet vindicated from the seemingly harsher judgment of being traitors. The guardians in these narratives thus play a very different role than the one they attribute to themselves in their own memories of catastrophes. One is, of course, also left to wonder what conversation, if any, different generations of Palestinian refugees in Syria are having now in light of the war and the unprecedented death and displacement it has wrought on the post-Palestine generations.

CONCLUSION

Second- and third-generation Palestinian refugees' imaginative investment in their postmemories revolves around the guardians' memories of loss. These powerful postmemories, which are imagined as memories of one's own, are informed by the narration and transmission of the communities and worlds of the guardians' former lives, envisioned as Palestine. In view of this, the Nakba does not figure as a postmemory; it figures in the post-Palestine generations' narratives on what they understand to constitute Nakba memory. These narratives engage the memories that circulate in the guardians' communities as well as the Nakba's myriad significations in its Arab and Palestinian universes of discourse examined throughout this book.

The meanings of 1948 in the post-Palestine generation's narratives are shared insofar as the Nakba is understood to revolve around its repercussions. There are also important generationally dependent differences in what constitutes Nakba memory. For the second generation, the Nakba is seen as extending into their own lives. In addition, their own temporal proximity to the generation of Palestine and this generation's memories of catastrophes means that their narratives more closely and sympathetically engage these memories when making meaning of the Nakba. In contrast, the third generation's temporal distance to the generation of Palestine's memories means that they prioritize the Nakba's myriad patriotic and nationalist significations when articulating their own understandings of 1948. Invoking those who remained and the implicit notion of the "ongoing Nakba" in occupied Palestine, third-generation narratives on Nakba memory challenge the guardians' self-ascribed role, especially insofar as the question of leaving is concerned.

Thus, the Nakba has undergone numerous historically and politically contingent shifts in meaning and signification. While the Nakba was first conceptualized within the context of the ascendant Arab nationalist liberation project of the post–World War II era, geopolitical regional transformation led to the eclipse of this Arab nationalist universe of discourse in 1967. The Nakba's contemporary emergence as a Palestinian catastrophe meant that it took on particular patriotic and memorial dimensions in light of the transformation of the Palestinian liberation movement. After Oslo, Palestinian refugee activists in Syria, as in other countries, mobilized memories of the Nakba primarily to refute the Palestinian leadership's separation of Palestinian liberation from return. In commemorating 1948 and mobilizing for the eventual return, activists also created pervasive popular memory discourses in their communities. In these discourses, the Nakba came to occupy a singular importance in terms of marking their communities' times and spaces, and the idea of memory itself took on a newfound political value.

In addition to the newfound meanings of the Nakba in its contemporary Palestinian universe of discourse, its memories and significations also circulate in various ways and with different competing and sometimes contradictory connotations in Palestinian refugee communities. In telling about the narration and transmission of memories in these communities, the post-Palestine generations emphasized that in their families, the generation of Palestine narrated memories that revolved around all that was lost, and what was transmitted to them was therefore loss itself. As shown in this chapter, these generations' postmemories imagine this loss as Palestine, while the Nakba figures in their narratives on what is understood to constitute Nakba memory. These narratives engage the generation of Palestine's memories and the Nakba's contingent, fluid, and shifting nationalist, patriotic, and memory discourses' significations that have been in circulation since the making of the Nakba.

The Palestine generation, whose members I theorized as the guardians of memory, given their real or purported roles in the narration and transmission of memories that are also intended to ensure the return, is the only generation with memories of both Palestine and the Nakba. Nevertheless, given the social nature of memory-making, the guardians related their memories in conversation with the various meanings of the Nakba examined throughout this book. Most important, the common memories that circulate in the guardians' communities of memories and loss are testament to yet another meaning of the Nakba today, one embodied in the very possibility of their communities existing in light of and despite the complete devastation of 1948. The guardians' communities today have been devastated and shattered for the final time through war, and only time will tell what is to become of their larger Syrian Palestinian refugee communities.

CONCLUSION

THE CATASTROPHES OF TODAY, THE CATASTROPHE OF 1948

I was thinking to myself, when our families left Palestine in 1948 and settled in Khan Eshieh, their intention was to be close to their homelands. A place from where they could immediately return once their crisis was over, a place from where every single one of them could immediately return to their own home. But unfortunately, their crisis was to be prolonged, it took a long time, and they began to yearn and to miss their homeland. And unfortunately, the dream of return did not realize itself, and so they decided to remain in the camp and to turn it into a little Palestine or a little homeland. They began to work on the farms and the lands and inside homes, and they did in fact succeed and managed to turn the camp into a little and very beautiful homeland. And they became attached to it and made us attached to it as well without anyone realizing this. And now the crisis of our age has unfolded, and we also left, and people started renting apartments close to the camp in 'Artuz, Jdayda, and Sahnaya, and here we are sitting and waiting to return to our homes. And what I fear is the length of the crisis and for everyone to create his own personal homeland because we Palestinians cannot live without a homeland. But did you see how they thought it too much for us to remain in a little homeland that is three kilometers by four kilometers? This little homeland that is in fact very, very large. . . . [The generation of Palestine] are the ones who created this homeland for us, most of them are now gone, and this is why we may remain without a homeland for the rest of our lives. Because we are weak and our worries have broken us, while their worries made them strong.

AHLAM, NOW A MOTHER DISPLACED FROM KHAN ESHIEH TO A
DAMASCUS SUBURB, DECEMBER 2014

enquired about the fate of Abu Samih, who at the beginning of 2013 had withstood what seemed to be the new Nakba by not leaving Rejeh Square after the majority of Yarmouk Camp's inhabitants had left in December 2012. By early 2015, the square and camp were unrecognizable even to those who knew the camp's every alleyway and corner. The rubble, the ruins of bombed buildings, tired and hungry people, and haunted alleyways and streets are the painful remains of a shattered community. Yarmouk is not the only Palestinian locality in Syria, of course, but it was in many ways the Palestinians' social, cultural, political, and even symbolic heart. It has therefore become emblematic of the catastrophe of the Palestinians in Syria whose communities may neither survive nor heal.

Whatever remained of the camp after the exodus of its people in December 2012 was leveled in the wake of the April 2015 appearance of the Islamic State of Iraq and Syria (ISIS) fighters as yet another armed group in and within its vicinity (AM 2013; Murphy 2015). Three years later, the army began a concerted aerial and ground offensive against the camp in a bid to drive out ISIS. A relief worker with access to the environs of the camp privately noted that of the estimated 18,000 who remained in Yarmouk following the December 2012 exodus, only 2,000–4,000 remained after ISIS. Today, the numbers are substantially lower. Abu Samih and his family, I was told by the activists who captured his photo at the end of 2012, did eventually leave, but they were scattered within Syria, in Egypt, and beyond. The Qadsayya suburb of Damascus, to which some members of Abu Samih's family, like many other families of Yarmouk, were displaced, has a market that reminds one of the previous bustling markets of Yarmouk's Lubya Street, I was told by a former resident of Yarmouk in Beirut. Lubya Street, named after a village in the Tiberias subdistrict, is today a devastated shadow of its former self, destroyed sixty-four years after the destruction of its namesake.

Qadsayya is no longer a safe haven from the conflict, like most areas meant to be safe havens in the Damascus and the Rural Damascus Governorates. Nothing new, a friend in Qadsayya told me at the beginning of 2014. The "problems" have also arrived here, and the area is under lockdown. People cannot leave, as rents have skyrocketed and landowners are asking for a year's rent in advance. A year later, she tells me that they no longer know how things are and do not keep up with word-of-mouth news; they simply try to get on with their lives. I ask her about the new Lubya Street in Qadsayya, and she sends photos of it that are worlds away from the Lubya Street of Yarmouk. She tells me that it is in fact a sight that makes her cry: zinc shacks erected by the people of Yarmouk in order to sell rationed vegetables and secondhand clothes.

It is from the inbetween of the imagined and the actual "Lubya Street" of Qadsayya and the Lubya Street of Yarmouk that I frequented daily all those years ago, that the conclusion of a book on memories and histories of the 1948 Nakba in Syria is now written. It is also written from the inbetween of images of the rubble that is Lubya Street in Yarmouk today and memories of Lubya in Palestine. What does it mean to conclude a book meant to examine Nakba memories of shattered communities five years into the beginning of their shattering anew? And what implications does this have for the arguments that were made, and the conclusions that can be reached? The communities of which I wrote, and the Syria that made their memories and histories possible, no longer exist as they did before 2011, and they tragically continue to be devastated. While this ongoing devastation has clear implications for the arguments made in the book, I can neither write a conclusion to the unfolding events nor provide a conclusive summary of the new meanings of the Nakba in post-2011 Syria.

In what follows, I bring the book to an end by moving between the past and the present. This is the past that made memories of 1948 possible, and of which I wrote, and the present marked by a catastrophe that the displaced post-Palestine generations now insist far exceeds the Nakba of 1948.

* * *

al-Dhiyabiyya, April 22, 2008

During an unusually hot, scorching spring day, the sun mercilessly beat down on a friend, her friend whom I had interviewed earlier in the day, and I as we made our way through the alleyways of Dhiyabiyya, an urban sprawl that houses the people who were uprooted from Golan some fifty years ago, and who have now been uprooted yet again . . . Inside one of the houses, we were welcomed by the family, and served cold drinks . . . I asked whether I could meet the late Umm Nimr, the interviewee's grandmother, and I was told that she lay inside the room, too frail to leave the mattress where she spends most of her days. . . . I walked into the room with my friend who is eager to listen to stories of al-hajje, literally, "the bolt" or "the dash," a name that many guardians from the tribes of Safad and Tiberias, both of settled-Bedouin and Ghawarina origins in Palestine,[1] use in order to connote the Nakba, and a name that I heard used yet again after the 2013 uprooting to Lebanon . . . At one point Umm Nimr lost her patience with my clear difficulty in understanding her dialect and reproached me... I was lost as I tried to make meaning of her unfamiliar expression, but I did pick up the story of the killing of the people in the fields of Akrad al-Baqqara, and their multiple wanderings from one place to another until the final hajje of 1956 . . . After we bring our interview to an end, she continued narrating the multiple wanderings after the occupation of the Golan, and their departure yet again . . . to different refugee camps, and the setting up of new homes and lives that were repeatedly disrupted. . . . "We have become gypsies, my daughter," she said as she reflected on her life's story . . . These words come back to me as I think of her natural passing before her family was displaced all over yet again, and one of her grandchildren and his wife disappeared at the hands of security men, and her great-grandchildren now orphans in the ongoing Syrian nightmare . . .

I accidently ran into an acquaintance from Yarmouk Camp in Beirut two weeks after the appearance of ISIS as a new actor in the camp in April 2015. He shared photos of Yarmouk's Palestine Street, which is no longer a street at all, and related the names of some of the unquantifiable number of armed leaders and groups within and around Yarmouk. He also described the realities of life in the greater Damascus metropolitan area for those who, like him, remain within a patchwork of areas controlled by the regime and armed groups. I interrupt to remind him of the research project that I undertook all those years ago. I note that talking about memories and histories of 1948 now feels as far removed from the present as did the days in which we would spend numerous evenings in Dar al-Shajara discussing Palestine, memory, and the return. Those evenings were shared with a number of common friends and acquaintances who are no longer with us, I remarked as I recalled their names. He insists that all those active in community relief efforts like himself have not given up on the patriotic education of community members, but that the priorities have now changed. People's everyday worries revolve around making ends meet, getting aid, and, above all, getting out of Syria. What does it mean, he tells me, when the Nakba for people has been transformed into the return to a limited geographical locality like Yarmouk Camp?

The Nakba, as I have argued, has always been a historically and politically contingent signifier. This has been the case through its Arab and Palestinian universes of discourse, and through first-, second-, and third-generation Palestinian refugees' memories, histories, and narratives, and the very possibility of their communities as such. That the Nakba has today gained different meanings and significations for Palestinians in light of the Syrian war therefore comes as no surprise.

The importance of the Nakba before 2011, as demonstrated, lay in the ways in which the temporal and spatial referents of the guardians' Nakba memories provided the symbolic contours around which communities would come to crystallize from the ruins of the devastation 1948 wrought. This meaning of the Nakba is being invoked today by the post-Palestine generations but implicated in a reverse process. The Nakba is in many ways now also about the destruction of the seventy-year-old Palestinian communities in Syria that were constituted anew in the aftermath of 1948. The near-universal insistence by the post-Palestine generations that this current catastrophe far exceeds the one of 1948 is rooted in the fear, perhaps even reality, that unlike 1948, this devastation may be final, given the relentlessness of the Syrian war.

Another important meaning of the Nakba before 2011 in Syria, as highlighted in this book, was implicated in the ways in which Right of Return Movement (RoRM) activists tied the Nakba's memory and the imperative to remember to political claims. These claims refuse to accept the Palestine Liberation Organization's (PLO) institutionalization of the separation between liberation and return through its moribund Oslo statist project. What this means is an insistence that the liberation of Palestinians from Israeli military occupation in 1967-occupied Palestine is not possible without the implementation of the Palestinian refugees' right to return to their lands in historic Palestine, or present day Israel. The Oslo Accords has transformed Palestine into the West Bank and the Gaza Strip. In addition, liberation and return have become about the "right of return," and this right has become negotiable and limited to the Occupied Palestinian Territories (OPT). This reality continues to be seen as not fulfilling the refugees' political rights and aspirations. Israel has in any case consistently refused to allow the refugees to return regardless of to where this return is supposed to take place.

Linking memories of the Nakba and pre-1948 Palestine more generally with the imperative to remember in order to return was a strategy RoRM activists used to mobilize in their communities. This mobilization was ultimately a political project formulated in a Palestinian national arena of contention. This political project both contested the Israeli state's settler-colonial division of historic Palestine into different geographic, political, and legal areas, and first the PLO's, and later the Palestinian Authority's, complicity in this. Although RoRM activism may have been substantially curtailed or suspended as a result of the Syrian war, what activists did through community-based mobilization continues to provide the possibility of thinking beyond the failed two-state solution that is today a cover for the Israeli settler-colonial status quo. Their political vision considers Palestinians' settler-colonized and stateless present synchronously. This present is represented by the refugees denied the right to return to their lands, which became a part of the Jewish state in 1948, because they are not Jewish. It is also represented by the second-class, non-Jewish Palestinian citizens of the Israeli state that defines itself as a Jewish state. Finally, it is also represented by the noncitizens living under a five-decade, brutal military settler-colonial regime allowing limited self-rule in a few areas under the authority of a complacent, unrepresentative, and corrupt leadership in the OPT.

The memory/return matrix at the heart of RoRM activists' mobilization of Nakba memories could therefore be read as a radical political project that calls for the decolonization of the Israeli state. The Israeli state is today for all intents and purposes one settler-colonial state that rules over all Palestinian communities that remained within the borders of British-ruled Palestine. It is radical because it dares to think beyond what the PLO or PA can ever offer by way of a coherent anticolonial liberation project. It is also radical in refusing to accept Israel's divide-and-conquer settler-colonial status-quo imposed upon all Palestinian lives since the Nakba. It therefore provides room to imagine alternative futures in which fragmented Palestinian communities under Israeli rule or in exile could finally live as equals alongside Israeli Jews in a nonsectarian state.

What are the implications for these alternative futures when the return today has had to be reprioritized, as related through my chance encounter in Beirut with the acquaintance from Yarmouk? When the return to Palestine has to take a backseat to the war in Syria and the urgent need of return to Palestinian camps and communities in the face of the relentless destruction of both? These questions are neither meant to absolve the Israeli state from the crimes it committed in 1948 nor to deny that according to international humanitarian law, refugees have an enshrined right to return to where they come from if they wish to do so. Nor are they meant to absolve Israel of its primary responsibility for blocking the Palestinian refugees' right of return or their ability to live as equal citizens alongside Israeli Jews in Israel and its constituent OPT. Indeed, these questions amplify the need to acknowledge Palestinian refugees' rights and Israel's obligation to provide restitution at a time when all exits have been closed to them in Syria.

With that said, these questions are also meant to provide an opening for thinking beyond this logic of recognition, as the latter has clearly not been able to translate the right of return into reality. This is not to deny that the demand for acknowledgment, justice, and restitution for the Israeli crimes of the 1948 Nakba continue to be important. Rather, it is to underscore that the Israeli state, as the power-wielding party against a stateless Palestinian population, has simply refused to cede this recognition since 1948 while

Palestinian refugee communities have been devastated as a matter of fact in different Arab countries. This has taken place in Lebanon, Kuwait, Libya, Iraq, and now Syria. In addition, Palestinians in the OPT and Israel have been subjected to unchecked military belligerence and colonial brutality, the latest in the Gaza Strip in the summer of 2014. To be sure, the United States, European Union, Arab states, and PLO have all been complicit in Israel's refusal to recognize its historical and contemporary injustices against Palestinians, to implement the right of return, and to end the occupation. In view of these factors, how can one begin to think through moving beyond a recognition whose structural realities have allowed Israel to continue its denial and violence as well as the de facto repeated destruction of various Palestinian communities in both Israel and the Arab world?

I consider the possibility of moving beyond this recognition by returning to the realities of the communities in Syria, whose memories and histories I have explored throughout this book, and to the tragic reality of their shattering anew. I visited Rashidieh Camp in the south of Lebanon, the southernmost UNRWA refugee camp in the country, in April 2015. Sitting in the room of the family of a friend who came to Lebanon from one of the more remote Damascus camps, we were by the sea to the west and farmlands to the south. Of course, there somewhere beyond the farmlands, we were also by the source of Nakba memories and histories and Palestinians' political claims and aspirations. This is the historic Palestine of the people of Rashidieh as well as the newcomers from Syria, the present-day Israel by whom and to which the return has been consistently denied.

Our conversations centered on the catastrophe in Syria and the hardships of those seeking a safe haven in Lebanon, where the family were living in legal limbo after Palestinians from Syria were blocked from entering the country. I was also told stories of the unhappiness of relatives who finally made it to Europe at the price of being cut off from their families and communities. Historic Palestine, so near yet so far from Rashidieh Camp, was recalled to underscore the extent of the calamity in Syria. The catastrophe of today is incomparable—indeed, it dwarfs—the Nakba of 1948, I was told. In terms of available options, hope of return was expressed through prayers for the return of Syria as a country and to homes left behind in it, whether they were still standing or in ruins. The northern European promise of access to a life of permanence and banal normality that was so abruptly ended by the war was emphatically no substitute for the dream of the return of Syria as it existed prior to the war and the return to it. Education, medical care, housing, work, and the social safety net of Europe were, after all, benefits enjoyed by all in Syria.

These are therefore hopes and aspirations of return that give new meanings to the Nakba as past and present catastrophe in light of the Syrian war. They are, I contend, fundamentally tied to the historical, social, and political experiences of the Palestinian refugee community in Syria. More specifically, they are tied to the possibilities and realities these different experiences have engendered. Syria allowed for multiple belongings, among them a belonging to the Palestine that informed the narration and transmission of memories of loss in families. At the same time, these belongings were concretely rooted in communities in Syria, as explored through their common memories, postmemories, and narratives on memories in this book, that were formed as a result of the 1948 Nakba but were nevertheless communities of Syria. It is true that these belongings may have been ambivalent, especially as related by the post-Oslo generations' sense of both belonging and not belonging in the country. They were nevertheless an important component of what made common memories, histories, and realities of shared communities possible. In addition, it is the multiple, rather than ambivalent, belongings that have taken precedence as a result of the war. In other words, as a result of the destruction of communities in Syria and the displaced Palestinians' yearning for these lost worlds, the dream of the return of the country to its previous self and their return to it is very strongly articulated. So much so, that it glosses over the realities of the ambivalence that may have existed before 2011.

References to the current catastrophe, which far exceeds that of 1948, are therefore being invoked from within these multiple sites of belonging. These are the different and multiple belongings to Palestine and Syria, as explored here through Nakba memories, histories, and communities. They are also different and multiple belongings to a Palestine within Syria, which is the belonging that is now most strongly articulated in light of the war. It is both limiting and short-sighted to translate these belongings into superficially understanding Palestinians from Syria as being really Syrians, a notion used as the basis of petty and at times institutional discrimination against them by Palestinians in Lebanon. It is similarly limiting and short-sighted to set up the two as competing political demands—the return to Palestine and now to Syria—of seeing the latter as taking away from the ultimate patriotic demand for the return to Palestine or as absolving Israel from the Palestinians' statelessness.

Palestinian communities belonging to both Palestine and Syria, the source of the demand of a return to them, challenges us to think beyond the British and French colonial era–carved nation-states that have so violently failed in the Arab East. These colonial relics and their consolidation through Israeli settler-colonialism and Arab absolute monarchist or totalitarian republican rule have failed to deliver on Palestinian self-determination. These states also fell apart, first in Lebanon, later Iraq, and now Syria. It is these modern nation-states, which are also the source of the logic of recognition, and their structural realities that have allowed Israel to maintain the status quo while refusing to cede the return.

Palestinians' different belongings and their articulation through the shifting meanings of the 1948 Nakba in light of the Syrian war point to the realities of the Palestinians' communities in Syria as transcending these colonial and settler-colonial modern nation-states of the Arab East. They are belongings to a historic Palestine whose geography transcends present-day settler-colonial Israel through these communities' embodiment of the 1948 Nakba. They are also belongings to a Syria that transcends its modern French colonial–carved borders, as most clearly expressed through invocation of the catastrophes of today and yesterday in light of the renewed devastation and shattering. They are therefore also belongings to an idea of a Palestine and a Syria of the past, during which their borders did not exist, and also of their potential future. The realities of Palestinian refugee communities in Syria as explored through Nakba memories and histories in this book could be said to embody political potentialities that may have been a product of, but also clearly transcend, the nation-state order left behind by the British and the French in the Arab East.

NOTES

PREFACE AND ACKNOWLEDGMENTS

1. There is a discrepancy in references to the number of localities destroyed and Palestinians expelled in 1948. I use Ilan Pappe's cited groundbreaking work on the 1948 Nakba for statistics that pertain to the war on the Palestinians.
2. The Peruvian sociologist Aníbal Quijano argues that the contemporary hegemonic global distribution of power has an element of "coloniality" insofar as its origins lie in a specific modern/colonial racialized Eurocentered system of capitalism. This system was established through the conquest and settler-colonization of the Americas, the extermination of the Indigenous population and slavery. The coloniality of knowledge is this power configuration's epistemic dimension based on the logic of coloniality or Eurocentrism.
3. UNRWA is the UN agency established in 1950 to provide immediate relief and assistance to the Palestinian refugees on a temporary mandate that has been renewed annually ever since (UNGA 1949). GAPAR is the main state body responsible for the Palestinians in Syria (GAPAR n/a). I return to both bodies in more detail in chapter 2.
4. Most interviewees consented to the use of their real names, done so unless indicated otherwise. I have used interviewees' first names or titles in a way that is recognizable and accountable to them. In order to provide context, I have included brief background information, like the generation, village of origin, and profession of the interviewee, as well as the date and place of the interview. In addition, although I met and interviewed most activists and UNRWA and GAPAR staff in a public capacity, I have similarly referred to the interviews, especially of activists, in a way that is recognizable only to the interviewees or their group. Ultimately, the conclusions derived from these interviews are mine.

INTRODUCTION

1. Khalid Bakrawi was a community activist who wrote about the historic 2011 Nakba Day March (Dawla 2013). In this march, Palestinian refugee youths

crossed into the Israeli-occupied Syrian Golan Heights. I return to the March and Bakrawi's article below.

2. Hassan Hassan was an actor, film and theater producer and a member of the artists' collective al-Tajamu' al-Falastini lil-Ibda' (The Palestinian Assembly of Creativity). The Assembly was a Yarmouk Camp-based collective that produced an online social commentary show, "Rad Fi'l" (Reaction), about everyday life in the camp. The show is available to view on YouTube. Private Communication with a member of the Assembly, March 22, 2015.

    The interview with the late Hassan was conducted as part of the Axel Salvatori-Sinz–directed film *The Shebabs of Yarmouk* (2013). I wish to thank Axel Salvatori-Sinz for making his film available to me.

3. Yarmouk Camp News seems to have moved to a new Facebook page in August 2013, and as a result, links to images and text on the old page no longer work. The aftermath of the bombing can still be seen as captured on camera and uploaded to YouTube (al-Keswani 2013).

4. Al-Husayni was of an old Jerusalem family that had long held religious-judicial posts in the Ottoman administration of their town. He was appointed grand mufti of Jerusalem and presided over the Supreme Muslim Council under British colonial role. Using his positions and influence, he played an important role in Palestinian national politics. An arrest warrant by the colonial authorities forced him to flee during the 1936–1939 popular uprising known as Thawrat Falastin al-Kubra (The Great Palestine Revolution, often translated as "Revolt") (Pappe 1997; 2006b, 85–107).

5. In Arabic, "nationalism" (*al-qawmiyya*) is reserved for the Arab nation. State-based "nationalism," such as Palestinian, Iraqi, Syrian, or Egyptian, is referred to as "patriotism" (*al-wataniyya*). Where relevant, I refer to (Palestinian) patriotism in order to draw a clear distinction from (Arab) nationalism. When discussing the making of the Palestinian national (patriotic) refugee community in Syria as well as the Palestinian national (patriotic) movement without reference to Arab nationalism, I refer to Palestinian nationalism rather than patriotism as per its common English translation.

6. The Oslo Accords refer to agreements between the Palestine Liberation Organization (PLO) and the Israeli state that began with the signing of a "Declaration of Principles" in 1993. These were based on granting the PLO limited self-rule in parts of the 1967 Occupied Palestinian Territories, through the accords-created Palestinian Authority, in exchange for the recognition of Israel's right to exist on the parts of Palestine occupied in 1948. Also known as the "Peace Process," these accords ushered in a period of negotiations on "final status issues" that were meant to eventually result in a Palestinian state (Chomsky 1999, 533–565).

7. See UNRWA's Syria Crises page for up-to-date statistics that pertain to the Palestinian refugee community in Syria (http://www.unrwa.org/syria-crisis).

8. The only other Palestinian refugee community that maintained its refugee status while enjoying substantial rights was the small Palestinian refugee community in Iraq. However, most Palestinian refugees left Iraq after their persecution in the civil war that followed the American invasion and destruction of the country.

The minority that remains has now been stripped of the right to permanently live in Iraq (see Al-Hardan 2009).

9. This echoes a similar argument made by the Marxist professor of philosophy Sadik Jalal al-Azm some forty years ago, to which I turn in the next chapter.

10. The ANM was important in terms of early Palestinian political organizing and preoccupation with the Nakba in relation to the resolution of the Palestine question within the context of the larger Arab liberation question. It was inspired by Constantine Zurayk's variant of revolutionary pan-Arab nationalism. What distinguished the ANM was the strong, though not exclusive, Palestinian element that in 1951 coalesced around the American University of Beirut and founded the group. Nevertheless, the ANM, like other nationalist movements and currents at the time, continued to advocate Arab unity as the path toward the liberation of Palestine. This approach was encapsulated in its early slogan "No dignity without revenge, and no solution without unity." The movement would come to change its course during the 1950s and to advocate for organizing the "displaced" (i.e., Palestinian refugees) for the Arab liberation battle. It was also the precursor of the Palestinian guerrilla Marxist group the Popular Front for the Liberation of Palestine, and its splinter group, the Democratic Front for the Liberation of Palestine. The Ba'th Party, in contrast, was first founded as the Resurrection Party by Michel 'Aflaq and Salah al-Bitar in Damascus in 1940. The Ba'th joined forces with the Arab Socialist Party in 1953 and became the Arab Socialist Resurrection Party, most commonly known as the Ba'th (Resurrection) Party. As the Ba'thist slogan "One Arab nation with an immortal mission" suggests, the Ba'th eventually became a pan-Arab nationalist party with regional country-based branches that espoused pan-Arab unity and an Arab variant of socialism. It prioritized nationalism over internationalism, as well as anticolonialism, all goals to be achieved through revolutionary means (Y. Sayigh 1991b; al-Sharif 1995, 48–56).

11. Fatah is the reverse acronym of the Palestinian Patriotic (National) Liberation Movement, established in 1957 (Y. Sayigh 2004, 80–87).

12. The June War (Harb Huzayran), often referred to in English by its Hebrew "Six-Day War," saw the Israeli defeat and occupation of parts of Egypt (Sinai Peninsula and Egyptian-controlled Gaza Strip), Syria (Golan Heights), and Jordan (Jordanian-controlled West Bank) in six days in June 1967 (Shlaim and Louis 2012).

13. The Arabic- and English-language literature on the Palestinians in Syria is very limited (see, e.g., Abdul-Rahim 2005; Al-Mawed 1999, 2002; Badwan 2004; Bin Khadra' 1999; Brand 1988c; Chatty 2010, 220–230; Gabiam 2009, 2012, 2014, 2016; Hanafi 1996, 2003, 2011; Kodmani-Darwish 1997, 93–108; Napolitano 2011, 2012, 2013; Rizqallah 1998; al-Sahli 2001; Sarhan 2005; Suleiman 1994; Tiltnes 2006).

14. In view of this, the deadlier Naksa Day march that took place three weeks later, on the forty-fourth anniversary of the June War, faced greater opposition within the camp. However, it was Palestinian youths who marched to the border yet again and who ultimately paid the price with their lives. The late Khalid Bakrawi (2012), who did not take part in the first Nakba march, took part in the Naksa march, and was shot by Israeli soldiers. See his article, cited in the opening epigraph of the chapter, which discusses his motives for taking part in the march. There is another firsthand account of both marches written by a former Syrian Arab Red Crescent worker (Bitari 2013).

15. The Action Group for Palestinians of Syria (AGPS) is a Palestinian Return Center initiative founded in London in October 2012 in order to document and raise awareness of the Palestinians' human rights situation in Syria. It is predominantly composed of Palestinian refugees from Syria in London and a network of activists on the ground in Syria and in the surrounding states, most of whom were also active in the RoRM. Private communication with AGPS activist, November 19, 2013.

16. According to Tarek Hamoud (2012), who carried out research in the camp shortly after the neighborhood adjacent to it was attacked by the Syrian army in August 2011, the camp was not subjected to shelling by the Syrian navy, as mainstream media narratives suggested. Most residents left the camp after warnings by the Syrian army, and the damage and fatalities that ensued were a result of the attack on the adjacent neighborhood rather than the camp itself.

17. The website of AGPS (http://www.actionpal.org.uk/en/) provides up-to-date statistics and reports on the current situation in Syria.

1. THE NAKBA IN ARAB THOUGHT

1. The works examined in this chapter are limited to this group, given the importance of Arab nationalism and its derivative ideologies and political currents for the period in question. The work of the Marxist Sadik Jalal al-Azm in the post-1967 period is included here for comparison with the nationalist position on the new defeat as yet another catastrophe or setback (*naksa*). The works of Islamists is beyond the scope of this chapter.

2. There have been recent reviews of some of this literature (see, e.g., Gluck 2008, 2012; Slyomovics 2013). The literature is multilingual and interdisciplinary (see, e.g., 'Abd al-Da'im 1998; Abdel Jawad 2008; Allan 2005, 2013; Ben-Ze'ev 2011; Damir-Geilsdorf 2009; Esmeir 2003; Hammami 2010; Hill 2005; Kabha 2006b; Kassem 2011; Khader 2008; Masalha 2005, 2012; Sa'di 2002, 2008; Sa'di and Abu-Lughod 2007; Saloul 2012; Schnieper 2012; al-Sharif 2008).

3. I wish to thank Huda Zurayk for her input on her late father's biography.

4. According to Benny Morris (2004, 111), al-Hawwari may have been a Haganah Intelligence Agency agent.

5. UN General Assembly Resolution 181 adopted the partition of Palestine into an Arab and a Jewish state (UNGA 1947).

6. The fifth volume is the appendix to the first four; the sixth is a compilation of the names of the war dead on the Arab side, including soldiers and irregular volunteers, Palestinians and non-Palestinians, listing the place and the circumstances of their death when known. There is an additional volume, *Al-Nakba fi Suwar: Nakbat al-'Arab fi Falastin* (The catastrophe in pictures: The Arabs' catastrophe in Palestine) (1961). It comprises Nakba photographs but does not seem to be a part of the six core historical volumes of *Nakba*.

7. Al-Tal (1959, 587–599) does, however, state that as early as December 1948 he began plotting a military coup that never materialized.

8. It seems that a second part never materialized, even though al-Tal states that the second part was to include the historical sections removed from the first. He intended to cover topics such as the history of the East Bank of the Jordan River

and how it was founded by Winston Churchill in order to serve Zionist interests, a study of John Glubb, the British commander of Transjordan's army, the Arab Legion, a study of the Legion, and a study of Palestine from the ancient era and until the UN Partition Resolution of 1947.

9. The Suez War—or the Tripartite Aggression (al-'Udwan al-Thulathi), as it is known in Arabic—saw Israel, Britain, and France invade Egypt in October 1956, shortly after Nasser nationalized the Suez Canal in July 1956. US and Soviet diplomatic and economic interventions, however, led to their withdrawal. This gave a major boost to Nasser and Nasserism (Y. Sayigh 2004, 19).

10. Nasserism refers to the broad political current associated with Nasser, the July Revolution, and Nasser's regional policies and actions during the 1950s and 1960s. Nasserism was a powerful contender for regional leadership after the Suez War. It espoused revolutionary pan-Arab nationalism based on socialism that distinguished itself from the former East Bloc by being a distinctly Arab variant of socialism attuned to the Arab world's pan-Arab nationalist desired ends. These ends included social and economic modernization, industrialization, anticolonialism, anti-imperialism, and ultimately unification. The person of Nasser and Nasserism more generally gained further prominence in the wake of the short-lived unification of Egypt and Syria in the United Arab Republic (UAR) (1958–1961). Nasser was also a leading founder and member of the Non-Aligned Movement (Kerr 1971; Torrey and Delvin 1965).

11. The October War refers to the joint Egyptian-Syrian attempt to liberate their respective territories occupied by Israel during the June War. They did this through a surprise attack on Israeli positions in these territories in 1973. Although they initially made military gains, these were reversed by Israel (see Bordeaux 2001).

12. She also notes that the first professional attempt to record the Nakba was that of a Palestinain graduate student (see Nazzal 1978).

13. See note 2.

14. The publication of this exchange led to an ideologically driven controversy among international genocide scholars. This involved the US-born director of the Israel-based Institute of the Holocaust and Genocide, Israel Charny, who posted public ad hominem attacks against Shaw on the listserv of the International Association of Genocide Scholars (IAoGS). The attacks included charges of anti-Semitism, Holocaust denial, and the psychopathologization of Shaw. Charny, a past president of the academic association, was censured by the IAoGS, which also issued an apology to Shaw (Beckerman 2011, Shaw 2013).

2. THE PALESTINIAN REFUGEE COMMUNITY IN SYRIA

1. Abu Subhi, interviewed by the author, June 2008, Qabr Essit Camp.

2. A number of camps received an influx of the internally displaced Palestinians from the Golan. In some camps, like Qabr Essit and Dera'a, there are old (1948) and new (1967) established quarters.

3. GAPAR Personal Affairs and Statistics Department civil servant, interviewed by the author, July 2008, Damascus.

4. Umm Ya'rub, interviewed by the author, February 2008, Damascus.

5. Abu Ahmad, interviewed by the author, June 2008, Damascus.
6. Abu Samih, interviewed by the author, May 2008, Yarmouk Camp.
7. Umm Rim, interviewed by the author, April 2008, Damascus.
8. Abu Khalil, interviewed by the author, March 2008, Khan Eshieh Camp.
9. Umm 'Izz al-Din, interviewed by the author, May 2008, Yarmouk Camp.
10. GAPAR Personal Affairs and Statistics Department interview.
11. UNRWA Eligibility and Registration Office employee, interviewed by the author, June 2008, Damascus. In 2008 the number of UNRWA-registered Palestinian refugees living in Ramadan was 1,000. According to the Action Group for Palestinian of Syria, by February 2013 this number had risen to 4,000 residents in addition to an influx of 200 internally displaced families from Yarmouk Camp (AGPS 2013a). UNRWA estimates that, as of February 2018, there are 393 families and 1,600 individuals in hard-to-reach Ramadan (UNRWA 2018).
12. GAPAR Personal Affairs and Statistics Department interview.
13. The Palestinians' lack of internal mobility within Syria before the war, as the authors of the survey argue, may have indeed been tied to private home ownership and equal access to state services regardless of place of abode. Their lack of external mobility, however, cannot be explained only by lack of labor market competitiveness, as the analysts of the survey do. The policies of Arab states regarding Palestinian refugees more generally need to be taken into account. This is particularly the case with regards to the difficulty Palestinian refugees from Syria had migrating to Gulf Arab states for job opportunities prior to the war. This lack of access to Arab states has become particularly acute during the war, as Palestinians have been unable to leave Syria legally.
14. The reasons that can explain the exceptional state policies that marked the Palestinian community in the country can be summarized in terms of size (Palestinians composing less than 3 percent of the population), history (kinship and trade ties between what would become the north of Palestine and southern Syria), and Arab nationalist sentiment (Arab nationalism as an important force in modern Syrian history).
15. UNRWA Education Program employee interview.
16. GAPAR Personal Affairs and Statistics Department interview; UNRWA Field Administration Office employee, interviewed by the author, July 2008, Damascus.
17. UNRWA Field Relief and Social Services Program employee, interviewed by the author, July 2008, Damascus; UNRWA Eligibility and Registration Office interview; UNRWA Education Program employee, interviewed by the author, June 2008, Damascus; UNRWA Health Program employee, interviewed by the author, July 2008, Damascus; UNRWA Logistics and Procurement Program employee, interviewed by the author, July 2008, Damascus.
18. This full-fledged Palestinian refugee integration into Syrian society, as well the international presence in the camps through UNRWA, led many Syrians in the areas that surround the camps to initially seek refuge in them and their UNRWA facilities. However, the international connection has not spared the camps from becoming war zones.
19. While plenty of anecdotal evidence can be related to support this claim, an example of this sentiment can be seen in the 2014 Carol Mansour–directed film *We Cannot Go There Now, My Dear*. In her documentary film, Mansour interviews young

Palestinian refugee artists and community activists from Syria displaced to Lebanon, and now beyond. During the interview, all interviewees articulated their feelings of belonging and yearnings for their communities in Syria. The director also asks her interviewees whether they identify as Syrian or Palestinian. The audience does not hear this question because it is cut out, but the interviewees' unanimous response, that they see themselves as Palestinian, underscores the cut-out question.

20. For example, I visited the PLO's Palestinian Central Bureau of Statistics in order to do archival research only to find that the archives are incomplete because some had been moved to Ramallah. Whatever statistics remained were out of date because no recent statistical surveys had been carried out.

21. The PLO adopted the "Declaration of Independence" in an extraordinary nineteenth session in Algiers in November 1988. The document declared the establishment of an independent Palestinian state in the areas of Palestine occupied in 1967 and under Israeli military rule. A month later, the United States and the PLO began a dialogue following the PLO's acceptance of US conditions. These included accepting the right of Israel to peace and security, UN Security Council Resolution 242 as the basis of negotiations, and the renunciation of the armed struggle. The latter resolution, adopted in the wake of the June War, calls for Israel's return to its 1949 armistice lines (Y. Sayigh 1989).

3. THE RIGHT OF RETURN MOVEMENT AND MEMORIES FOR THE RETURN

1. 194 Group activist, interviewed by the author, June 2008, Yarmouk Camp.
2. Wajeb activist, interviewed by the author, June 2008, Yarmouk Camp.
3. The late Ghassan Shihabi, director of Dar al-Shajara, interviewed by the author, February 2008, Yarmouk Camp.
4. The horrific details of Shihabi's murder and the sniper's attempt to kill his accompanying wife and twin daughters, as well as the intentional destruction of Dar al-Shajara, were related to me by the late Shihabi's wife, Siham Abu-Sitta. He is survived by Siham, two daughters, and two stepchildren.
5. Interview with the late Shihabi.
6. Ai'doun activist, interviewed by the author, May 2008, Damascus.
7. RRRC activist, interview by the author, July 2008, Yarmouk Camp.
8. Ibid.
9. Ai'doun activist interview.
10. Wajeb activist interview.
11. Ai'doun activist interview.
12. Ibid.
13. I wish to thank David Landy, who in a reading of an earlier draft of this chapter stressed the relationship between RoRM activists' roles as activists and their perception in the community.
14. I wish to thank Helga Tawil Souri, who raised the question of the exchange value for activists at a presentation of an earlier draft of this chapter at the Third World Congress for Middle Eastern Studies at the Universitat Autònoma de Barcelona in July 2010.
15. Ai'doun activist interview.

16. RRRC activist interview.
17. An Ottoman system of land measurement in which one *dunam* equaled approximately 1,000 square meters in Palestine (El-Eini 2006, xiii).
18. Aïdoun activist interview.
19. Interview with the late Shihabi.
20. Wajeb activist interview.
21. Aïdoun activist interview.
22. Aïdoun activist interview.
23. Wajeb activist interview.
24. Public memory narration by the generation of Palestine was also carried out by women and for an audience of women. One such event was organized by the DFLP's Women's Center in March 2008.
25. Muhamad, interviewed by the author, June 2008, Yarmouk Camp.
26. Abu Muhamad, interviewed by the author, June 2008, Yarmouk Camp.
27. Wajeb activist interview.

4. NARRATING PALESTINE, TRANSMITTING ITS LOSS

1. Abu Durra was one of the leading commanders of the 1936–1939 Palestinian uprising (Swedenburg 2003, 104).
2. The Salvation Army was a League of Arab States irregular force composed of mostly Arab volunteers who operated in Palestine before the entry of the regular Arab armies (Pappe 2006, 127).
3. Abu Subhi, interviewed by the author, June 2008, Qabr Essit Camp.
4. *Fida'i* is the singular masculine form of *fida'iyyin*. Umm 'Izz al-Din, interviewed by the author, May 2008, Yarmouk Camp.
5. Umm Nimr, interviewed by the author, April 2008, Dhiyabiyya.
6. Abu Khalil, interviewed by the author, March 2008, Khan Eshieh Camp.
7. Abu Nidal, interviewed by the author, June 2008, Yarmouk Camp.
8. Suzanne, interviewed by the author, May 2008, al-Hajar al-Aswad.
9. Abu Shadi, interviewed by the author, June 2008, Damascus.
10. Ibid.
11. Ibid.
12. Umm Ghassan (not her real name), interviewed by the author, May 2008, Yarmouk Camp.
13. Ibid.
14. Khawla, interviewed by the author, May 2008, al-Hajar al-Aswad.
15. *'Ataba* is an Arab folk song.
16. Bassam, interviewed by the author, June 2008, Dhiyabiyya.
17. Muhammad-Khayr, interviewed by the author, June 2008, Yarmouk Camp.
18. 'Ammar, interviewed by the author, May 2008, Yarmouk Camp.
19. Abu Shadi interview.
20. Ahlam, interviewed by the author, February 2008, Khan Eshieh Camp.
21. Ibid.
22. Muhammad-Khayr interview.

23. Ayman, interviewed by the author, May 2008, Yarmouk Camp.
24. Suzanne interview.
25. Abu Nidal interview.
26. Maha, interviewed by the author, April 2008, al-Hajar al-Aswad.
27. Buthayna, interviewed by the author, June 2008, Yarmouk Camp.

5. THE GUARDIANS' COMMUNITIES AND MEMORIES OF CATASTROPHES

1. Fu'ad Hijazi was one of the three men sentenced to death and hanged by the British in 1930 following the 1929 Buraq Wall, known as Wailing Wall in English, uprising in Jerusalem. The three have been commemorated as heroes and martyrs in folk songs and poetry (see, e.g., Boullata 1997).
2. Abu Ahmad, interviewed by the author, June 2008, Damascus.
3. Umm Ya'rub, interviewed by the author, February 2008, Damascus.
4. Living in tents was also a characteristic of their earlier lives. Umm 'Abdul 'Aziz told me that in Jubb Yusuf, some people, including her father, had already begun to build concrete housing structures by 1948. She recalled how, after having fled the village to a safe distance, they watched from afar as Zionist militia men began dynamiting her relatives' concrete homes.
5. Umm 'Abdul 'Aziz, interviewed by the author, May 2008, al-Hajar al-Aswad.
6. Abu Kamal, interviewed by the author, May 2008, Khan Eshieh Camp.
7. Ibid.
8. Abu Subhi and Abu Fu'ad, interviewed by the author, June 2008, Qabr Essit Camp.
9. Ibid.
10. This was most likely a reference to the body of King Faysal I of Iraq that was en route to Iraq from Europe, where he had passed away in 1933. An image of the event can be seen in Walid Khalidi's *Before Their Diaspora* (2010), as digitized on the Institute for Palestine Studies website.
11. Umm Hasan, interviewed by the author, April 2008, al-Hajar al-Aswad.
12. Abu Samih, interviewed by the author, May 2008, Yarmouk Camp.
13. Abu Khalil, interviewed by the author, March 2008, Khan Eshieh Camp.
14. Abu Hind, interviewed by the author, April 2008, Damascus.
15. Umm 'Izz al-Din, interviewed by the author, May 2008, Yarmouk Camp.
16. Abu Samih interview.
17. Umm Ya'rub interview.
18. Abu Hind interview.
19. Umm 'Izz al-Din interview.
20. Abu 'Imad (not his real name), interviewed by the author, June 2008, Yarmouk Camp.
21. Umm Ahmad, interviewed by the author, June 2008, Damascus.
22. Umm 'Izz al-Din interview.
23. Abu 'Imad interview.
24. Umm Rim, interviewed by the author, April 2008, Damascus.
25. Umm 'Izz al-Din interview.

26. Sharon refers to the late Ariel Sharon, Israeli general, politician and Prime Minister during the second intifada responsible for numerous Palestinian massacres throughout his long career. See for example note 19 in the next chapter on his role in the Qibya massacre. Umm Hasan seems to have mixed pre- with post-1948 Zionist leaders.
27. Umm Hasan interview.
28. Umm 'Izz al-Din interview.

6. SECOND- AND THIRD-GENERATION POSTMEMORIES OF PALESTINE AND NARRATIVES ON NAKBA MEMORY

1. Manal, interviewed by the author, May 2008, al-Hajar al-Aswad.
2. Tahani, interviewed by the author, April 2008, al-Husayniyya.
3. Ibid.
4. Muhamad-Khayr, interviewed by the author, June 2008, Yarmouk Camp.
5. Abu Muhammad, interviewed by the author, June 2008, Yarmouk Camp.
6. Umm Muhammad, interviewed by the author, June 2008, Yarmouk Camp.
7. Buthayna, interviewed by the author, June 2008, Yarmouk Camp.
8. *Kufiyya* refers to an embroidered scarf that is traditionally worn as a headdress by Arab men. It was popularized by different Palestinian nationalist leaders, chief among them Yasser Arafat, as a symbol of Palestinian identity. The *kufiyya*, in its white and black checkered guise, is today also worn as a scarf outside the Arab world in solidarity with Palestinians.
9. Muhammad-Khayr interview. B's name has been withheld
10. Mayada, interviewed by the author, May 2008, al-Hajar al-Aswad.
11. Khawla, interviewed by the author, May 2008, al-Hajar al-Aswad.
12. Fatima, interviewed by the author, February 2008, Khan Eshieh Camp.
13. Buthayna interview.
14. Abu Shadi, interviewed by the author, June 2008, Damascus.
15. Fatima interview.
16. Abu Shadi interview.
17. Abu Bassam, interviewed by the author, April 2008, al-Dhiyabiya.
18. Umm Shadi, interviewed by the author, April 2008, Damascus.
19. Qibya is a village close to Ramallah that was the site of a gruesome 1953 massacre led by Ariel Sharon. In that massacre, sixty-nine civilians were murdered by forcing them to remain in their homes, which were subsequently blown up (Shlaim 2001, 90–94). It was not uncommon for interviewees to mix 1948 and post-1948 massacres.
20. Abu 'Ammar, interviewed by the author, May 2008, Yarmouk Camp.
21. Abu Nidal, interviewed by the author, June 2008, Yarmouk Camp.
22. Suzanne, interviewed by the author, May 2008, al-Hajar al-Aswad.
23. Sarab, interviewed by the author, May 2008, Khan Eshieh Camp.
24. Niyazi, interviewed by the author, March 2008, Khan Eshieh Camp.
25. Ibid.
26. 'Ammar interviewed by the author, May 2008, Yarmouk Camp.
27. Ayman, interviewed by the author, May 2008, Yarmouk Camp.

CONCLUSION

1. Ghawarina were peasant farming communities that inhabited the Hula Valley in northern Palestine and the Jordan Valley. They descended from peasants who were brought from the southern Ottoman provinces to work the land in semifeudal conditions (Y. Sayigh 2004, 49).

BIBLIOGRAPHY

ARABIC

'Abd al-Da'im, Abdullah. 1970. "Min Harakat al-Muqawama al-Falastiniyya ila Harakat al-Muqawama al-'Arabiyya" [From the Palestinian resistance movement to the Arab resistance movement]. *Mawaqif* 2 (8): 29–41. Republished in CAUS (Center for Arab Unity Studies, Markaz Dirasat al-Wihda al-'Arabiyya). 1996. *Qira'at fi al-Fikr al-Qawmi: al-Qawmiyya al-'Arabiyya wa Falastin wa al-Amn al-Qawmi wa Qadaya al-Taharrur* [Readings in nationalist thought: Arab nationalism, Palestine, national security and questions of liberation]. Vol. 5. Beirut Center for Arab Unity Studies.

——. 1998. *Nakbat Falastin 'Am 1948: Usuluha wa Asbabuha wa Atharuha al-Siyasiyya wa al-Fikriyya wa al-Adabiyya fi al-Hayat al-'Arabiyya* [The Palestine catastrophe of 1948: Its origins, causes and political, intellectual and literary aftermath in Arab life]. Beirut: Dar al-Tali'a.

Abdel Jawad, Saleh ('Abd al-Jawwad, Salih). 2006a. "Limatha la Nastati' Kitabat Tarikhina al-Mu'asir min dun Istikhdam al-Masadir al-Shafawiyya? Harb 1948: Dirasat Hala" [Why can't we write our modern history without the use of oral sources? The war of 1948: a study of a condition]. In *Nahwa Siyaghat Riwaya Tarikhiyya lil-Nakba: Ishkaliyyat wa Tahaddiyat* [Toward a historical narrative of the Nakba: Complexities and challenges], ed. Mustafa Kabha, 25–55. Haifa: Mada al-Carmel.

——. 2008. "Hal Hunak Thakira Jam'iyya lil-Nakba?" [Is there a Palestinian collective memory of the Nakba?]. Paper presented at al-Bina' al-Watani al-Falastini: Situna 'Aman 'ala al-Nakba [Palestinian national construction: Sixty years after the Nakba]. Conference of Institut Français du Proche-Orient, Damascus, April 16–17, 2008.

Abu-Lughud, Ibrahim. 1972. "Min al-Nakba ila al-Naksa: Ta'biran li-Hawadith Jisam" [From the catastrophe to the setback: Two expressions of grave events]. *Shu'un Falastiniyya* 11: 49–57.

Abu Rashid, Amin. 2013. "Jawla Midaniyya fi 'Asimat al-Shatat'" [A field trip in "The Diaspora Capital"]. *Al-'Awda Magazine*. Last updated March 2013. http://www.alawda-mag.com/default.asp?issueID=67&MenuID=153.

AGPS (Action Group for Palestinians of Syria, Majmuʻat al-ʻAml min Ajl Falastiniyyi Suriyya). 2013a. "Al-Taqrir al-Yawmi al-Khas bi-Awdaʻ al-Lajʼin al-Falastiniyyin fi Suriyya, al-ʻAdad 102" [Daily report pertaining to the situation of Palestinian refugees in Syria, no. 102]. *Action Group for Palestinians of Syria*. Last updated February 14, 2013. http://www.actionpal.org.uk/ar/reports/daily/14-2-2013.pdf.

——. 2013b. "Al-Taqrir al-Yawmi al-Khas bi-Awdaʻ al-Lajʼin al-Falastiniyyin fi Suriyya, al-ʻAdad 135" [Daily report pertaining to the situation of Palestinian refugees in Syria, no. 135]. *Action Group for Palestinians of Syria*. Last updated March 19, 2013. http://www.actionpal.org.uk/ar/reports/daily/19-3-2013.pdf.

——. 2014. "Al-Taqrir al-Yawmi al-Khas bi-Awdaʻ al-Lajiʼin al-Falastiniyyin fi Suriyya, al-ʻAdad 573" [Daily report pertaining to the situation of Palestinian refugees in Syria, no. 573]. *Action Group for Palestinians of Syria*. Last updated June 8, 2014. http://actionpal.org/phocadownloadpap/6-2014/8-6-2014.pdf.

——. 2015. "Falastiniyyu Suriyya . . . Ihsaʼiyyat wa Arqam Hata 25 Adhar/Maris 2015" [Palestinians in Syria . . . statistics and numbers up to March 25, 2015]. *Action Group for Palestinians of Syria*. Last updated March 25, 2015. http://www.actionpal .org.uk/ar/post.php?id=1213.

——. 2018. "Al-Taqrir al-Yawmi al-Khas bi-Awdaʻ al-Lajʼin al-Falastiniyyin fi Suriyya, al-ʻAdad 2006" [Daily report pertaining to the situation of Palestinian refugees in Syria, no. 2006]. *Action Group for Palestinians of Syria*. Last updated May 2, 2018. http://www.actionpal.org.uk/ar/reports/daily/02-05-2018.pdf.

AJA (Al Jazeera Arabic). 2011. "Al-Mufawadat al-Falastiniyya maʻ Israʼil" (*Bila Hudud* TV show) [Palestinian negotiations with Israel (*Without Limits* TV show)]. *Al-Jazeera*. Last updated January 27, 2011. http://www.aljazeera.net/NR/exeres /CA184112-2445-4853-A2F0-23D44ADD73F0.htm.

Alami, Musa (ʻAlami, Musa al-). 1949. *ʻIbrat Falastin* [The lesson of Palestine]. Beirut: Dar al-Kashaf.

ʻAllush, Naji. 1964. *al-Masira ila Falastin* [The march to Palestine]. Beirut: Dar al-Taliʻa.

AM (*Al-ʻAwda Magazine, Majallat al-ʻAwda*). 2012. "Al-Shaykh Mahmud Ibrahim al-Samadi Mithal al-Lajiʼ al-Falastini al-Muthaqaf" [Shaykh Mahmud Ibrahim al-Samadi, an example of a learned Palestinain refugee]. *Al-ʻAwda Magazine*. Last updated January 2012. http://www.alawda-mag.com/default.asp?issueID=53&MenuID=18.

——. 2013. "Mukhayyam al-Yarmuk ʻala Khat al-Nar: al-Hisar wa al-Waqiʻ al-Maʻishi al-Munhar" [Yarmouk Camp on the firing line: The siege and devastated living reality]. *Al-ʻAwda Magazine*. Last updated March 2013. http://www.alawda-mag .com/default.asp?issueID=67&MenuID=33.

ʻArif, ʻArif al-. 1956. *Al-Nakba: Nakbat Bayt al-Maqdis wa al-Firdaws al-Mafqud, 1947–1952* [The catastrophe: The catastrophe of Jerusalem and the lost paradise, 1947–52]. Vol 1. Sidon: Manshurat al-Maktaba al-ʻAsriyya.

——. 1956–1962. *Al-Nakba: Nakbat Bayt al-Maqdis wa al-Firdaws al-Mafqud, 1947–1955* [The catastrophe: The catastrophe of Jerusalem and the lost paradise, 1947–55]. Vols 1–6. Sidon: Manshurat al-Maktaba al-ʻAsriyya.

——. 1961. *al-Nakba fi Suwar: Nakbat al-ʻArab fi Falastin* [The catastrophe in pictures: The Arabs' catastrophe in Palestine]. Beirut: Dar al-ʻIlm lil-Malayin.

——. 1962. *Sijil al-Khulud: Asmaʼ al-Shuhadaʼ al-Ladhina Istashhadu fi Maʻarik Falastin, 1947–1952* [The registry of immortality: The names of the martyrs who fell during the battles for Palestine, 1947–1952]. Vol 6. Beirut: Manshurat al-Maktaba al-ʻAsriyya.

As'ad, Muhammad al-. 1990. *Atfal al-Nada* [Children of the dew]. London: Dar Riyad al-Rayyis.

——. 1999. "Nas al-Laji'" [The refugee's text]. *Al-'Usur al-Jadida Magazine*, December.

'Ayid, Khalid. 2012. "Al-Nazihun al-Falastiniyyun min Suriyya ila al-Urdun: Ma ba'd al-Hudud al-Akhira!" [The Palestinians displaced from Syria to Jordan: What lies after the final borders!]. *Institute for Palestine Studies*. Last updated n/a. Accessed April 23, 2014. http://www.palestine-studies.org/sites/default/files/uploads/files /ayed4.pdf.

'Aziza, Tariq. 2012. "Al-Falastiniyyun fi Suriyya Bayna Matraqat al-Thawra wa Sindan al-Nizam" [The Palestinians in Syria between the hammer of the revolution and the anvil of the regime]. *Institute for Palestine Studies*. Last updated n/a. Accessed April 23, 2015. http://www.palestine-studies.org/sites/default/files/uploads/files /Aziza2.pdf.

Azm, Sadik Jalal al- ('Azm, Sadiq Jalal al-). 1968. *Al-Naqd al-Dhati Ba'd al-Hazima* [Self-criticism after the defeat]. Beirut: Dar al-Tali'a.

——. 2007. *Al-Naqd al-Dhati Ba'd al-Hazima* [Self-criticism after the defeat]. Damascus: Dar Mamduh 'Adwan.

'Azma, 'Aziz al-. 2003. *Qustantin Zurayq: 'Arabiyyun lil-Qarn al-'Ishrin* [Constantine Zurayk: An Arab for the twentieth century]. Beirut: Institute for Palestine Studies.

Badwan, 'Ali. 2004. *Al-Laji'un al-Falastiniyyun fi Suriyya: al-Su'ud Nahwa al-Watan* [The Palestinian refugees in Syria: The ascension toward a homeland]. Damascus: Mu'assasat al-Manara.

Bakrawi, Khalid. 2012. "Hilm 'Awda" [Dream of return]. *Shabakat Yarmuk*. Last updated February 22, 2012. http://www.yarmouk.org/news/616?language=arabic.

Bin Khadra', Zafir. 1999. *Suriyya wa al-Laji'un al-Falastiniyyun al-'Arab al-Muqimun* [Syria and the resident Palestinian Arab refugees]. Damascus: Dar Kan'an.

Bitar, Nadim al-. [1965] 1973. *Al-Fa'aliyya al-Thawriyya fi al-Nakba* [The revolutionary potential of the catastrophe]. 2nd ed. Beirut: Dar al-Tali'a.

——. 1968. *Min al-Naksa ila al-Thawra* [From the setback to the revolution]. Beirut: Dar al-Tali'a.

Bitari, Nidal. 2012. "Al-Laji'un al-Falastiniyyun fi Suriyya: Qalaq al-Wujud wa Jahim al-Nuzuh" [The Palestinian refugees in Syria: Existential anxiety and the inferno of displacement]. *Assafir*. Last updated April 21, 2012. http://assafir.com/Article .aspx?EditionID=2131&ChannelID=50904&ArticleID=1879.

CAUS (Center for Arab Unity Studies, Markaz Dirasat al-Wihda al-'Arabiyya). 1993. *Qira'at fi al-Fikr al-Qawmi: al-Wihda al-'Arabiyya* [Readings in nationalist thought: Arab unity]. Vol. 2. Beirut Center for Arab Unity Studies.

——. 1996. *Qira'at fi al-Fikr al-Qawmi: al-Qawmiyya al-'Arabiyya wa Falastin wa al-Amn al-Qawmi wa Qadaya al-Taharrur* [Readings in nationalist thought: Arab nationalism, Palestine, national security and questions of liberation]. Vol. 5. Beirut Center for Arab Unity Studies.

CPE (Committee of the Palestinian Encyclopedia, Hay'at al-Mawsu'a al-Falastiniyya). 1984a. "'Arif al-'Arif (1892–1973)." In *Al-Mawsu'a al-Falastiniyya* [The Palestinian encyclopedia]. Vol 3. Damascus: Committee of the Palestinian Encyclopedia.

——. 1984b. "Al-Nakba, ('Ilm -)" [The catastrophe (science of -)]. In *Al-Mawsu'a al-Falastiniyya* [The Palestinian encyclopedia]. Vol 4. Damascus: Committee of the Palestinian Encyclopedia.

Darwaza, Muhammad. 1959. *Al-Qadiyya al-Falastiniyya fi Mukhtalafi Marahiliha* [The Question of Palestine through its different stages]. Vol 1. 2nd ed. Sidon: Manshurat al-Maktaba al-'Asriyya.

——. 1960. *Al-Qadiyya al-Falastiniyya fi Mukhtalafi Marahiliha* [The Question of Palestine through its different stages]. Vol 2. Sidon: Manshurat al-Maktaba al-'Asriyya.

Dawla, Zuhayr. 2013. "Al-Falastini Khalid Bakrawi . . . Dahiyyat al-Ta'thib fi al-Sujun al-Suriyya" [The Palestinian Khalid Bakrawi . . . a victim of torture in Syrian jails]. *Al-Imarat al-Yawm*. Last updated September 16, 2013. http://www.emaratalyoum .com/politics/reports-and-translation/2013-09-16-1.606897.

Dayyub, Basil. 2013. "Mukhayyam Hindarat: Qusat Luju' Intahat bi-Luju'ayn!" [Hindarat Camp: The story of refuge that ended with being made refugees twice!]. *Al-Akhbar*. Last updated September 28, 2013. http://www.al-akhbar.com /node/192220.

Falah, Ghazi. 1993. *Al-Jalil wa Mukhattatat al-Tahwid* [Plans for the Judaization of the Galilee]. Translated by Mahmud Zayid. Beirut: Institute for Palestine Studies.

Fayyad, Ahmad. 2011. "Taharuk Shababi lil-'Awda al-Falastiniyya" [Youth initiative for the Palestinian return]. *Al-Jazeera*. Last updated n/a. Accessed September 19, 2012. http://www.aljazeera.net/news/pages/046424c0–0d7c-439d-990e-0806e352c7be.

Fu'ad, Fu'ad. 2014. "N/A." Paper presented at Rughma Kul al-Su'ubat: al-Mujtama' al-Madani al-Suri min Zaman ma Qabla al-Thawra [Against all odds: Syrian civil society before the revolution]. Panel at the Asfari Institute for Civil Society and Citizenship and Issam Fares Institute for Public Policy and International Affairs, American University of Beirut, May 16. Last updated June 5, 2014. https://www .youtube.com/watch?v=WzidI7BUE4Q.

GAPAR (General Authority for Palestinian Arab Refugees, al-Hay'a al-'Ama lil-Laji'in al-Falastiniyyin al-'Arab). n/a. *Al-Hay'a al-'Ama lil-Laji'in al-Falastiniyyin al-'Arab wa al-Laji'un al-Falastiniyyun fi al-Jumhiriyya al-'Arabiyya al-Suriyya: Qawanin, Marasim, Qararat, Khadamat, Bayanat, Ihsa'iyyat* [The General Authority for Palestine Arab Refugees and the Palestinian Refugees in the Syrian Arab republic: Laws, protocols, resolutions, services, statements, statistics]. Damascus: General Authority for Palestine Arab Refugees, Ministry of Social Affairs and Labor, Syrian Arab Republic.

Ghuri, Imil al-. 1955. *Al-Mu'amara al-Kubra: Ightiyal Falastin wa Mahq al-'Arab* [The great plot: Palestine's assassination and the Arabs' extermination]. Cairo: Dar al-Nil.

——. 1959. *15 Ayyar 1948: Dirasa Siyasiyya 'Ilmiyya Murakkaza 'an al-Asbab al-Haqiqiyya li-Nakbat Falastin* [May 15, 1948: A condensed scientific-political study of the real reasons for Palestine's catastrophe]. Beirut: al-Kitab al-'Arabi.

Ghubari, Omar al-. 2012. *Dhakirat al-Tira, Haifa* [al-Tira's memory, Haifa]. Tel Aviv-Jaffa: Zochrot. Last updated May 2012. http://zochrot.org/uploads /uploads/5407e1b89d03e7a473f6dbe7c0915726.pdf.

Hafiz, Yasin al-. 1979. *Al-Hazima wa al-Aidyulujiyya al-Mahzuma* [The defeat and the defeated ideology]. Beirut: Dar al-Tali'a.

Hanafi, Sari. 1996. "Al-Falastiniyyun fi Suriyya wa 'Amaliyat al-Salam" [The Palestinians in Syria and the peace process]. *Majallat al-Dirasat al-Falastiniyya* 7, 28 (Autumn): 85–103.

Hanna, Jurj. 1948. *Tariq al-Khalas: Tahlilun Wad'iyyun li-Mihnat Falastin* [Salvation's path: A positivist analysis of Palestine's calamity]. Beirut: Dar al-Ahd.

Hawwari, Muhammad al-. 1955. *Sir al-Nakba* [The catastrophe's secret]. Nazareth: Matba'at al-Hakim.

Husayni, Muhammad al-. 1956. *Haqa'iq 'an Qadiyyat Falastin* [The Question of Palestine facts]. 2nd ed. Cairo: Arab Higher Committee Press.

Hut, Bayan Nuwayhid al-. 1981. *Al-Qiyadat wa al-Mu'assasat al-Siyasiyya fi Falastin, 1917–1948* [Political leaderships and institutions in Palestine, 1917–1948]. Beirut: Institute for Palestine Studies.

Jabiri, Muhammad al-. 1982. *Al-Khitab al-'Arabi al-Mu'asir: Dirasa Tahliliyya Naqdiyya* [Contemporary Arab discourse: A critical-analytical study]. Casablanca: Arab Cultural Center.

Jammal, Gabi al-. 2012. "Al-Laji'un al-Falastiniyyun fi Suriyya . . . Ba'da Sitat 'Uqud min al-Luju', al-Khuruj ila Luju'in Jadid" [The Palestinian refugees in Syria . . . after six decades of refuge, leaving for a new one]. *Institute for Palestine Studies.* Last updated n/a. Accessed March 8, 2013. http://www.palestine-studies.org/sites /default/files/uploads/files/Jammal3.pdf.

Kabha, Mustafa. 2006a. "Ishkaliyyat Kitabat al-Tarikh al-Falastini al-Hadith wa Darurat Siyaghat Riwaya Tarikhiyya Mutakamila" [The problems of writing modern Palestinian history and the importance of an integral historical narrative]. In *Nahwa Siyaghat Riwaya Tarikhiyya lil-Nakba: Ishkaliyyat wa Tahaddiyat* [Toward a historical narrative of the catastrophe: Complexities and challenges], ed. Mustafa Kabha, 5–23. Haifa: Mada al-Carmel.

——, ed. 2006b. *Nahwa Siyaghat Riwaya Tarikhiyya lil-Nakba: Ishkaliyyat wa Tahaddiyat* [Toward a historical narrative of the catastrophe: Complexities and challenges]. Haifa: Mada al-Carmel.

Kassem, Fatma (Qasim, Fatima). 2007. "Al-Lugha wa al-Tarikh wa al-Nisa': Nisa' Falastiniyyat fi Isra'il Yasifna Ahdath al-Nakba" [Language, history and women: Palestinian women in Israel describe the Nakba]. In *Kitabat Nisawiyya: Ma Bayna al-Qam' wa Aswat Falastiniyya Muqawima* [Feminist writings: Between oppression and Palestinian resistance voices], ed. Nadera Shalhoub-Kevorkian, 105–144. Haifa: Mada al-Carmel.

Kayyal, Majd. 2013. "Falastin: al-Nakba al-Mustamirra" [Palestine: The ongoing Nakba]. *Assafir.* Last updated May 15, 2013. http://arabi.assafir.com/Article .asp?aid=882&refsite=assafir&reftype=leftmenu&refzone=switcher.

Keswani, Ward al-. 2013. "Mukhayyam al-Yarmuk: Athar al-Damar al-Ladhi Sabbabathu al-Sayyara al-Mufakhkhakha" [Yarmouk Camp: The aftermath of the booby-trapped car's destruction]. *YouTube.* Last updated December 28, 2013. https://www.youtube.com/watch?v=MGiWkbkjSiM&feature=youtu.be.

Khalidi, Walid (Khalidi, Walid al-). 2009. "Muqaddima" [Introduction]. In *Nakbat 1948: Asbabuha wa Subul 'Ilajiha* [The Nakba of 1948: Causes and solutions], by Qustantin Zurayq, Jurj Hanna, Musa al-'Alami, and Qadri Tuqan (Constantine Zurayk, George Hanna, Musa Alami, and Qadri Tuqan), xi–xlii. Edited and introduced by Walid Khalidi. Beirut: Institute for Palestine Studies.

Khatib, Husam al-. 1971. "Al-Thawra al-Falastiniyya: Ila Ayn?" [The Palestinian revolution: Where is it heading?]. *Shu'un Falastiniyya* 4: 5–30.

Khatib, Muhammad Nimr al-. 1951. *Min Athar al-Nakba* [The catastrophe's aftermath]. Damascus: al-Matba'a al-'Umumiyya.

——. 1967. *Ahdath al-Nakba aw Nakbat Falastin* [The events of the catastrophe or Palestine's catastrophe]. Damascus: al-Matba'a al-'Umumiyya.

Ma'an. 2013a. "Nas Muqabalat al-Ra'is Ma' Qanat al-Mayadin" [Transcript of president's interview with Al-Mayadeen channel]. *Ma'an News Agency*. Last updated January 25, 2013. http://maannews.net/arb/ViewDetails.aspx?ID=559196.

Mawed, Hamad Al- (Maw'id, Hamad al-). 2002. *Mukhayyam al-Yarmuk* [Yarmouk Camp]. Damascus: Dar al-Shajara.

Mukhayyam al-Yarmuk Nuyuz [Yarmouk Camp news]. Facebook Page. Updated daily. https://www.facebook.com/yarmok.news?fref=ts.

Munawwar, Hisham. 2012. "Al-Laji'un al-Falastiniyyun fi Suriyya: al-Nakba al-Thaniya'" [The Palestinian refugees in Syria: "The second catastrophe"]. *Institute for Palestine Studies*. Last updated n/a. Accessed April 29, 2015. http://www .palestine-studies.org/sites/default/files/uploads/files/Mnawarı.pdf.

Munjid, Salah al-Din al-. 1968. *A'midat al-Nakba: Bahthun 'Ilmiyyun fi Asbab Hazimat 5 Huzayran* [The pillars of the catastrophe: A scientific study of the reasons for the June 5 defeat]. 2nd ed. Beirut: Dar al-Kitab al-Jadid.

Nasser, Gamal Abdel ('Abd al-Nasir, Jamal). [1954] 2005. *Falsafat al-Thawra* [The philosophy of the revolution]. Cairo: Maktabat Madbuli.

Qamhawi, Walid. 1956. *Al-Nakba wa al-Bina': Nahwa Ba'th al-Watan al-'Arabi* [The catastrophe and construction: Toward resurrecting the Arab homeland]. Beirut: Dar al-'Ilm lil-Malayin.

Rizqallah, Hala. 1998. *Al-Falastiniyyun fi Lubnan wa Suriyya: Dirasa Dimughrafiyya Muqarina, 1948–1995* [The Palestinians in Lebanon and Syria: A comparative demographic study, 1948–1995]. Beirut: Dar al-Jadid.

Sahli, Nabil al-. 2001. "Al-Laji'un al-Falastiniyyun fi Suriyya: Mu'tayat Asasiyya" [The Palestinian refugees in Syria: Basic data]. *Majallat al-Dirasaat al-Falastiniyya* 12 (45–46): 119–129.

Salayma, Bilal. 2012. "Al-Laji'un al-Falastiniyyun fi Suriyya wa al-Thawra al-Suriyya" [Palestinain refugees in Syria and the Syrian revolution]. Unpublished diploma thesis in refugee studies, Academy of Refugee Studies, London. Last updated n/a. Accessed June 9, 2013. http://www.alzaytouna.net/arabic/data/attachments /ReportsZ/2012/Pal_Refugees_Syria_Events_7–12.pdf.

Samadi, Khalil al-. 2007. "Al-'Alim al-Da'iya al-Mujahid Tilmidh al-Qassam" [The scholar, preacher, warrior student of al-Qassam]. *Mu'assasat Falastin lil-Thaqafa*. Last updated March 3, 2007. http://www.thaqafa.org/site/pages/details.aspx-?itemid=2107#.VBxKoUvldZg.

——. 2013. "Mawasim al-Hijra ila Mukhayyam al-Yarmuk" [Seasons of migration to Yarmouk Camp]. *Al-'Awda Magazine*. Last updated September 2013. http://www .alawda-mag.com/Default.asp?ContentID=2369&menuID=8.

Sarhan, Basim. 2005. *Tahawwulat al-Usra al-Falastiniyya fi al-Shatat: Dirasa Susyulujiyya Muqarina* [Transformations of the Palestinian family in the diaspora: A comparative sociological study]. Beirut: Institute for Palestine Studies.

Sawwah, Wa'il, and Salam Kawakibi. 2013. "Zuhur wa Tatawur al-Mujtama' al-Madani fi Suriyya" [The emergence and development of civil society in Syria]. In *Aswat*

Suriyya min Zaman ma Qabla al-Thawra: al-Mujtama' al-Madani Rughma Kul al-Su'ubat [Pre-revolution Syrian voices: Syrian civil society against all odds], ed. Salam Kawakibi, 15–34. Damascus: Bayt al-Muwatan and Atlasu.

Sayf al-Dawla, 'Ismat. 1970. "Al-Muqawama min Wijhat Nazar Qawmiyya" [The resistance from a nationalist perspective]. *Al-Adab* 18 (1): 2–10 and 54–63. Republished in CAUS (Center for Arab Unity Studies, Markaz Dirasat al-Wihda al-'Arabiyya). 1996. *Qira'at fi al-Fikr al-Qawmi: al-Qawmiyya al-'Arabiyya wa Falastin wa al-Amn al-Qawmi wa Qadaya al-Taharrur* [Readings in nationalist thought: Arab nationalism, Palestine, national security and questions of liberation]. Vol. 5. Beirut: Center for Arab Unity Studies.

Sharif, Mahir al-. 1995. *Al-Bahth 'an Kiyan: Dirasa fi al-Fikr al-Siyasi al-Falastini, 1908–1993* [In search of an entity: A study in Palestinian political thought, 1908–1993]. Nicosia: Center for Socialist Studies and Research in the Arab World.

——. 2008. "Al-Nakba wa Ma'naha fi Mir'at al-'Aql al-Naqdi" [The Nakba and its meaning as reflected in critical thought]. *Majallat al-Dirasat al-Falastiniyya* 19 (74–75): 15–23.

Suleiman, Jaber (Sulayman, Jabir). 1994. "Al-Falastiniyyun fi Suriyya: Bayanat wa Shahadat" [The Palestinians in Syria: Statements and testimonies]. *Majallat al-Dirasat al-Falastiniyya* 5 (20): 136–162.

Tal, Abdullah al-. 1959. *Karithat Falastin: Mudhakkarat 'Abdu Allah al-Tal, Qa'id Ma'rakat al-Quds* [Palestine's disaster: Memoirs of Abdullah al-Tal, leader of the Battle of Jerusalem]. Vol 1. Cairo: Dar al-Qalam.

Tu'ma, Hadi. 1969. "Harb al-Tahrir al-'Arabiyya al-Falastiniyya: Intilaqatuha wa Ab'aduha" [The Palestinian Arab Liberation War: Its beginnings and scope]. *Al-Adab* 7 (8): 24–29. Republished in CAUS (Center for Arab Unity Studies, Markaz Dirasat al-Wihda al-'Arabiyya). 1996. *Qira'at fi al-Fikr al-Qawmi: al-Qawmiyya al-'Arabiyya wa Falastin wa al-Amn al-Qawmi wa Qadaya al-Taharrur* [Readings in nationalist thought: Arab nationalism, Palestine, national security and questions of liberation]. Vol. 5. Beirut: Center for Arab Unity Studies.

Tuqan, Qadri. 1950. Ba'd al-Nakba [*After the Catastrophe*]. Beirut: Dar al-'Ilim lil Malayyin.

Wajeb (Tajamu' al-'Awda al-Falastini, Palestinian Return Community). 2010. "Mahrajan Yawm al-Qarya al-Falastiniyya al-Thamin 'Ashar: Qaryat Saffuriyya" [Eighteenth Palestinian Village Day festival: Saffuriyya village]. *Palestine Poster Project Collection.* Last updated n/a. Accessed April 22, 2015. http://www.palestineposterproject.org/poster/the-village-of-safuria.

——. n/a. "al-Tarikh al-Shafawi" [Oral history]. *Palestinian Return Community— Wajeb.* Last updated n/a. Accessed April 22, 2015. http://www.wajeb.org/index .php?option=com_content&task=blogsection&id=22&Itemid=320.

Zua'iter, Akram (Zu'aytar, Akram). 1955. *Al-Qadiyya al-Falastiniyya* [The Question of Palestine]. Cairo: Dar al-Ma'arif.

Zurayk, Constantine (Zurayq, Qustantin). [1948] 2001. "Ma'na al-Nakba" [The meaning of the catastrophe]. In *Al-A'mal al-Fikriyya al-'Amma lil-Duktur Qustantin Zurayq* [The general intellectual works of Doctor Constantine Zurayk], 193–260. Vol 1. Beirut: Centre for Arab Unity Studies.

——. [1967] 2001. "Maʿna al-Nakba Mujaddadan" [The meaning of the catastrophe anew]. In *Al-Aʿmal al-Fikriyya al-ʿAmma lil-Duktur Qustantin Zurayq* [The general intellectual works of Doctor Constantine Zurayk], 985–1035. Vol 2. Beirut: Centre for Arab Unity Studies.

ENGLISH, FRENCH, AND GERMAN

Abbasi, Mustafa. 2004. "The Battle for Safad in the War of 1948: A Revised Study." *International Journal of Middle East Studies* 36 (1): 21–47. doi:10.2307/3880136.

——. 2008. "The End of Arab Tiberias: The Arabs of Tiberias and the Battle for the City in 1948." *Journal of Palestine Studies* 37 (3): 6–29. doi:10.1525/jps.2008.37.3.6.

Abdel Jawad, Saleh. 2006b. "The Arab and the Palestinian Narratives of the 1948 War." In *Israeli and Palestinian Narratives of Conflict: History's Double Helix*, ed. Robert Rotberg, 72–114. Bloomington: Indiana University Press.

——. 2007. "Zionist Massacres: The Creation of the Palestinian Refugee Problem in the 1948 War." In *Israel and the Palestinian Refugees*, ed. Eyal Benvenisti, Chaim Gans, and Sari Hanafi, 59–127. Berlin: Springer.

Abdul-Rahim, Adnan. 2005. "Palestinian Refugee Children and Caregivers in Syria." In *Children of Palestine: Experiencing Forced Migration in the Middle East*, ed. Dawn Chatty and Gillian Lewando Hundt, 58–86. New York: Berghahn Books.

Abu-Lughod, Lila. 2007. "Return to Half-Ruins: Memory, Postmemory and Living History in Palestine." In *Nakba: Palestine, 1948 and the Claims of Memory*, ed. Ahmad Saʿdi and Lila Abu-Lughod, 77–104. New York: Columbia University Press.

Abu-Lughod, Lila, and Ahmad Saʿdi. 2007. "Introduction: The Claims of Memory." In *Nakba: Palestine, 1948 and the Claims of Memory*, ed. Ahmad Saʿdi and Lila Abu-Lughod, 1–24. New York: Columbia University Press.

Abunimah, Ali. 2011a. "Jordan, PLO Clash on Refugee Issue." *Al-Jazeera English*. Last Updated January 24, 2011. Accessed September 28, 2015: http://www.aljazeera.com /palestinepapers/2011/01/2011124122125339673.html.

——. 2011b. "Dramatic Video Shows Palestinians, Syrians Entering Israeli-Occupied Golan Heights." *Electronic Intifada*. Last updated May 15, 2011. Accessed September 19, 2012. http://electronicintifada.net/blog/ali-abunimah/dramatic -video-shows-palestinians-syrians-entering-israeli-occupied-golan-heights.

——. 2011c. "Video: Interview with Hassan Hijazi, Who Returned to Jaffa from Syria." *Electronic Intifada*. Last updated May 16, 2011. Accessed September 19, 2012. http:// electronicintifada.net/blogs/ali-abunimah/video-interview-hassan-hijazi-who -returned-jaffa-syria.

AFP (Agence France-Presse). 2012. "Over 30 Killed in 24 Hours at Damascus Palestinian Camp." *Relief Web: United Nations Office for the Coordination of Humanitarian Affairs*. Last updated n/a. Accessed March 4, 2013. http://reliefweb .int/report/syrian-arab-republic/over-30-killed-24-hours-damascus-palestinian -camp.

AI (Amnesty International). 2013. "Refugees from Syria Face Further Suffering If Jordan Closes Border." *Amnesty International—USA*. Last updated January 18, 2013. http://www.amnestyusa.org/news/news-item/refugees-from-syria-face-further -suffering-if-jordan-closes-border.

——. 2014. "Lebanon: Denied Refuge: Palestinians from Syria Seeking Safety in Lebanon." *Amnesty International*. Last updated July 1, 2014. https://www.amnesty .org/en/documents/MDE18/002/2014/en.

——. 2015. "'Hello, I Am Still Alive!'—Voices from Yarmouk." *Syria: Voices in Crises. A Monthly Insight Into the Human Rights Crises in Syria* (Amnesty International Newsletter). Last updated April 2015. http://reliefweb.int/sites/reliefweb.int/files /resources/MDE2415252015ENGLISH.pdf.

Al-Achi, Dalia. 2010. "End of Long Ordeal for Palestinian Refugees as Desert Camp Closes." *United Nations High Commissioner for Refugees*. Last updated February 1, 2010. http://www.unhcr.org/cgi-bin/texis/vtx/search?page=search&docid =4b67064c6&query=al%20hol%20camp.

Alami, Musa. 1949b. "The Lesson of Palestine." *Middle East Journal* 3 (4): 373–405. doi:10.2307/4322113.

Al-Hardan, Anaheed. 2008. "Remembering the Catastrophe: Uprooted Histories and the Grandchildren of the Nakba." In *Auto/Biography Yearbook*, ed. Andrew Sparkes, 153–170. Southampton, UK: Clio.

——. 2009. "Iraq's Palestinian Refugees Back at Square One." *Electronic Intifada*. Last updated March 5, 2009. http://electronicintifada.net/v2/article10372.shtml.

——. 2012a. "The Right of Return Movement in Syria: Building a Culture of Return, Mobilizing Memories for the Return." *Journal of Palestine Studies* 41 (2): 62–79. doi:10.1525/jps.2012.XLI.2.62.

——. 2012b. "A Year On: The Palestinians in Syria." *Syrian Studies Association Newsletter* 17 (1): 3–9.

——. 2014. "Decolonizing Research on Palestinians: Toward Critical Epistemologies and Research Practices." *Qualitative Inquiry* 20 (1): 61–71. doi:10.1177/1077800413508534.

Al-Husseini, Jalal. 2000. "UNRWA and the Palestinian Nation-Building Process." *Journal of Palestine Studies* 29 (2): 51–64. doi:10.2307/2676536.

Al-Husseini, Jalal, and Ricardo Bocco. 2009. "The Status of the Palestinian Refugees in the Near East: The Right of Return and UNRWA in Perspective." In "UNRWA and the Palestinian Refugees 60 Years Later." Special issue, *Refugee Survey Quarterly* 28 (2–3): 260–285. doi:10.1093/rsq/hdp036.

Allan, Diana. 2005. "Mythologizing Al-Nakba: Narratives, Collective Identity and Cultural Practice Among Palestinian Refugees in Lebanon." *Oral History* 33 (1): 47–56. doi:10.2307/40179820.

——. 2007. "The Politics of Witness: Remembering and Forgetting 1948 in Shatila Camp." In *Nakba: Palestine, 1948 and the Claims of Memory*, ed. Ahmad Sa'di and Lila Abu-Lughod, 253–282. New York: Columbia University Press.

——. 2013. "Commemorative Economies and the Politics of Solidarity in Shatila Camp." *Humanity: An International Journal of Human Rights, Humanitarianism, and Development* 4 (1): 133–148. doi:10.1353/hum.2013.0000.

——. 2014. *Refugees of the Revolution: Experiences of Palestinian Exile*. Stanford, CA: Stanford University Press.

Al-Mawed, Hamad. 1999. "The Palestinian Refugees in Syria: Their Past, Present and Future." *International Development Research Centre*. Last updated n/a. Accessed January 11, 2010. http://cmsweb.idrc.ca/uploads/user-S/12075964281Syria_Past _Present_.al-mawed.pdf.

Al-Rasheed, Madawi. 2007. "Saudi Arabia and the 1948 Palestine War: Beyond Official History." In *The War for Palestine: Rewriting the History of 1948*, ed. Eugene Rogan and Avi Shlaim, 228–247. 2nd ed. Cambridge: Cambridge University Press.

Anderson, Benedict. 2006. *Imagined Communities: Reflections on the Origin and Spread of Nationalism*. 3rd ed. London: Verso.

Andrews, Molly, Corinne Squire, and Maria Tamboukou, eds. 2013. *Doing Narrative Research*. 2nd ed. London: Sage Publications.

Aruri, Naseer, ed. 2001a. *Palestinian Refugees: The Right of Return*. London: Pluto Press.

——. 2001b. "Towards Convening a Congress of Return and Self-Determination." In *Palestinian Refugees: The Right of Return*, ed. Naseer Aruri, 260–271. London: Pluto Press.

Azm, Sadik Jalal al-. 2011. *Self-criticism After the Defeat*. Translated by George Stergios. London: Saqi Books.

——. 2012. "Civil Society, the Arab Spring and th Return of Islam." Paper presented at Wissenscaftskolleg zu Berlin, October 17, 2012.

Badeau, John. 1959. "Introduction." In *The Philosophy of the Revolution*, by Gamal Abdul Nasser, 13–23. Introduced by John Badeau. Biographical Sketch by John Gunther. Buffalo, NY: Smith, Keynes and Marshall.

Bal, Mieke. 1999. "Introduction." In *Acts of Memory: Cultural Recall in the Present*, ed. Mieke Bal, Leo Spitzer, and Jonathan Crewe, vii–xvi. Hanover, NH: University Press of New England.

Bal, Mieke, Leo Spitzer, and Jonathan Crewe, eds. 1999. *Acts of Memory: Cultural Recall in the Present*. Hanover, NH: University Press of New England.

Barad, Karen. 2007. *Meeting the Universe Halfway: Quantum Physics and the Entanglement of Matter and Meaning*. Durham, NC: Duke University Press.

Beckerman, Gal. 2011. "Top Genocide Scholars Battle over How to Characterize Israel's Actions." *Forward*. Last updated February 16, 2011. http://forward.com/news/135484/top-genocide-scholars-battle-over-how-to-character.

Beinin, Joel, and Frederic Vairel. 2011. "Introduction: The Middle East and North Africa Beyond Social Movement Theory." In *Social Movements, Mobilization and Contestation in the Middle East and North Africa*, ed. Joel Beinin and Frederic Vairel, 1–23. Stanford, CA: Stanford University Press.

Bellah, Robert, Richard Madsen, William Sullivan, Ann Swidler, and Steven Tipton. 2007. *Habits of the Heart: Individualism and Commitment in American Life*. 3rd ed. Berkeley: University of California Press.

Benvenisti, Meron. 2000. *Sacred Landscape: The Buried History of the Holy Land Since 1948*. Berkeley: University of California Press.

Ben-Ze'ev, Efrat. 2005. "Transmission and Transformation: The Palestinian Second Generation and the Commemoration of the Homeland." In *Homelands and Diasporas: Holy Lands and Other Places*, ed. Andre Levy and Alex Weingrod, 123–139. Stanford, CA: Stanford University Press.

——. 2011. *Remembering Palestine in 1948: Beyond National Narratives*. Cambridge: Cambridge University Press.

Berlant, Lauren. 2008. "Thinking About Feeling Historical." *Emotion, Space and Society* 1 (1): 4–9.

Bitari, Nidal. 2013. "Yarmuk Refugee Camp and the Syrian Uprising." *Journal of Palestine Studies* 43 (1): 61–78. doi:10.1525/jps.2013.43.1.61.

Bocco, Ricardo, and Lex Takkenberg, eds. 2009. "UNRWA and the Palestinian Refugees 60 Years Later." Special issue, *Refugee Survey Quarterly* 28, nos. 2–3, http://rsq .oxfordjournals.org/content/28/2-3.toc.

Bordeaux, Richard. ed. 2001. *The October War: A Retrospective.* Gainesville: University Press of Florida.

Boullata, Issa. 1997. "Ibrahim Tuqan's Poem 'Red Tuesday.'" In *Tradition and Modernity in Arabic Literature*, ed. Issa Boullata and Terri DeYoung, 87–100. Fayetteville: University of Arkansas Press.

Bowker, Robert. 2003. *Palestinian Refugees: Mythology, Identity, and the Search for Peace.* Boulder, CO: Lynne Rienner.

Brand, Laurie. 1988a. "Nasir's Egypt and the Reemergence of the Palestinian National Movement." *Journal of Palestine Studies* 17 (2): 29–45. doi:10.2307/2536862.

——. 1988b. *The Palestinians in the Arab World: Institution Building and the Search for State.* New York: Columbia University Press.

——. 1988c. "The Palestinians in Syria: The Politics of Integration." *Middle East Journal* 42 (4): 621–637. doi:10.2307/4327836.

——. 1990. "Asad's Syria and the PLO: Coincidence or Conflict of Interests?" *Journal of South Asian and Middle Eastern Studies* 14 (2): 22–42.

Browers, Michaelle. 2006. *Democracy and Civil Society in Arab Political Thought: Transcultural Possibilities.* Syracuse, NY: Syracuse University Press.

Bruner, Jerome. 1991. "The Narrative Construction of Reality." *Critical Inquiry* 18 (1): 1–21. doi:10.2307/1343711.

——. 2004. "Life as Narrative." *Social Research* 71 (3): 691–710. doi:10.2307/40970444.

Buehrig, Edward. 1971. *The UN and the Palestinian Refugees: A Study in Non-territorial Administration.* Bloomington: Indiana University Press.

Butler, Judith. 1997. *The Psychic Life of Power: Theories in Subjection.* Stanford, CA: Stanford University Press.

——. 2003. "Afterword: After Loss, What Then?" In *Loss: The Politics of Mourning*, ed. David Eng and David Kazanjian, 467–473. Berkeley: University of California Press.

Challand, Benoît. 2008. "The Evolution of Western Aid for Palestinian Civil Society: Bypassing Local Knowledge and Resources." *Middle Eastern Studies* 44 (3): 397–417. doi:10.1080/00263200802021566.

——. 2009. *Palestinian Civil Society: Foreign Donors and the Power to Promote and Exclude.* London: Routledge.

Chatty, Dawn. 2010. *Displacement and Dispossession in the Modern Middle East.* Cambridge: Cambridge University Press.

Chomsky, Noam. 1999. *Fateful Triangle: The United States, Israel and the Palestinians.* 2nd ed. London: Pluto Press.

Chow, Rey. 2008. "Translator, Traitor; Translator, Mourner (Or, Dreaming of Intercultural Equivalence)." *New Literary History* 39 (3): 565–580. doi:10 .2307/20533102.

Cohen, Anthony. 1985. *The Symbolic Construction of Community.* London: Ellis Horwood and Tavistock Publications. Cited in Gerard Delanty. 2010. *Community*. 2nd ed. London: Routledge.

Collins, Patricia Hill. 2008. *Black Feminist Thought: Knowledge, Consciousness and the Politics of Empowerment*. 2nd ed. London: Routledge.

Connerton, Paul. 1989. *How Societies Remember*. Cambridge: Cambridge University Press.

Coser, Lewis. 1992. "Introduction: Maurice Halbwachs, 1877–1945." In *On Collective Memory*, by Maurice Halbwachs, 1–34. Edited, translated, and introduced by Lewis Coser. Chicago: University of Chicago Press.

Cronin, David. 2010. *Europe's Alliance with Israel: Aiding the Occupation*. London: Pluto Press.

Damir-Geilsdorf, Sabine. 2009. *Die "Nakba" Erinnern: Palästinensische Narrative des ersten arabisch-israelischen Krieges 1948* [Remembering the "Nakba:" Palestinian narratives of the first 1948 Arab-Israeli war]. Wiesbaden: Reichert Verlag.

Davis, Rochelle. 2007. "Mapping the Past, Re-creating the Homeland: Memories of Village Places in Pre-1948 Palestine." In *Nakba: Palestine, 1948 and the Claims of Memory*, ed. Ahmad Sa'di and Lila Abu-Lughod, 53–75. New York: Columbia University Press.

——. 2010. *Palestinian Village Histories: Geographies of the Displaced*. Stanford, CA: Stanford University Press.

Davis, Uri. 1983. *The Golan Heights Under Israeli Occupation, 1967–1981*. Edited by John Dwedney and Heather Bleaney. Occasional Paper Series. Durham, UK: Centre for Middle Eastern and Islamic Studies, University of Durham. Last updated 18 May 2006: http://dro.dur.ac.uk/138/1/18CMEIS.pdfUlt

Day Sclater, Shelley. 2003. "What Is the Subject?" *Narrative Inquiry* 13 (2): 317–330.

Delanty, Gerard. 2010. *Community*. 2nd ed. London: Routledge.

Della Porta, Donatella, and Mario Diani. 2006. *Social Movements: An Introduction*. 2nd ed. Oxford: Blackwell.

Docker, John. 2012. "Instrumentalising the Holocaust: Israel, Settler-Colonialism, Genocide (Creating a Conversation Between Raphaël Lemkin and Ilan Pappe)." *Holy Land Studies* 11 (1): 1–32. doi:10.3366/hls.2012.0027.

Douglas, Mary. 1980. "Introduction: Maurice Halbwachs (1877–1945)." In *Collective Memory*, by Maurice Halbwachs, 1–19. Introduced by Mary Douglas. Translated by Francis Didder Jr. and Vida Ditter. New York: Harper and Row.

Dussel, Enrique. 2000. "Europe, Modernity and Eurocentrism." Translated by Javier Krauel and Virginia Tuma. *Nepantla: Views from the South* 1 (3): 465–478. http://muse.jhu.edu/journals/nep/summary/v001/1.3dussel.html.

El-Eini, Roza. 2006. *Mandated Landscape: British Imperial Rule in Palestine, 1929–1948*. London: Routledge.

Ellis, Carolyn. 2004. *The Ethnographic I: A Methodological Novel About Autoethnography*. Walnut Creek, CA: AltaMira Press.

——. 2009. *Revision: Autoethnographic Reflections on Life and Work*. Walnut Creek, CA: Left Coast Press.

El-Nimr, Sonia. 1993. "Oral History and Palestinian Collective Memory." *Oral History* 21 (1): 54–61. doi:10.2307/40179316.

Elvira, Laura Ruiz de, and Tina Zintl. 2012. *Civil Society and the State in Syria: The Outsourcing of Social Responsibility*. Edited and introduced by Raymond

Hinnebusch. Fife, Scotland: University of St. Andrews Centre for Syrian Studies.

Eng, David, and David Kazanjian. eds., 2003a. "Introduction: Mourning Remains." In *Loss: The Politics of Mourning*, ed. David Eng and David Kazanjian, 1–25. Berkeley: University of California Press.

——. 2003b. *Loss: The Politics of Mourning*. Berkeley: University of California Press.

Erll, Astrid, Ansgar Nünning, and Sara Young. 2008. *Cultural Memory Studies: An International and Interdisciplinary Handbook*. Berlin: Walter de Gruyter.

Esmeir, Samera. 2003. "Law, History, Memory." *Social Text* 21 (2): 25–48. http://muse.jhu.edu/journals/soc/summary/v021/21.2esmeir.html.

——. 2007. "Memories of Conquest: Witnessing Death in Tantura." In *Nakba: Palestine, 1948 and the Claims of Memory*, ed. Ahmad Sa'di and Lila Abu-Lughod, 229–250. New York: Columbia University Press.

EU (European Union). 2009. "Water Supply and Sanitation for Khan Eshieh and Khan Dannoun Palestine Refugee Camps and Adjacent Areas." In *Delegation of the European Union to Syria Annual Report*. Last updated n/a. Accessed April 25, 2015. http://www.eeas.europa.eu/delegations/syria/documents/content/more_info/annual_report_en.pdf.

Farah, Randa. 1997. "Crossing Boundaries: Reconstruction of Palestinian Identities in al-Baq'a Refugee Camp, Jordan." In *Palestine, Palestiniens: Territoire National, Espaces Communautaires* [Palestine, Palestinians: National territory, community spaces], ed. Ricardo Bocco, Blandine Destremau, and Jean Hannoyer, 259–298. Beirut: Centre d'Etudes et de Recherches sur le Moyen-Orient Contemporain.

——. 2003. "Palestinian Refugee Camps: Reinscribing and Contesting Memory and Space." In *Isolation: Places and Practices of Exclusion*, ed. Carolyn Strange and Alison Bashford, 191–207. London: Routledge.

——. 2006. "Palestinian Refugees: Dethroning the Nation at the Crowning of the 'Statelet'?" *Interventions: International Journal of Postcolonial Studies* 8 (2): 228–252. doi:10.1080/13698010600781040.

——. 2009a. "Refugee Camps in the Palestinian and Sahrawi National Liberation Movements: A Comparative Perspective." *Journal of Palestine Studies* 38 (2): 76–93. doi:10.1525/jps.2009.38.2.76.

——. 2009b. "UNRWA: Through the Eyes of Its Refugee Employees in Jordan." In "UNRWA and the Palestinian Refugees 60 Years Later." Special issue, *Refugee Survey Quarterly* 28 (2–3): 389–411. doi:10.1093/rsq/hdp046.

Feldman, Ilana. 2012. "The Challenge of Categories: UNRWA and the Definition of a 'Palestine Refugee.'" *Journal of Refugee Studies* 25 (3): 387–406. doi:10.1093/jrs/fes004.

Fentress, James, and Chris Wickham. 1992. *Social Memory*. Oxford: Blackwell.

Finkelstein, Norman. 1991. "Myths, Old and New." *Journal of Palestine Studies* 21 (1): 66–89. doi:10.2307/2537366.

——. 2003. *Image and Reality of the Israel-Palestine Conflict*. 2nd ed. London: Verso Books.

Fischbach, Michael. 2003. *Records of Dispossession: Palestinian Refugee Property and the Arab-Israeli Conflict*. New York: Columbia University Press.

Fivush, Robyn. 2008a. "Remembering and Reminiscing: How Individual Lives Are Constructed in Family Narratives." *Memory Studies* 1 (1): 49–58.

——. 2008b. "The Intergenerational Self: Subjective Perspective and Family History." In *Self Continuity: Individual and Collective Perspectives*, ed. Fabio Sani, 131–143. New York: Psychology Press.

Foucault, Michel. 1991. *Discipline and Punish: The Birth of the Prison*. Translated by Alan Sheridan. London: Penguin Books.

——. 2005. *The Archaeology of Knowledge*. Translated by A. M. Sheridan Smith. London: Routledge.

Freud, Sigmund. ([1915], [1917] 2001). "Mourning and Melancholia." In *Complete Psychological Works of Sigmund Freud*. Vol. 14, *On the History of the Psycho-Analytic Movement, Papers on Metapsychology and Other Works, 1914–1916*, 239–258. Translated by James Strachey, Anna Freud, Alix Strachey, and Alan Tyson. London: Vintage Books.

——. ([1923] 2001). "The Ego and the Id." In *Complete Psychological Works of Sigmund Freud*. Vol. 19, *The Ego and the Id and Other Works, 1923–1925*, 3–66. Translated by James Strachey, Anna Freud, Alix Strachey, and Alan Tyson. London: Vintage Books.

Gabiam, Nell. 2006. "Negotiating Rights: Palestinian Refugees and the Protection Gap." *Anthropological Quarterly* 79 (4): 717–730. doi:10.1353/anq.2006.0049.

——. 2009. "Rethinking Camps: Palestinian Refugees in Damascus." In *Urban Life: Readings in Anthropology of the City*, ed. George Gmelch, Robert Kemper, and Walter Zenner, 144–156. 5th ed. Long Grove, IL: Waveland Press.

——. 2012. "When 'Humanitarianism' Becomes 'Development': The Politics of International Aid in Syria's Palestinian Refugee Camps." *American Anthropologist* 114 (1): 95–107. doi:10.1111/j.1548–1433.2011.01399.x.

——. 2014. "Implementing the Neirab Rehabilitation Project: UNRWA's Approach to Development in Syria's Palestinian Refugee Camps." In *UNRWA and Palestinian Refugees: From Relief and Works to Human Development*, ed. Sari Hanafi, Leila Hilal, and Lex Takkenberg, 221–239. London: Routledge.

——. 2016. *The Politics of Suffering: Syria's Palestinian Refugee Camps*. Bloomington: Indiana University Press.

Gatti, Fabrizio. 2013. "Lampedusa, Passing the Buck of Responsibilities: This Is How They Left the Syrian Children Drown." *L'Espresso*. Last updated November 28, 2013. http://espresso.repubblica.it/internazionale/2013/11/28/news/lampedusa-buck-passing-on-the-massacre-so-they-left-syrians-children-drown-1.143363.

Georgakopoulou, Alexandra. 2006. "Thinking Big with Small Stories in Narrative and Identity Analysis." *Narrative Inquiry* 16 (1): 122–130.

Gerges, Fawaz. 2007. "Egypt and the 1948 War: Internal Conflict and Regional Ambition." In *The War for Palestine: Rewriting the History of 1948*, ed. Eugene Rogan and Avi Shlaim, 150–175. 2nd ed. Cambridge: Cambridge University Press.

Gluck, Sherna Berger. 2008. "Oral History and al-Nakbah." *Oral History Review* 35 (1): 68–80. doi:10.1093/ohr/ohn001.

——. 2012. "New Directions in Palestinian Oral History." *Oral History Review* 39 (1): 100–111. doi:10.1093/ohr/ohr112.

Goodwin, Jeff, James M. Jasper, and Jaswinder Khattra. 1999. "Caught in a Winding, Snarling Vine: The Structural Bias of Political Process Theory." *Sociological Forum* 14 (1): 27–54. doi:10.2307/685013.

Gordon, Neve. 2008. *Israel's Occupation.* Berkeley: University of California Press.

Gray, Peter, and Kendrick Oliver, eds. 2004. *The Memory of Catastrophe.* Manchester, UK: Manchester University Press.

Gregg, Melissa, and Gregory Seigworth. 2010. *The Affect Theory Reader.* Durham, NC: Duke University Press.

Grosfoguel, Ramon. 2011. "Decolonizing Postcolonial Studies and Paradigms of Political-Economy: Transmodernity, Decolonial Thinking and Global Coloniality." *TRANSMODERNITY: Journal of Peripheral Cultural Production of the Luso-Hispanic World*, vol. 1, no. 1. http://escholarship.org/uc/item/21k6t3fq.

——. 2012. "Decolonizing the Holocaust." Lecture delivered at Third Genocide Memorial Day Conference, Islamic Human Rights Commission, School of Oriental and African Studies, University of London, January 22. Last updated March 11, 2012. https://www.youtube.com/watch?v=1PwG9fb6oEA.

Gunther, John. 1959. "Biographical Note: Nasser and Naguib." In *The Philosophy of the Revolution*, by Gamal Abdul Nasser, 81–90. Introduced by John Badeau. Biographical Sketch by John Gunther. Buffalo, NY: Smith, Keynes and Marshall.

Halbwachs, Maurice. 1980. *Collective Memory.* Introduced by Mary Douglas. Translated by Francis Didder Jr. and Vida Ditter. New York: Harper & Row.

——. 1992a. *On Collective Memory.* Edited, translated, and introduced by Lewis Coser. Chicago: University of Chicago Press.

——. [1925] 1992b. "The Social Frameworks of Memory." In *On Collective Memory*, by Maurice Halbwachs, 37–189. Edited, translated, and introduced by Lewis Coser. Chicago: University of Chicago Press.

Hammami, Rema. 2010. "Gender, Nakba and Nation: Palestinian Women's Presence and Absence in the Narration of 1948 Memories." In *Across the Wall: Narratives of Israeli-Palestinian History*, ed. Ilan Pappe and Jamil Hilal, 235–268. London: I. B. Tauris.

Hamoud, Tareq. 2012. "The Impact of the Syrian Revolution on Palestinian Refugees." *Journal of Palestinian Refugee Studies* 2 (2): 7–22. http://www.prc.org.uk/portal/images/stories/pdfs/JPRS-4_Small.pdf.

Hanafi, Sari. 2003. "Rethinking the Palestinians Abroad as a Diaspora: The Relationship Between the Diaspora and the Palestinian Territories." *HAGAR: International Social Science Review* 4 (1–2): 157–182.

——. 2011. "Governing the Palestinian Refugee Camps in Lebanon and Syria: The Cases of Nahr el-Bared and Yarmouk Camps." In *Palestinian Refugees: Identity, Space and Place in the Levant*, ed. Are Knudsen and Sari Hanafi, 29–49. London: Routledge.

Hanafi, Sari, Leila Hilal, and Lex Takkenberg, eds. 2014. *UNRWA and Palestinian Refugees: From Relief and Works to Human Development.* London: Routledge.

Haraway, Donna. 1991. *Simians, Cyborgs and Women: The Reinvention of Nature.* London: Routledge.

——. 1997. *Modest_Witness@Second_Millennium.FemaleMan©_Meets_OncoMouse™: Feminism and Technoscience.* London: Routledge.

Hasso, Frances. 2000. "Modernity and Gender in Arab Accounts of the 1948 and 1967 Defeats." *International Journal of Middle East Studies* 32 (4): 491–510. doi:10.2307/259422.

Hijab, Nadia. 2011. "The 'Palestine Papers': An Alternative Analysis for Action." *Al-Shabaka: The Palestinian Policy Network*. Last updated February 2, 2011. http://al-shabaka.org/commentaries/the-palestine-papers-an-alternative-analysis-for-action.

Hill, Tom. 2005. "Historicity and the *Nakba* Commemorations of 1998." European University Institute Working Papers, Robert Schuman Centre for Advanced Studies No. 2005/33. Mediterranean Program Series. Last updated December 2005. http://cadmus.iue.it/dspace/bitstream/1814/3768/1/2005_33 Hill.pdf.

——. 2008. "1948 After Oslo: Truth and Reconciliation in Palestinian Discourse." *Mediterranean Politics* 13 (2): 151–170. doi:10.1080/13629390802127505.

Hinnebusch, Raymond. 2002. *Syria: Revolution from Above*. London: Routledge.

——. 2014. "The Foreign Policy of Syria." In *The Foreign Policies of Middle East States*, ed. Raymond Hinnebusch and Anoushiravan Ehteshami, 207–232. 2nd ed. Boulder, CO: Lynne Rienner.

Hirsch, Marianne. 1997. *Family Frames: Photography, Narrative, and Postmemory*. Cambridge, MA: Harvard University Press.

——. 2012. *The Generation of Postmemory: Writing and Visual Culture After the Holocaust*. New York: Columbia University Press.

Hirsch, Marianne, and Valerie Smith. 2002. "Gender and Cultural Memory." Special issue, *Signs: Journal of Women and Culture in Society* 28, no. 1: 1–19, doi:10.1086/340890.

Hodgkin, Katharine and Susannah Radstone. 2003. "Introduction: Contested Pasts." In *Contested Pasts: The Politics of Memory*, ed. Katharine Hodgkin and Susannah Radstone, 1–21. London: Routledge.

Hourani, Albert. 1988. "Musa 'Alami and the Problem of Palestine, 1933–1949." In *Studia Palaestina: Studies in Honor of Constantine K. Zurayk*, ed. Hisham Nashabe, 23–41. Beirut: Institute for Palestine Studies.

Howard, Harry. 1966. "UNRWA, the Arab Host Countries and the Arab Refugees." *Middle East Forum* 42 (3): 29–42.

HRW (Human Rights Watch). 2012. "Jordan: Bias at the Syrian Border." *Human Rights Watch*. Last updated July 4, 2012. http://www.hrw.org/news/2012/07/04/jordan-bias-syrian-border.

——. 2013. "Egypt: Syria Refugees Detained, Coerced to Return." *Human Rights Watch*. Last updated November 11, 2013. http://www.hrw.org/news/2013/11/10/egypt-syria-refugees-detained-coerced-return.

Humphries, Isabelle, and Laleh Khalili. 2007. "Gender of Nakba Memory." In *Nakba: Palestine, 1948 and the Claims of Memory*, ed. Ahmad Sa'di and Lila Abu-Lughod, 207–227. New York: Columbia University Press.

Hutton, Patrick. 1993. *History as an Art of Memory*. Hanover, NH: University Press of New England.

——. 1997. "Mnemonic Schemes in the New History of Memory." *History and Theory* 36 (3): 378–391. doi: 10.1111/0018-2656.00021.

——. 2000. "Recent Scholarship on Memory and History." *The History Teacher* 33 (4): 533–548. doi: 10.2307/494950

Huyssen, Andreas. 1995. *Twilight Memories: Marking Time in a Culture of Amnesia.* London: Routledge.

——. 2003. *Present Pasts: Urban Palimpsests and the Politics of Memory.* Stanford, CA: Stanford University Press.

Jaradat, Ingrid Gassner. 2001. "A Programme for an Independent Rights Campaign." In *Palestinian Refugees: The Right of Return,* ed. Naseer Aruri, 252–259. London: Pluto Press.

Jayyusi, Lena. 2007. "Iterability, Cumulativity, and Presence: The Relational Figures of Palestinian Memory." In *Nakba: Palestine, 1948 and the Claims of Memory,* ed. Ahmad Sa'di and Lila Abu-Lughod, 107–133. New York: Columbia University Press.

JPS (Journal of Palestine Studies). 2001. "The Tantura Massacre, 22–23 May 1948." *Journal of Palestine Studies* 30 (3): 5–18. doi:10.1525/jps.2001.30.3.5.

Juneja, Monica. 2009. "Architectural Memory Between Representation and Practice: Rethinking Pierre Nora's *Les Lieux de mémoire.*" In "Memory, History and Colonialism: Engaging with Pierre Nora in Colonial and Postcolonial Contexts." Special issue, *German Historical Institute London Bulletin,* suppl. 1, pp. 11–36.

Kabha, Mustafa. 2007. "A Palestinian Look at the New Historians and Post-Zionism in Israel." In *Making Israel,* ed. Benny Morris, 299–318. Ann Arbor: University of Michigan Press.

Kanaana, Sharif, and Bassam Al-Ka'bi. 1986. *Destroyed Palestinian Villages: Ein Houd.* Ramallah: Bir Zeit University Research and Documentation Center. Cited in Susan Slyomovics. 1991. "Destroyed Palestinian Villages: Ein Houd by Sharif Kanaana, Bassām al-kbī; Destroyed Palestinian Villages: Majdal Asgalan by Sharif Kanaana, Rashād al-Madanī; Destroyed Palestinian Villages: Salameh by Sharif Kanaana, Lubna Abd al-Hādī; Destroyed Palestinian Villages: Deir Yassin by Sharif Kanaana, Nihād Zaytawī; Destroyed Palestinian Villages: Innabeh by Sharif Kanaana, Muhammad Ishtayeh; Destroyed Palestinian Villages: Lajun by Sharif Kanaana, Umar Mahāmīd; Destroyed Palestinian Villages: Al-Falujah by Sharif Kanaana, Rashād al-Madanī." *Journal of American Folklore* 104 (413): 385–387. doi:10.2307/541468.

Kanaaneh, Rhoda. 1995. "We'll Talk Later." *Cultural Anthropology* 10 (1): 125–135. doi:10.2307/656235.

Kanaaneh, Rhoda, and Isis Nusair, eds. 2010. *Displaced at Home: Ethnicity and Gender Among Palestinians in Israel.* Albany: State University of New York Press.

Kanafani, Ghassan. [1969] 2000. "Returning to Haifa." In *Palestine's Children: Return to Haifa and Other Stories,* by Ghassan Kanafani, 149–196. Translated and edited by Barbara Harlow and Karen Riley. Boulder, CO: Lynne Rienner.

Kansteiner, Wulf. 2002. "Finding Meaning in Memory: A Methodological Critique of Collective Memory Studies." *History and Theory* 41 (2): 179–197. doi:10.1111/0018 -2656.00198.

Kassab, Elizabeth Suzanne. 2010. *Contemporary Arab Thought: Cultural Critique in Comparative Perspective.* New York: Columbia University Press.

Kassem, Fatma. 2010. "Counter-Memory: Palestinian Women Naming Historical Events." In *Displaced at Home: Ethnicity and Gender Among Palestinians in Israel,* ed. Rhoda Kanaaneh and Isis Nusair, 93–108. Albany: State University of New York Press.

——. 2011. *Palestinian Women: Narrative Histories and Gendered Memory*. London: Zed Books.

Kerr, Malcolm. 1965. *The Arab Cold War, 1958–1964: A Study of Ideology in Politics*. Oxford: Oxford University Press.

——. 1971. *The Arab Cold War: Gamal 'Abd al-Nasir and His Rivals, 1958–1970*. 3rd ed. Oxford: Oxford University Press.

Khader, Hassan. 1998. "One Event, Two Signs." *Al-Ahram Weekly*. April 2–8.

Khader, Jamil. 2008. "After Tantura/After Auschwitz: Trauma, Postcoloniality and the (Un)Writing of the Nakbah in the Documentary Film *Paradise Lost*." *Journal of Postcolonial Writing* 44 (4): 355–365. doi:10.1080/17449850802410473.

Khalidi, Rashid. 1984. "The Asad Regime and the Palestinian Resistance." *Arab Studies Quarterly* 6 (4): 259–266.

——. 1992. "Observations on the Right of Return." *Journal of Palestine Studies* 21 (2): 29–40. doi:10.2307/2537217.

——. 1996. *Palestinian Identity: The Construction of a Modern National Consciousness*. New York: Columbia University Press.

——. 2006. *The Iron Cage: The Story of the Palestinian Struggle for Statehood*. Boston: Beacon Press.

——. 2007. "The Palestinians and 1948: The Underlying Causes of Failure." In *The War for Palestine: Rewriting the History of 1948*, ed. Eugene Rogan and Avi Shlaim, 12–36. 2nd ed. Cambridge: Cambridge University Press.

——. 2013. *Brokers of Deceit: How the US Has Undermined Peace in the Middle East*. Boston: Beacon Press.

Khalidi, Walid, ed. 1992. *All That Remains: The Palestinian Villages Occupied and Depopulated by Israel in 1948*. Washington, DC: Institute for Palestine Studies.

——. 2008. "The Fall of Haifa Revisited." *Journal of Palestine Studies* 37 (3): 30–58. doi:10.1525/jps.2008.37.3.30.

——. ed. 2010. *Before Their Diaspora: A Photographic History of the Palestinians, 1876–1948*. 4th ed. Washington, DC: Institute for Palestine Studies. Last updated 2009. http://btd.palestine-studies.org/content/digital-edition.

Khalili, Laleh. 2004. "Grass-Roots Commemorations: Remembering the Land in the Camps of Lebanon." *Journal of Palestine Studies* 34 (1): 6–22. doi:10.1525/jps.2004.34.1.6.

——. 2005. "Commemorating Contested Lands." In *Exile and Return: Predicaments of Palestinians and Jews*, ed. Ann Mosely Lesch and Ian Lustick, 19–40. Philadelphia: University of Pennsylvania Press.

——. 2007. *Heroes and Martyrs of Palestine: The Politics of National Commemoration*. Cambridge: Cambridge University Press.

Khoury, Elias. 2012. "Rethinking the Nakba." *Critical Inquiry* 38 (2): 250–266. doi:10.1086/662741.

Kirk, George. 1959. "Arab Nationalism and Nasser." In *The Philosophy of the Revolution*, by Gamal Abdul Nasser, 97–102. Introduced by John Badeau. Biographical Sketch by John Gunther. Buffalo, NY: Smith, Keynes and Marshall.

Klein, Kerwin. 2000. "On the Emergence of Memory in Historical Discourse." In "Grounds for Remembering," Special Issue, *Representations*, no. 69, pp. 127–150. doi:10.2307/2902903.

Kodmani-Darwish, Basma. 1997. *La diaspora palestinienne* [The Palestinain diaspora]. Paris: Presses Universitaires de France.

Kritzman, Lawrence. 1996. "In Remembrance of Things French." In *Realms of Memory: Rethinking the French Past*, under the direction of Pierre Nora. Edited and foreword by Lawrence Kritzman. Translated by Arthur Goldhammer. New York: Columbia University Press.

Kuhn, Annette. 2002. *Family Secrets: Acts of Memory and Imagination.* 2nd ed. London: Verso Books.

Landis, Joshua. 2007. "Syria and the Palestine War: Fighting King 'Abdullah's 'Greater Syria Plan.'" In *The War for Palestine: Rewriting the History of 1948*, ed. Eugene Rogan and Avi Shlaim, 176–203. 2nd ed. Cambridge: Cambridge University Press.

Langbehn, Volker, and Mohammad Salama. 2011. *German Colonialism: Race, the Holocaust, and Postwar Germany.* New York: Columbia University Press.

LAS (League of Arab States). 1965. "League of Arab States' Protocol on the Treatment of Palestinian Refugees ('Casablanca Protocol')." *United Nations Information System on the Question of Palestine.* Last updated n/a. Accessed July 7, 2010. http://unispal .un.org/unispal.nsf/0145a8233e14d2b585256cbf005af141/e373eb5c166347ae85256e 36006948ba?OpenDocument.

Le Goff, Jacques. 1992. *History and Memory.* New York: Columbia University Press.

Lentin, Ronit. 2010. *Co-memory and Melancholia: Israelis Memorialising the Palestinian Nakba.* Manchester, UK: Manchester University Press.

Leydesdorff, Selma, Luisa Passerini, and Paul Thompson. 1996. "Introduction." In *International Yearbook of Oral History and Life Stories*, ed. Selma Leydesdorff, Luisa Passerini, and Paul Thompson, 1–16. Oxford: Oxford University Press.

Ma'an. 2013b. "Israel Denies West Bank Deal for Refugees Fleeing Syria." *Ma'an News Agency—English.* Last updated January 28, 2013. http://www.maannews.net/eng /ViewDetails.aspx?ID=559225.

Mannheim, Karl. [1923] 2007. "The Problem of Generations." In *Essays on the Sociology of Knowledge*, ed. Paul Kecskemeti, 276–322. Collected Works Vol 5. 5th ed. London: Routledge.

Mansour, Carol, dir. 2014. *We Cannot Go There Now, My Dear* (film). Forward Film Production. (Arabic/English).

Masalha, Nur. 1991. "A Critique of Benny Morris." *Journal of Palestine Studies* 21 (1): 90–97. doi:10.2307/2537367.

——. 1992. *Expulsion of the Palestinians: The Concept of "Transfer" in Zionist Thought, 1882–1948.* Washington, DC: Institute for Palestine Studies.

——. 1997. *A Land Without a People: Israel, Transfer and the Palestinians, 1949–96.* London: Faber and Faber.

——. 2003. *The Politics of Denial: Israel and the Palestinian Refugee Problem.* London: Pluto Press.

——, ed. 2005. *Catastrophe Remembered: Palestine, Israel and the Internal Refugees: Essays in Memory of Edward W. Said (1935–2003).* London: Zed Books.

——. 2008. "Remembering the Palestinian Nakba: Commemoration, Oral History and Narratives of Memory." *Holy Land Studies* 7 (2): 123–156. https://doi.org/10.3366/ E147494750800019X.

——. 2011. "New History, Post-Zionism and Neo-colonialism: A Critique of the Israeli 'New Historians.'" *Holy Land Studies* 10 (1): 1–53. doi:10.3366/hls.2011.0002.

——. 2012. *The Palestine Nakba: Decolonising History, Narrating the Subaltern, Reclaiming Memory.* London: Zed Books.

Mason, Victoria. 2007. "Children of the 'Idea of Palestine': Negotiating Identity, Belonging and Home in the Palestinian Diaspora." *Journal of Intercultural Studies* 28 (3): 271–285. doi:10.1080/07256860701429709.

Massad, Joseph. 1995. "Conceiving the Masculine: Gender and Palestinian Nationalism." *Middle East Journal* 49 (3): 467–483. doi:10.2307/4328835.

——. 2000. "Palestinians and Jewish History: Recognition or Submission?" *Journal of Palestine Studies* 30 (1): 52–67. doi:10.2307/2676481.

McAdam, Doug, John McCarthy, and Mayer Zald, eds. 1996. *Comparative Perspectives on Social Movements: Political Opportunities, Mobilizing Structures, and Cultural Framings.* Cambridge: Cambridge University Press.

McCarthy, John, and Mayer Zald. 1977. "Resource Mobilization and Social Movements: A Partial Theory." *American Journal of Sociology* 82 (6): 1212–1241. doi:10.2307/2777934.

Melucci, Alberto. 1996. *Challenging Codes: Collective Action in the Information Age.* Cambridge: Cambridge University Press. Cited in Gerard Delanty. 2010. *Community.* 2nd ed. London: Routledge.

Mignolo, Walter. 2011. *The Darker Side of Western Modernity: Global Futures, Decolonial Options.* Durham, NC: Duke University Press.

Misselwitz, Philipp, and Sari Hanafi. 2009. "Testing a New Paradigm: UNRWA's Camp Improvement Programme." In "UNRWA and the Palestinian Refugees 60 Years Later." Special issue, *Refugee Survey Quarterly* 28 (2–3): 360–388. doi:10.1093/rsq/hdp039.

Mondoweiss. 2012. "Abbas Tells Israeli TV He Has No Right to Live on Land He Was Displaced From" (interview clip). *Mondoweiss.* Last updated November 2, 2012. http://mondoweiss.net/2012/11/abbas-tells-israeli-tv-he-has-no-right-to-live-on-land-he-was-displaced-from.html.

Moreton-Robinson, Aileen. 2004. "Whiteness, Epistemology and Indigenous Representation." In *Whitening Race: Essays in Social and Cultural Criticism*, ed. Aileen Moreton-Robinson, 75–88. Canberra: Australian Studies Press.

Morris, Benny. 1991. "Response to Finkelstein and Masalha." *Journal of Palestine Studies* 21 (1): 98–114. doi:10.2307/2537368.

——. 2001. *Righteous Victims: A History of the Zionist-Arab Conflict, 1881–1999.* New York: Vintage Books.

——. 2004. *The Birth of the Palestinian Refugee Problem Revisited.* 2nd ed. Cambridge: Cambridge Univeristy Press.

Muhawi, Ibrahim, and Sherif Kanaana. 1989. *Speak Bird, Speak Again: Palestinian Arab Folktales.* Berkeley: University of California Press.

Murphy, Maureen. "'Catastrophe' in Yarmouk as ISIS Seizes Camp." *Electronic Intifada.* Last updated April 4, 2015. http://electronicintifada.net/blogs/maureen-clare-murphy/catastrophe-yarmouk-isis-seizes-camp.

Napolitano, Valentina. 2011. "Recompositions sociopolitiques dans le camp de réfugiés palestiniens de Yarmouk: La montée en puissance du Hamas depuis la fin des années 1990" [Sociopolitical rearrangements in the Palestinian refugee camp of

Yarmouk: Hamas's rise in power since the 1990s]. *Confluences Méditerranée* 1 (76): 71–88. doi:10.3917/come.076.0071.

——. 2012. "La mobilisation des réfugiés palestiniens dans le sillage de la 'révolution' syrienne: s'engager sous contrainte" [The mobilization of the Palestinian refugees in the wake of the Syrian "revolution": Mobilizing under constraint]. *Cultures et Conflits*, no. 87: 119–137. http://conflits.revues.org/18489.

——. 2013. "Hamas and the Syrian Uprising: A Difficult Choice." *Middle East Policy* 20 (3): 73–85. doi:10.1111/mepo.12034.

Nasser, Cilina. 2013. "To My Valentine: Death Will Not Part Us." *Amnesty International*. Last updated February 14, 2013. https://www.amnesty.org/en/articles/blogs/2013/02 /to-my-valentine-death-will-not-part-us.

Nasser, Gamal Abdel. 1959. *The Philosophy of the Revolution*. Introduced by John Badeau. Biographical Sketch by John Gunther. Buffalo, NY: Smith, Keynes and Marshall.

Nayel, Moe. 2013. "Yarmouk Activist Describes 'Atrocious' State of War-Torn Camp in Syria." *Electronic Intifada*. Last updated February 26, 2013. http://electronicintifada .net/content/yarmouk-activist-describes-atrocious-state-war-torn-camp-syria /12231.

Nazzal, Nafez. 1978. *Palestinian Exodus from Galilee, 1948*. Beirut: Institute for Palestine Studies.

Nora, Pierre. 1989. "Between Memory and History: *Les Lieux de Memoire*," in "Memory and Countermemory," special issue, *Representations*, no. 26: 7–24, doi:10.2307/2928520.

——. 1996a. "From *Lieux de mémoire* to Realms of Memory." In *Realms of Memory: Rethinking the French Past*. Vol. 1, *Conflicts and Divisions*, xv–xxiv. Under the direction of Pierre Nora. Edited by Lawrence Kritzman. Translated by Arthur Goldhammer. New York: Columbia University Press.

——. 1996b. "General Introduction: Between Memory and History." In *Realms of Memory: Rethinking the French Past*. Vol. 1, *Conflicts and Divisions*, 1–20. Under the direction of Pierre Nora. Edited by Lawrence Kritzman. Translated by Arthur Goldhammer. New York: Columbia University Press.

——, dir. 1996c. *Realms of Memory: Rethinking the French Past*. Vol. 1, *Conflicts and Divisions*. Edited by Lawrence Kritzman. Translated by Arthur Goldhammer. New York: Columbia University Press.

——, dir. 1997. *Realms of Memory: Rethinking the French Past*. Vol. 2, *Traditions*. Edited by Lawrence Kritzman. Translated by Arthur Goldhammer. New York: Columbia University Press.

——, dir. 1998. *Realms of Memory: Rethinking the French Past*. Vol. 3, *Symbols*. Edited by Lawrence Kritzman. Translated by Arthur Goldhammer. New York: Columbia University Press.

——. 2001. "General Introduction." In *Rethinking France: Les lieux de mémoire*. Vol. 1, *The State*, vii–xxii. Under the direction of Pierre Nora. Translation directed by David Jordan. Translated by Mary Trouille. Chicago: University of Chicago Press.

——, dir. 2006. *Rethinking France: Les lieux de mémoire*. Vol. 2, *Space*. Translation directed by David Jordan. Translated by Mary Trouille. Chicago: University of Chicago Press.

——, dir. 2009. *Rethinking France: Les lieux de mémoire*. Vol. 3, *Legacies*. Translation directed by David Jordan. Translated by Mary Trouille. Chicago: University of Chicago Press.

——, dir. 2010. *Rethinking France: Les lieux de mémoire*. Vol. 4, *Histories and Memories*. Translation directed by David Jordan. Translated by Mary Trouille. Chicago: University of Chicago Press.

Olick, Jeffrey. 2008. "'Collective Memory': A Memoir and Prospect." *Memory Studies* 1 (1): 23–28. doi:10.1177/1750698007083885.

Olick, Jeffrey, and Joyce Robbins. 1998. "Social Memory Studies: From 'Collective Memory' to the Historical Sociology of Mnemonic Practices." *Annual Review of Sociology* 24: 105–140. doi:10.2307/223476.

Olick, Jeffrey, Vered Vinitzky-Seroussi, and Daniel Levy, eds. 2011. *The Collective Memory Reader*. Oxford: Oxford University Press.

Pappe, Ilan. 1992. *The Making of the Arab-Israeli Conflict, 1947–51*. London: I. B. Tauris.

——. 1997. "The 'Politics of the Notables' to the 'Politics of Nationalism': The Husayni Family, 1840–1922." In *Middle Eastern Politics and Ideas: A History from Within*, ed. Ilan Pappe and Moshe Maʿoz, 163–207. London: Tauris Academic Studies.

——, ed. 1999. *The Israel/Palestine Question (Rewriting Histories)*. London: Routledge.

——. 2001. "The Tantura Case in Israel: The Katz Research and Trial." *Journal of Palestine Studies* 30 (3): 19–39. doi:10.1525/jps.2001.30.3.19.

——. 2006a. *The Ethnic Cleansing of Palestine*. Oxford: Oneworld.

——. 2006b. *A History of Modern Palestine: One Land, Two Peoples*. 2nd ed. Cambridge: Cambridge University Press.

——. 2011. *The Forgotten Palestinians: A History of the Palestinians in Israel*. New Haven, CT: Yale University Press.

Passerini, Luisa. 2011. "A Passion for Memory." *History Workshop Journal*, no. 72, pp. 241–250. doi:10.2307/41306849.

Perks, Robert, and Alistair Thomson, eds. 2006. *The Oral History Reader*. 2nd ed. London: Routledge.

Peteet, Julie. 2005. *Landscape of Hope and Despair: Palestinian Refugee Camps*. Philadelphia: University of Pennsylvania Press.

——. 2007. "Problematizing a Palestinian Diaspora." *International Journal of Middle East Studies* 39 (4): 627–646. doi:10.1017/S0020743807071450.

Quijano, Aníbal. 2002. "Coloniality of Power, Eurocentrism and Latin America." Translated by Michael Ennis. *Nepantla: Views from the South* 1 (3): 533–580. http://muse.jhu.edu/journals/nep/summary/v001/1.3quijano.html.

Radstone, Susannah. 2000. "Working with Memory: An Introduction." In *Memory and Methodology*, ed. Susannah Radstone, 1–22. Oxford: Berg.

Radstone, Susannah, and Bill Schwarz, eds. 2010. *Memory: Histories, Theories, Debates*. New York: Fordham University Press.

Radstone, Susannah and Katharine Hodgkin. 2002. "Regimes of Memory: An Introduction." In *Regimes of Memory*, ed. Susannah Radstone and Katharine Hodgkin, 1–22. London: Routledge.

Rashed, Haifa, and Damien Short. 2012. "Genocide and Settler Colonialism: Can a Lemkin-Inspired Genocide Perspective Aid Our Understanding of the Palestinian Situation?" *International Journal of Human Rights* 16 (8): 1142–1169. doi:10.1080/13642987.2012.735494.

Rashed, Haifa, Damien Short, and John Docker. 2014. "Nakba Memoricide: Genocide Studies and the Zionist/Israeli Genocide of Palestine." *Holy Land Studies* 13 (1): 1–23. doi:10.3366/hls.2014.0076.

Reed-Danahay, Deborah, ed. 1997. *Auto/ethnography: Rewriting the Self and the Social.* New York: Berg Press.

Ricoeur, Paul. 2004. *Memory, History, Forgetting.* Chicago: University of Chicago Press.

Robinson, Richard. 1959. "What Is Nasser Like?" In *The Philosophy of the Revolution,* by Gamal Abdul Nasser, 91–96. Introduced by John Badeau. Biographical Sketch by John Gunther. Buffalo, NY: Smith, Keynes and Marshall.

Robinson, Shira. 2013. *Citizen Strangers: Palestinians and the Birth of Israel's Liberal Settler State.* Stanford, CA: Stanford University Press.

Rogan, Eugene. 2007. "Jordan and 1948: The Persistence of an Official History." In *The War for Palestine: Rewriting the History of 1948,* ed. Eugene Rogan and Avi Shlaim, 104–124. 2nd ed. Cambridge: Cambridge University Press.

Rogan, Eugene, and Avi Shlaim, eds. 2007. *The War for Palestine: Rewriting the History of 1948.* 2nd ed. Cambridge: Cambridge University Press.

Rossington, Michael, and Anne Whitehead, eds. 2007. *Theories of Memory: A Reader.* Edinburgh: Edinburgh University Press.

Rothberg, Michael. 2009. *Multidirectional Memory: Remembering the Holocaust in the Age of Decolonization.* Stanford, CA: Stanford University Press.

Roy, Sara. 2007. *Failing Peace: Gaza and the Palestinian-Israeli Conflict.* London: Pluto Press.

Sa'di, Ahmad. 2002. "Catastrophe, Memory and Identity: Al-Nakbah as a Component of Palestinian Identity." *Israel Studies* 7 (2): 175–198. http://muse.jhu.edu/journals/is /summary/v007/7.2saadi.html.

——. 2008. "Remembering al-Nakba in a Time of Amnesia: On Silence, Dislocation and Time." *Interventions: International Journal of Postcolonial Studies* 10 (3): 381–399. doi:10.1080/13698010802445006.

Sa'di, Ahmad, and Lila Abu-Lughod, eds. 2007. *Nakba: Palestine, 1948 and the Claims of Memory.* New York: Columbia University Press.

Said, Edward. 2003. *Orientalism.* 5th ed. London: Penguin Books.

——. 1997. *Beginnings: Intention and Method.* 3rd ed. London: Granta Books.

——. 1998. "New History, Old Ideas." *Al-Ahram Weekly.* May 21–27.

Said, Edward, and Christopher Hitchens, eds. 2001. *Blaming the Victims: Spurious Scholarship and the Palestinian Question.* 2nd ed. London: Verso Books.

Salamanca, Omar Jabary, Mezna Qato, Kareem Rabie, and Sobhi Samour. 2012. "Past Is Present: Settler Colonialism in Palestine." In "Past Is Present: Settler Colonialism in Palestine." Special issue, *Settler Colonial Studies* 2 (1): 1–8. doi:10.1080/220147 3X.2012.10648823.

Salameh, Salim. 2013. "On Hassan Hassan, or the Most Beautiful Place on Earth, Yarmouk Camp!" *Oxymity.* Last updated December 17, 2013. https://www.oximity .com/article/On-Hassan-Hassan-or-the-most-beautiful-1.

Saloul, Ihab. 2012. *Catastrophe and Exile in the Modern Palestinian Imagination: Telling Memories.* New York: Palgrave Macmillan.

Salvatori-Sinz, Axel, dir. 2013. *The Shebabs of Yarmouk* (film). Adalios, Taswir Films, Maritima TV, and 2M (Maroc). (Arabic/English).

Sanbar, Elias. 2001. "Out of Place, Out of Time." *Mediterranean Historical Review* 16 (1): 87–94. doi:10.1080/714004568.

Sayegh, Fayez. 2012. "Zionist Colonialism in Palestine (1965)." In "Past Is Present: Settler Colonialism in Palestine." Special issue, *Settler Colonial Studies* 2 (1): 206–225. doi:10.1080/2201473X.2012.10648833.

Sayigh, Rosemary. 1998. "Palestinian Camp Women as Tellers of History." *Journal of Palestine Studies* 27 (2): 42–58. doi:10.2307/2538283.

——. 2007a. "Women's Nakba Stories: Between Being and Knowing." In *Nakba: Palestine, 1948 and the Claims of Memory*, ed. Ahmad Sa'di and Lila Abu-Lughod, 135–158. New York: Columbia University Press.

——. 2007b. *Voices: Palestinian Women Narrate Displacement*. Al-Mashriq e-book. http://almashriq.hiof.no/palestine/300/301/voices.

——. 2008a. *The Palestinians: From Peasants to Revolutionaries*. 2nd ed. London: Zed Books.

——. 2008b. "Palestinians: From Peasants to Revolutionaries a Quarter of a Century On. Unexplored Problems of Palestinian Identity." In *Time and Space in Palestine: The Flows and Resistances of Identity*, ed. Roger Heacock, 247–257. Beirut: Institut français du Proche-Orient. Last updated May 26, 2009. http://books.openedition.org/ifpo/495.

——. 2012. "Palestinian Refugee Identity and Identities: Strategy, Generation, Class, Region." In *Palestinian Refugees: Different Generations but One Identity Conference Proceedings*. Ibrahim Abu Lughod Center for International Studies, Birzeit University. Last updated December 2012. http://ialiis.birzeit.edu/fmru/userfiles/Palestinian-Refugees-Different-Generations-But-one-Identity.pdf.

——. 2013. "On the Exclusion of the Palestinian Nakba from the 'Trauma Genre.'" *Journal of Palestine Studies* 43 (1): 51–60. doi:10.1525/jps.2013.43.1.51.

——. 2015. "Oral History, Colonialist Dispossession and the State: The Palestinian Case," in "Settler-Colonial Studies and Israel-in Palestine," special issue, *Settler Colonial Studies* 5, no. 3: 193–204, doi:10.1080/2201473X.2014.955945.

Sayigh, Yezid. 1983a. "Israel's Military Performance in Lebanon, June 1982." *Journal of Palestine Studies* 13 (1): 24–65. doi:10.2307/2536925.

——. 1983b. "Palestinian Military Performance in the 1982 War." *Journal of Palestine Studies* 12 (4): 3–24. doi:10.2307/2536242.

——. 1986. "Palestinian Armed Struggle: Means and Ends." *Journal of Palestine Studies* 16 (1): 95–112. doi:10.2307/2537024.

——. 1989. "Struggle Within, Struggle Without: The Transformation of PLO Politics Since 1982." *International Affairs* 65 (2): 247–271. doi:10.2307/2622071.

——. 1991a. "The Gulf Crisis: Why the Arab Regional Order Failed." *International Affairs* 67 (3): 487–507. doi:10.2307/2621948.

——. 1991b. "Reconstructing the Paradox: The Arab Nationalist Movement, Armed Struggle, and Palestine, 1951–1966." *Middle East Journal* 45 (4): 608–629. doi:10.2307/4328352.

——. 1992. "Turning Defeat Into Opportunity: The Palestinian Guerrillas After the June 1967 War." *Middle East Journal* 46 (2): 244–265. doi:10.2307/4328432.

——. 1998. "Escalation or Containment? Egypt and the Palestine Liberation Army, 1964–67." *International Journal of Middle East Studies* 30 (1): 97–116. doi:10.2307/164206.

———. 2004. *Armed Struggle and the Search for State: The Palestinian National Movement, 1948–1993*. Cambridge: Cambridge University Press.

Schnieper, Marlène. 2012. *Nakba—die offene Wunde: Die Vertreibung der Palästinenser 1948 und ihr Folgen* [Nakba—the open wound: The 1948 expulsion of the Palestinians and its consequences]. Zurich: Rotpunktverlag.

Schwartz, Barry. 1996. "Introduction: The Expanding Past." *Qualitative Sociology* 19 (3): 275.

Scott, Joan. 1992. "Experience." In *Feminists Theorize the Political*, ed. Judith Butler and Joan Scott, 22–40. London: Routledge.

Shadid, Anthony. 2011. "Syrian Elite to Fight Protests to 'the End.'" *New York Times*. Last updated May 10, 2011. http://www.nytimes.com/2011/05/11/world/middleeast /11makhlouf.html?pagewanted=all&_r=0.

Shadid, Mohammed. 1981. *The United States and the Palestinians*. London: Croom Helm.

Shammas, Anton. 1992. "Then How Will the Poem Come?" In *Anthology of Modern Palestinian Literature*, ed. Salma Khadra Jayyusi, 300–301. New York: Columbia University Press.

Shavit, Ari. 2004. "Survival of the Fittest? An Interview with Benny Morris." *Counterpunch*. Last updated January 16–18, 2004. http://www.counterpunch.org /shavit01162004.html.

Shaw, Martin. 2010. "Palestine in an International Historical Perspective on Genocide." *Holy Land Studies* 9 (1): 1–24. doi:10.3366/hls.2010.0001.

———. 2013. "Palestine and Genocide: An International Historical Perspective Revisited." *Holy Land Studies* 12 (1): 1–7. doi:10.3366/hls.2013.0056.

Shaw, Martin, and Omer Bartov. 2010. "The Question of Genocide in Palestine, 1948: An Exchange Between Martin Shaw and Omer Bartov." *Journal of Genocide Research* 12 (3–4): 243–259. doi:10.1080/14623528.2010.529698.

Sherwood, Harriet. 2012. "Mahmoud Abbas Outrages Palestinian Refugees by Waiving His Right to Return." *Guardian*. Last updated November 4, 2012. http://www .guardian.co.uk/world/2012/nov/04/mahmoud-abbas-palestinian-territories.

Shlaim, Avi. 1986. "Husni Za'im and the Plan to Resettle Palestinian Refugees in Syria." *Journal of Palestine Studies* 15 (4): 68–80. doi:10.2307/2536612.

———. 1988. *Collusion Across the Jordan: King Abdullah, the Zionist Movement and the Partition of Palestine*. Oxford: Clarendon Press.

———. 1995. "The Debate About 1948." *International Journal of Middle East Studies* 27 (3): 287–304. doi:10.1017/S0020743800062097.

———. 2001. *The Iron Wall: Israel and the Arab World*. New York: Norton.

———. 2007. "Israel and the Arab Coalition of 1948." In *The War for Palestine: Rewriting the History of 1948*, ed. Eugene Rogan and Avi Shlaim, 79–103. 2nd ed. Cambridge: Cambridge University Press.

Shlaim, Avi, and Wm. Roger Louis, eds. 2012. *The 1967 Arab-Israeli War: Origins and Consequences*. Cambridge: Cambridge University Press.

Slyomovics, Susan. 1998. *The Object of Memory: Arab and Jew Narrate the Palestinian Village*. Philadelphia: University of Pennsylvania Press.

———. 2007. "The Rape of Qula, a Destroyed Palestinian Village." In *Nakba: Palestine, 1948 and the Claims of Memory*, ed. Ahmad Sa'di and Lila Abu-Lughod, 27–51. New York: Columbia University Press.

———. 2013. "Memory Studies: Lebanon and Israel/Palestine." *International Journal of Middle East Studies* 45 (3): 589–601. doi:10.1017/S002074381300055X.

Smith, Linda Tuhiwai. 2012. *Decolonizing Methodologies: Research and Indigenous Peoples.* 2nd ed. London: Zed Books.

Sontag, Susan. 2003. *Regarding the Pain of Others.* New York: Farrar, Straus and Giroux.

Stanley, Liz. 1992. *The Auto/Biographical I: Theory and Practice of Feminist Autobiography.* Manchester, UK: Manchester University Press.

Stanley, Liz, and Helen Dampier. 2005. "Aftermaths: Post/Memory, Commemoration and the Concentration Camps of the South African War, 1899–1902." *European Review of History/Revue européenne d'histoire* 12 (1): 91–119. doi:10.1080/13507480500047860.

Stanley, Liz, and Sue Wise. 1993. *Breaking Out Again: Feminist Ontology and Epistemology.* 2nd ed. London: Routledge.

Steppat, Fritz. 1988. "Re-reading the Meaning of the Disaster in 1985." In *Studia Palaestina: Studies in Honor of Constantine K. Zurayk,* ed. Hisham Nashabe, 12–19. Beirut: Institute for Palestine Studies.

Strindberg, Anders. 2000. "The Damascus-Based Alliance of Palestinian Forces: A Primer." *Journal of Palestine Studies* 29 (3): 60–76. doi:10.2307/2676456.

Suleiman, Jaber. 2001. "The Palestinian Liberation Organization: From the Right of Return to Bantustan." In *Palestinian Refugees: The Right of Return,* ed. Naseer Aruri, 87–102. London: Pluto Press.

———. 2004. "The Right of Return Movement: Reality and Ambition." In *The Issue of Palestinian Refugees and International Law: The Proceedings of Damascus International Symposium: "A Just Solution for Palestinian Refugees?" Damascus, 6–7/9/2004,* ed. Jaber Suleiman and Raja Deeb, 265–273. Damascus: Aïdoun Group.

Swedenburg, Ted. 2003. *Memories of Revolt: The 1936–39 Rebellion and the Palestinian National Past.* Fayettville: University of Arkansas Press.

———. 2004. "The Role of the Palestinian Peasantry in the Great Revolt (1936–39)." In *The Modern Middle East: A Reader,* ed. Albert Hourani, Philip Khoury, and Mary Wilson, 467–502. 2nd ed. London: I. B. Tauris.

Swisher, Clayton. 2004. *The Truth About Camp David: The Untold Story About the Collapse of the Middle East Peace Process.* New York: Nation Books.

———. 2011. *The Palestine Papers: The End of the Road?* London: Hesperus Press.

Tabar, Linda. 2007. "Memory, Agency, Counter-Narrative: Testimonies from Jenin Refugee Camp." *Critical Arts* 21 (1): 6–31. doi:10.1080/02560040701398749.

———. 2012. "The 'Urban Redesign' of Jenin Refugee Camp: Humanitarian Intervention and Rational Violence." *Journal of Palestine Studies* 41 (2): 44–61. doi:10.1525/jps.2012.XLI.2.44.

Takkenberg, Lex. 1998. *The Status of Palestinian Refugees in International Law.* Oxford: Clarendon Press.

Talhami, Ghada. 1997. "An Interview with Sadik Al-Azm." *Arab Studies Quarterly* 19 (3): 113–126. doi:10.2307/41859000.

———. 1998. "Trends in Arab Thought: An Interview with Sadek Jalal al-Azm." *Journal of Palestine Studies* 27 (2): 68–80. doi:10.2307/2538285.

———. 2001. *Syria and the Palestinians: The Clash of Nationalisms.* Gainesville: University Press of Florida.

Tamboukou, Maria, Corinne Squire, and Molly Andrews. 2013. "Introduction: What Is Narrative Research?" In *Doing Narrative Research*, ed. Molly Andrews, Corinne Squire, and Maria Tamboukou, 1–22. 2nd ed. London: Sage Publications.

Terdiman, Richard. 1993. *Present Past: Modernity and the Memory Crisis*. Ithaca, NY: Cornell University Press.

Tiltnes, Åge, ed. 2006. *Palestinian Refugees in Syria: Human Capital, Economic Resources and Living Conditions*. Norway: Allkopu AS.

Torrey, Gordon, and John Delvin. 1965. "Arab Socialism." *Journal of International Affairs* 19 (1): 47–62.

Tripp, Charles. 2007. "Iraq and the 1948 War: Mirror of Iraq's Disorder." In *The War for Palestine: Rewriting the History of 1948*, ed. Eugene Rogan and Avi Shlaim, 125–149. 2nd ed. Cambridge: Cambridge University Press.

UN (United Nations). 2012. "UN Agency Calls on Parties to Syrian Conflict to Refrain from Fighting in Civilian Areas." *United Nations News Center*. Last updated September 9, 2012. http://www.un.org/apps/news/story.asp?NewsID=42835&Cr =palestine&Cr1#.UTTMRTfNEto.

UNGA (UN General Assembly). 1947. "181 (II). Future Government of Palestine." November 29, 1946. UN document A/RES/181 (II). *The United Nations Information System on the Question of Palestine*. Last updated n/a. http://unispal.un.org/unispal .nsf/0/7F0AF2BD897689B785256C330061D253.

——. 1948. "194 (III). Palestine—Progress Report of the United Nations Mediator." December 11, 1948. UN document A/RES/194 (III). *The United Nations Information System on the Question of Palestine*. Last updated n/a. http://unispal.un.org /UNISPAL.NSF/0/C758572B78D1CD0085256BCF0077E51A.

——. 1949. "Resolution 302 (IV) Assistance to Palestine Refugees." December 8, 1949. UN document A/RES/302 (IV). *The United Nations Information System on the Question of Palestine*. Last updated n/a. http://unispal.un.org/unispal.nsf/0 /AF5F909791DE7FB0852560E500687282.

——. 1967. "Report of the Secretary-General Under General Assembly Resolution 2252 (ES-V) and Security Council Resolution 237 (1967)." September 15, 1967. UN document A/6797. *United Nations Information System on the Question of Palestine*. Last updated n/a. http://unispal.un.org/UNISPAL.NSF/0 /CC2CFCFE1A52BDEC852568D20051B645.

UNRWA (UN Relief and Works Agency for Palestine Refugees in the Near East). 2012a. "The Situation in Syria." *United Nations Relief and Works Agency for Palestine Refugees in the Near East*. Last updated August 3, 2012. http://www.unrwa.org /etemplate.php?id=1410.

——. 2012b. "Statement by UNRWA on Today's Events in Yarmouk Camp, Syria." *United Nations Relief and Works Agency for Palestine Refugees in the Near East*. Last updated December 16, 2012. http://www.unrwa.org/etemplate.php?Id=1568.

——. 2012c. "Syria Humanitarian Response (Issue 10)." *United Nations Relief and Works Agency for Palestine Refugees in the Near East*. Last updated September 24, 2012. http://www.unrwa.org/etemplate.php?id=1437.

——. 2012d. "UNRWA in Figures." *United Nations Relief and Works Agency for Palestine Refugees in the Near East*. Last updated January 1, 2012. http://www.unrwa.org /userfiles/20120317152850.pdf.

——. 2012e. "UNRWA Statement on Palestine Refugees in Syria." *United Nations Relief and Works Agency for Palestine Refugees in the Near East*. Last updated July 22, 2012. http://www.unrwa.org/etemplate.php?id=1398.

——. 2012f. "UNRWA Syria Crisis Situation Update (Issue 23)." *United Nations Relief and Works Agency for Palestine Refugees in the Near East*. Last updated December 19, 2012. http://www.unrwa.org/etemplate.php?id=1576.

——. 2012g. "UNRWA Syria Crisis Situation Update (Issue 27)." *United Nations Relief and Works Agency for Palestine Refugees in the Near East*. Last updated December 28, 2012. http://www.unrwa.org/etemplate.php?id=1585.

——. 2012h. "Yarmouk, Syria: Humanitarian Needs Rising as Residents Flee Fighting, Seek Safety in UNRWA Schools." *United Nations Relief and Works Agency for Palestine Refugees in the Near East*. Last updated December 17, 2012. http://www.unrwa.org/etemplate.php?id=1573.

——. 2013a. "More than Half of the Palestinian Refugee Camps in Syria 'Theatres of War.'" *United Nations Relief and Works Agency for Palestine Refugees in the Near East*. Last updated June 16, 2013. http://www.unrwa.org/etemplate.php?id=1784.

——. 2013b. "Syria Crises Response Update (Issue No 66)." *United Nations Relief and Works Agency for Palestine Refugees in the Near East*. Last updated December 23, 2013. http://unrwatest.devcloud.acquia-sites.com/newsroom/emergency-reports/syria-crisis-response-update-issue-no-66.

——. 2013c. "UNRWA Calls on All Sides in Syria Not to Take Up Positions in Refugee Camps and to Respect Civilian Areas." *United Nations Relief and Works Agency for Palestine Refugees in the Near East*. Last updated January 16, 2013. http://www.unrwa.org/etemplate.php?id=1593.

——. 2013d. "UNRWA Condemns the Killing of Six Palestine Refugees in Khan Eshieh Camp Outside Damascus." *United Nations Relief and Works Agency for Palestine Refugees in the Near East*. Last updated June 21, 2013. http://www.unrwa.org/etemplate.php?id=1795.

——. 2014. "UNRWA Strongly Condemns School Explosion in Southern Syria." *United Nations Relief and Works Agency for Palestine Refugees in the Near East*. Last updated February 11, 2014. http://www.unrwa.org/newsroom/official-statements/unrwa-strongly-condemns-school-explosion-southern-syria.

——. 2015. "Syria Crises Response Update (Issue No 85)." *United Nations Relief and Works Agency for Palestine Refugees in the Near East*. Last updated March 18, 2015. http://www.unrwa.org/newsroom/emergency-reports/syria-regional-crisis-response-update-85.

——. 2018. "Syria: UNRWA—Overview of Hard-to-Reach and Besieged Areas as of February 2018." *United Nations Relief and Works Agency for Palestine Refugees in the Near East*. Last updated April 3, 2018. https://www.unrwa.org/resources/reports/syria-unrwa-overview-hard-reach-and-besieged-areas-february-2018.

——. n/a-a. "Palestine Refugees." *United Nations Relief and Works Agency for Palestine Refugees in the Near East*. Last updated n/a. http://www.unrwa.org/palestine-refugees.

——. n/a-b. "Where We Work (Camp Profiles)." *United Nations Relief and Works Agency for Palestine Refugees in the Near East*. Last updated n/a. http://www.unrwa.org/where-we-work/syria/camp-profiles?field=16.

——. n/a-c. "Who We Are." *United Nations Relief and Works Agency for Palestine Refugees in the Near East*. Last updated n/a. http://www.unrwa.org/who-we-are.

Vromen, Suzanne. 1975. "The Sociology of Maurice Halbwachs." Unpublished PhD diss., Department of Sociology, New York University.

Wasif Jawhariyya Collection. 2010. "King Faisal I of Iraq Funeral" (image). *Before Their Diaspora: A Photographic History of the Palestinians, 1876–1948*. Edited by Walid Khalidi. 4th ed. Washington, DC: Institute for Palestine Studies. Last updated 2009. http://btd.palestine-studies.org/content/pan-arabism-2.

Whitehead, Andrew. 2002. "'No Common Ground': Joseph Massad and Benny Morris Discuss the Middle East." *History Workshop Journal* 53 (1): 205–216. doi:10.2307/4289780.

Williams, Lauren. 2012. "Palestinian Camp Attack in Syria Sparks Fears of Factional Tensions." *The Daily Star*. Last updated August 4, 2012. http://www.dailystar.com .lb/News/Middle-East/2012/Aug-04/183385-palestinian-camp-attack-in-syria -sparks-fears-of-factional-tensions.ashx#axzz2MaS3DoQJ.

Winter, Jay. 2001. "The Memory Boom in Contemporary Historical Studies." *Raritan* 21 (1): 52–66.

Winter, Jay, and Emmanuel Sivan, eds. 2000. *War and Remembrance in the Twentieth Century*. Cambridge: Cambridge University Press.

Wolfe, Patrick. 2006. "Settler Colonialism and the Elimination of the Native." *Journal of Genocide Research* 8 (4): 387–409. doi:10.1080/14623520601056240.

——. 2012. "Purchase by Other Means: The Palestine Nakba and Zionism's Conquest of Economics," in "Past Is Present: Settler Colonialism in Palestine," special issue, *Settler Colonial Studies* 2, no. 1: 133–171, doi:10.1080/2201473x.2012.10648830.

Yates, Frances. 1999. *The Art of Memory*. London: Routledge.

Zarzar, Anas. 2012a. "Palestinian Camps in Syria: Pulled Into the Fray." *Al-Akhbar English*. Last updated July 17, 2012. http://english.al-akhbar.com/node/9911.

——. 2012b. "Syria: Armed Opposition Takes Yarmouk Refugee Camp." *Al-Akhbar English*. Last updated December 17, 2012. http://english.al-akhbar.com/node/14411.

Zimmerer, Jürgen. 2004. "Colonialism and the Holocaust: Towards an Archaeology of Genocide." Translated by Andrew Beattie. In *Genocide and Settler Society: Frontier Violence and Stolen Indigenous Children in Australian History*, ed. A. Dirk Moses, 49–76. New York: Berghahn Books.

Zua'iter, Akram. 1958. *The Palestine Question*. Translated by Musa Khuri. Damascus: Palestine Arab Refugees' Institution.

Zurayk, Constantine. 1956. *The Meaning of the Disaster*. Translated by R. Bayly Winder. Beirut: Khayat's College Book Cooperative.

Zureik, Elia. 2003. "Theoretical and Methodological Considerations for the Study of Palestinian Society." *Comparative Studies of South Asia, Africa and the Middle East* 23 (1–2): 152–162. http://muse.jhu.edu/journals/cst/summary/v023/23.1zureik.html.

INDEX

'Arif, 'Arif al-, 35, 72
art of memory, 24, 143
Asad, Hafiz al-, 68
As'ad, Muhammad al-, 96
Atfal al-Nada (al-As'ad), 96
Ayman, 120–121, 180–181
'Ayn Ghazal, 111, 124, 136–137, 138–140
Azm, Sadik Jalal al-, 42–43, 196*n*1

BADIL. *See* Resource Center for
    Palestinian Residency and Refugee
    Rights
Bakrawi, Khalid, 1, 7–8, 193*n*1, 194*n*14
Bal, Mieke, 115
barring, of refugees, 19
Bartov, Omer, 47–48
Bassam, 112, 113
Ba'th Party, 9, 40, 66, 195*n*10
begging, 148–149, 151
Bellah, Robert, 130–131
belonging: loss linked to, 131; refugee's
    multiple, 3, 65, 191–192, 198*n*19
betrayal: by Arabs, 147, 173–174, 175–176,
    178; of refugees by PLO, 11, 75, 82
Bin Khadra', Zafir, 65–66
Birzeit University, 44
Black September, 52, 58, 67–68
blaming, by third-generation refugees,
    176–181
Blandford, John B., Jr., 55
Blandford Plan, 55–56
boats, death, 19
books, of destroyed villages, 44, 45, 85–86
Buthayna, 122, 164, 165, 169–170
Butler, Judith, 118, 131

Camp David, 73, 79
camps: community created by, 60;
    depopulated, 20, 60, 61–62, 126;
    described, 54–55; Infrastructure and
    Camp Improvement Program for,
    64; names of official and unofficial,
    60–62; Syrian locations for, 60–64;
    Syrian War impacting, 19–20, 56,
    60–61; transportation to, 54. *See also*
    specific camps
Casablanca Protocol, 56–57

Castoriadis, Cornelius, 75–76
catastrophe. *See* Nakba
*Catastrophe's Aftermath, The (Min Athar
    al-Nakba)* (al-Khatib), 35
Catastrophe's Secret, The (Sir al-Nakba)
    (Hawwari), 32
Challand, Benoît, 75–77
children left behind, 137–140, 168, 172–173
Chow, Rey, 118
civil society, 75–76, 77, 84
collective memories, 23–24
Collective Memory, The (Halbwachs),
    23–24
colonialism: Arab Nakba linked to, 9; in
    Holocaust studies, 5; of Israel, 4, 11, 48,
    100, 127, 188–189, 191–192
community: camps creating, 60;
    definitions of, 14; demarcation of,
    51–60; guardians of memory as
    constituting, 124–131, 153–154; of
    memories, 13–14, 130–131; memories
    of death forming, 135; postmemories
    creating, 160–161; refugee experience
    of, 50–51, 58–59; RoRM enabling, 15
contentious narratives of, 176–181, 182
corner shop analogy, 82–83
counterhistory, 100, 111, 112, 127
countermemory, 100, 103, 106
coups, 9, 31, 36–38, 56
cultural memory, 115–116
culture of return, 74, 82–86, 88

Damascus, camps in, 60–64
Dar'a, 165–166
Dar al-Shajara publishing house, 78–79,
    80, 85–86, 187, 199*n*4
Dayr Yassin, 174–175
death: boats, 19; memories of, 131–137; of
    Palestinian refugees in Syria, 20
Declaration of Independence, PLO, 69,
    199*n*21
declassified Israeli government archives,
    27, 44, 45, 47
Delanty, Gerard, 14
demarcation of community, 51–60
Democratic Front for the Liberation of
    Palestine (DFLP), 78

depopulated camps, 20, 60, 61–62, 126
Dera'a camp, 60–61
destroyed villages books, 44, 45, 85–86
DFLP. *See* Democratic Front for the Liberation of Palestine
Dhiyabiyya, 186–187
diaspora, 15
dinya matat, el- (world died), 131–132, 134
disarming, of Palestinians, 142
disease, memory as, 167
displaced refugees, numbers of, 19
donors, civil society and, 75–76

education: about Nakba, 166; for refugees, 57–58; RoRM and, 60; UNRWA providing, 59, 60
Egypt: coup in, 37; July Revolution of, 9, 37–39, 197*n*10; liberation movements impacted by Syria's relations with, 66–67; Nasser in, 37, 38–39; Syria, UAR and, 197*n*10
Ein el-Tal camp, 61
employment, of refugees, 56–57
Eng, David, 118
entanglements of memories, 100, 103, 106
Erekat, Saeb, 93–94
European imperialism, 30, 39
European Jewish Holocaust, 5, 22, 85, 158, 197*n*14
European Union: Israel's injustices not recognized by, 190; refugees in, 19
evacuation, of PLO, 10, 68
Events of the Catastrophe or Palestine's Catastrophe, The (*Ahdath al-Nakba aw Nakbat Falastin*) (al-Khatib), 35
exchange value, 82

Facebook page, Yarmouk Camp News, 2, 3, 50, 194*n*3
"Falastin: al-Nakba al-Mustamirra" (Kayyal), 72
Falsafat al-Thawra (*The Philosophy of the Revolution*) (Nasser), 9, 26, 38–39
Faluja, al-, 26, 37, 39
family occasions, for memory narratives, 104–107, 117, 122–123

family separations, 52–53
fantastical memories, 127–128
Fatah, 9, 40, 66, 78; Syria's crackdown on, 68–69, 73, 75
Fatima, 168–169, 170, 171
first intifada, 69
forgetfulness, 72, 85–86, 87
Free Officers, 37
Free Syrian Army (FSA), 17–18
Freud, Sigmund, 118
FSA. *See* Free Syrian Army
funding, 77, 78

GAPAR. *See* General Authority for Palestine Arab Refugees
Gaza Strip, 5, 67, 188, 190
gendered hierarchy, in memories, 107–110 113
General Authority for Palestine Arab Refugees (GAPAR), 52, 55, 59, 61–62, 193*n*3
General Union of Palestine Students, 66
General Union of Palestinian Women, 66
generation: RoRM's targeted, 74, 83–85, 91–92; as social location, 99–100. *See also* generation of Palestine; second-generation refugees; third-generation refugees
generation of Palestine, 15, 21, 44; as guardians of memory, 97, 98, 103; loss experienced by, 98; as parochial, 179–180, 181; role of memories for, 11, 97–98, 100–103, 110, 123, 124
genocide, 47–48, 197*n*14
geographic realities, of Syrian Palestinian refugees, 60–65
Ghawarina, 186, 203*n*1
Ghul, Wisam al-, 17
Golan Heights, 52, 54, 64, 73, 127
grandmothers, 111–118, 160–161
grief, affects of, 117–122
guardians of memory: community constituted by, 124–131, 153–154; family occasions and, 104–107, 117, 122–123; generation of Palestine as, 97, 98, 103; grandmothers as, 111–118, 160–161; women's role as, 107–110

Palestinian refugees (*continued*)
population of, 5, 18–19, 51–52,
62–63, 198*n*11; property ownership
of, 57; resettlement plans for, 55–56,
57; rights of, 5, 56–59; shaming and
prejudice experienced by, 147–150;
from Suez War, 52; Syrian War
impacting, 16–20, 190–192, 198*n*18;
UNRWA role for, 51–60. *See also*
camps
Palestinian universe of discourse, 44, 70,
72, 136, 144, 182
pamphlets, air dropped by Israel, 26
PANU. *See* Palestinian Arab Nationalist
Union (al-Ittihad al-Qawmi
al-Falastini)
Pappe, Ilan, 46–47
PARI. *See* Palestine Arab Refugee
Institution
parochialism, 179–180, 181
patriotic signifier, 13, 97, 98, 104–107, 125,
177–181, 182
PFLP. *See* Popular Front for the
Liberation of Palestine
PFLP-GC. *See* Popular Front for the
Liberation of Palestine–General
Command
Philosophy of the Revolution, The (*Falsafat
al-Thawra*) (Nasser), 9, 26, 38–39
photographs, 164–165
PLA. *See* Palestine Liberation Army
Plan Dalet, 47
PLO. *See* Palestine Liberation
Organization
political autonomy, 75–78
Popular Front for the Liberation of
Palestine (PFLP), 77, 79
Popular Front for the Liberation of
Palestine–General Command
(PFLP-GC), 17–18, 61, 77, 78
postmemories: community created by,
160–161; Hirsch on, 158–159, 162, 164–
165; memories distinguished from,
161; Nakba as secondary to loss in, 4,
163–165, 168–170; of Palestine, 157–165;
photographs in, 164–165

post-Palestine generations. *See* second-
generation refugees; third-generation
refugees
prejudice, 147–150
property ownership, of refugees, 57

Qabr Essit camp, 20, 60, 64, 103–104, 133
Qadsayya, 185–186
Qasim, Abdul Karim, 37, 66
Qibya, 174, 202*n*19
Question of Palestine facts, The (*Haqa'iq
'an Qadiyyat Falastin*) (al-Husayni),
33–34

Ramadan camp, al-, 56, 61
Rashidieh Camp, 190
Red Cross, 53, 54, 135, 139, 145
Refugees and Right of Return Committee
(RRRC), 78, 79–80, 84. *See* Palestinian
refugees, in Syria; second-generation
refugees; third-generation refugees
reliability of memories, 91
Relief and Works Agency for Palestine
Refugees in the Near East, UN
(UNRWA): aid convoys of,
18; education provided by, 59,
60; Infrastructure and Camp
Improvement Program of, 64;
resettlement instead of, 55–56; Syrian
Palestinian refugees and, 51–60; in
Yarmouk camp, 185
resettlement, 55–56, 57
Resolution 181, UNGA, 34, 35, 54, 142,
196*n*5
Resolution 194, UNGA, 7, 73, 84
Resolution 513, UNGA, 55–56
Resource Center for Palestinian Residency
and Refugee Rights (BADIL), 45
return: "leave and you will return"
promise of, 152, 175, 179; liberation
linked to, 7, 8; liberation separated
from, 3–4, 70, 73, 97, 182; marches of,
6–8, 16–17, 99, 193*n*1, 195*n*14; memory
as guarantor of, 11, 85, 91, 97, 100, 189.
See also Right of Return Movement
Rhodes Armistice Agreements, 37

Ricoeur, Paul, 24
rifles, 141–144, 173
Right of Return Movement (RoRM), 50;
    Abbas on, 70–71; Ai'doun in, 78, 79,
    80, 83, 84–85, 87, 88–89; Camp David
    as impetus for, 73, 79; community
    enabled by, 15; constituent groups of,
    78–83; culture of return in, 74, 82–86,
    88; education and, 60; forgetfulness
    and, 72, 85–86, 87; funding for, 77, 78;
    as grassroots, 81; memories mobilized
    by, 11, 74–75, 86–93, 174, 188; new
    generation targeted by, 74, 83–85,
    91–92; Oslo Accords and, 11, 73, 79;
    PA countered by, 82; PFLP and, 79;
    PLO countered by, 74, 82; as social
    entrepreneurs, 82–83; Syrian War
    impacting, 188–189; Syria's tolerance
    of, 73–74; time working against, 84–85,
    87; as transnational, 79–80, 81–82;
    UNGA Resolution 194 and, 73, 84;
    Village Day Events for, 89–93; Wajeb
    in, 78, 81, 85, 87, 89–93; Yarmouk
    camp headquarters for, 77–78
rights, of refugees, 5, 56–59
"Right That Refuses Forgetfulness, A"
    (television series), 3
RoRM. See Right of Return Movement
RRRC. See Refugees and Right of Return
    Committee

Safad, 70, 125–126, 128–130, 159–161
Sa'iqa, al- (Vanguards of the Popular War
    of Liberation), 66
Salameh, Salim, 5–6
Salvation Army, 99, 104, 175–176, 200n2
Salvatori-Sinz, Axel, 194n2
Sarab, 176–177
Sayigh, Rosemary, 44
Sayigh, Yezid, 36
Sbeineh camp, 20, 60, 64
second-generation refugees, 116;
    intergenerational narrative differences
    for, 166, 170–172; as Nakba generation,
    171–172; Nakba's multiple meaning for,
    156–157, 181–182; narratives on Nakba

memory of, 170–176; shared narratives
    of, 166–170
second intifada, 73, 93, 202n26
second-personhood, 115–117, 129
self-criticism, for Nakba, 29–30, 32–34,
    42–43
Self-criticism After the Defeat (Al-Naqd
    al-Dhati Ba'da al-Hazima) (al-Azm),
    42–43
setback. See naksa
settler-colonialism, of Israel, 4, 11, 48, 100,
    127, 188–189, 191–192
Shajara Institute for Oral Memory,
    78, 80
shaming memories, 147–150
Shaml (Palestinian Diaspora and Refugee
    Center), 45
Shammas, Anton, 96
shared intergenerational narratives,
    166–170
Sharif, Mahir al-, 9
Sharon, Ariel, 153, 202n19, 202n26
Shaw, Martin, 47–48, 197n14
Shebabs of Yarmouk, The (film), 194n2
Shihabi, Ghassan, 6, 78–79, 199n4
shock, 167–168
silences, in memory narration, 120–121
Sir al-Nakba (The catastrophe's secret)
    (Hawwari), 32
Six-Day War. See June War
social entrepreneurs, 82–83
social location, generations as, 99–100
sociological memories, 22–24
solid waste collection, 61
sorrowful regret (hasra), 117, 119–121
Soviet influence, 36
space, memories linked to, 88
statelessness, 3, 4, 14, 15, 84, 102, 171,
    189–190
statist project, 7, 73, 82, 188
Suez War, 38, 52, 197nn9–10
survival memories, 144–147
survivor, of massacre, 126–128
Suzanne, 106–107, 121, 176
Syria: coups in, 37; Egypt, UAR and,
    197n10; Fatah and PLO crackdown

Syria (*continued*)
by, 68–69, 73, 75; Law 260 of,
57–58; Lebanon intervention of, 68;
liberation movements impacted
by Egypt's relations with, 66–67;
Palestinian liberation movements in,
65–70; PARI of, 55–56, 57; political
autonomy of refugees in, 75–78;
refugees integrated in, 3, 15–16, 55–56,
63–65, 198*n*18; RoRM tolerated by,
73–74. *See also* Palestinian refugees,
in Syria
Syrian War: camps embroiled in, 19–20,
56, 60–61; camps impacted by, 19–20,
56, 60–61; as Nakba, 3, 156, 187–188;
refugees impacted by, 16–20, 190–192,
198*n*18; RoRM impacted by, 188–189;
Yarmouk camp impacted by, 2–3,
17–19, 20, 61, 185, 187

Tahani, 161–162
Tal, Abdullah al-, 37, 196*nn*7–8
Tantura: massacre in, 35, 55, 148–149, 163,
165; Village Day Event, 91–93
technologies of memory, 112
tents, 132–133, 168, 201*n*4
Thawrat Falastin al-Kubra, 33, 194*n*4
"Then How Will the Poem Come?"
(Shammas), 96
third-generation refugees, 106; blaming
by, 176–181; contentious narratives
of, 176–181, 182; as Nakba generation,
171–172; Nakba's multiple meanings
for, 156–157, 181–182; Nakba's patriotic
signification for, 177–181, 182; shared
narratives of, 166–170
time, RoRM fighting against, 84–85, 87
Tira, al-, 26, 89–91
Transjordan, 32–33, 37–38, 45–46, 47, 54
transnational, RoRM as, 79–80, 81–82
transportation, to camps, 54
truth value, of memories, 127

UAR. *See* United Arab Republic
Umm 'Abdul 'Aziz, 126, 132, 134, 135
Umm Ahmad, 149

Umm Ghassan, 109–110
Umm Hasan, 124, 136–137, 138–140, 153
Umm 'Izz al-Din, 55, 101, 102, 114–115, 124,
144–146, 148, 150–153
Umm Muhammad, 163–164
Umm Nimr, 101–102, 186–187
Umm Rim, 54, 152
Umm Shadi, 173–174
Umm Ya'rub, 52–53, 129–130, 146–147
UN. *See* United Nations
United Arab Republic (UAR), 67, 197*n*10
United Nations (UN): UNGA Resolution
181 of, 34, 35, 54, 142, 196*n*5; UNGA
Resolution 194 of, 7, 73, 84; UNGA
Resolution 513 of, 55–56. *See also*
Relief and Works Agency for Palestine
Refugees in the Near East, UN
United States (US): imperialism of, 30,
39; Iraq invasion by, refugees from, 52,
63, 190, 194*n*8; Israel's injustices not
recognized by, 190
universe of discourse, 10; Arab
nationalist, 8, 25, 27, 41, 45, 49,
142–143, 173–174, 182; Palestinian, 44,
70, 72, 136, 144, 182
UNRWA. *See* Relief and Works Agency
for Palestine Refugees in the Near
East, UN
uprisings (2011), 6–8, 16–18, 186
US. *See* United States

Vanguards of the Popular War of
Liberation (al-Sa'iqa), 66
village day events, 89–93
villages, books of destroyed, 44, 45, 85–86

Wadi al-Raqqad, 131–137
Wadi al-T'in, 131–137
Wajeb, 78, 81, 85, 87, 89–93
Wa'ra al-Sawda' massacre, al-, 133
war crimes, 47, 48
West Bank, 5, 70, 188
winter, deaths during, 131–137
women, as guardians of memory, 107–110
"world died" phrase (*el-dinya matat*),
131–132, 134